THE HOME RUN
HORSE

THE HOME RUN HORSE

Inside America's Billion-Dollar
Racehorse Industry and the
High-Stakes Dreams that Fuel It

GLENYE CAIN

Published by
Daily Racing Form Press
100 Broadway, 7th Floor
New York, NY 10005

ISBN: 0-9726401-2-6
Library of Congress Control Number: 2004100441

Cover and jacket designed by Chris Donofry

Text design by Neuwirth and Associates

Printed in the United States of America

CONTENTS

To Charles and Myra Cain, who are the best company of all
and
to Jack Mann for setting the standard

1 The Gamble

ROGER KING, the chairman of King World Productions, is a player.

"Yeah, I gamble," he said. "Casinos, racetracks, stock market." King punctuated his list of favorite pastimes by stabbing at the air with a glowing cigarette, drawing smoky trails that wafted around his head in the humid summer night.

Like anyone in search of action, King will travel to find it. On this August evening in 2001 he was slouched on a green wooden park bench in one of America's historic gambling centers: Saratoga Springs, New York. But he wasn't at the races or playing cards.

Instead, King was at a place most people would have considered a strange sort of gambling hall: a Thoroughbred auction, across the road from Saratoga's fabled racetrack. The international horsey set has come to the Fasig-Tipton August select yearling sale since 1917, making it one of only three world-class Thoroughbred yearling sales on this side of the Atlantic. Traditionally, the two others have been held in July and September at Keeneland, a Thoroughbred racetrack and auction company in Lexington, Kentucky.

Before then—starting in 1898, when William Fasig and Edward Tipton met in New York City, shook hands, and founded the auction house—the company had built its business primarily on trotting-horse sales in Manhattan's Madison Square Garden, Chicago, Cleveland, San Francisco, and Kentucky. But their office assistant, a former stable boy named Enoch James Tranter who took over the company after Fasig died and Tipton bailed out, knew a good business opportunity when he saw one. He wisely decided to follow the money trail from New York City to Saratoga every August, when everyone who was anyone went upstate for sport and gambling, just as today's Roger Kings do.

Officially, turn-of-the-century Saratoga was a spa town with curative waters. Very likely that was a chief attraction for the robber barons' wives, who, like most of Saratoga's citizens, were banned from one of the primary sources of the town's fame: the Club House casino. But even after antigambling reformers in the local establishment shuttered the casino for good in 1907, Saratoga's other main attraction, the racetrack, survived. So did Tranter's little Thoroughbred sale, which had harnessed the sportsmen's passion for racehorses and turned it into a fantastically profitable business. By the time Roger King got there in 2001, Fasig-Tipton Company was about to have its best run ever. During three consecutive evenings, with buyers like King to push it along, the 2001 auction would sell 162 yearlings for more than $62 million, or an average price of more than $385,000 a horse.

If the sale's history was any guide, at least one of those horses might turn out to be a Man o' War, who sold at Saratoga in 1918. Figuring out *which* one that was, paying for him, and then sending him to a trainer to see what you really had . . . that was what made Fasig-Tipton's circular two-story sale pavilion a gambling hall after all.

King is a man who doesn't really give a damn about history, unless it comes in the form of *Daily Racing Form* past-performance lines. On that summer night, slumped against the park bench's slatted back, chin thrust forward and eyes half closed, he looked like a bored pool-hall player waiting for something—a fistfight, a pick-up game—just to break the monotony.

That expression and his dissipated-frat-boy wardrobe—baggy khakis, an untucked green-and-white bamboo-print shirt, and new white tennis shoes—made the 59-year-old King seem out of place at a Thoroughbred auction, where most attendees conform studiously to a *Town and Country* standard of elegance, heavily reliant on silk and linen. King may be from the paved-over pastureland of Asbury Park, New Jersey, but he commands the Turf set's respect by meeting its most important criterion: He has real money. King World Productions is the television-show syndicator that distributes such popular fare as *The Oprah Winfrey Show, Wheel of Fortune,* and *Jeopardy!* CBS bought the company for $2.5 billion in 1999, leaving King plenty of money to play with.

King's aggressiveness in Las Vegas and Atlantic City has made him what casino insiders call a whale, a player who routinely gambles $1 million a visit. He apparently is aggressive in other ways, too. The online site CasinoDealers.net once listed him as one of gaming's most obnoxious players, and not just because he is allegedly a bad tipper. In 1987, apparently overjoyed after winning a $20,000 bet at baccarat, King celebrated by picking the dealer up by the throat and holding him in midair until other players convinced him to put the man down. The dealer sued and won compensatory damages.

So far, none of his horse trainers has ever sued King for physical assault, but King's appetite for action puts a different kind of squeeze on them. A Hall of Fame trainer, the late Sonny Hine, once said of King after he had yanked 11 horses out of Hine's barn without warning, "When you're training his horses, he never bothers you. The only pressure was the pressure you put on yourself. You didn't want the horse to lose when you knew the owner had $30,000 or $40,000 bet on him."

In August 2001, King was looking for a few more horses for his West Coast racing stable. He shopped at Saratoga because it is one of the nation's best places to buy a "home run horse"—one that blooms into a champion with multimillion-dollar earnings and then goes to stud and makes millions more. It is the Thoroughbred sport's equivalent of hitting the lottery. If the owner can cash some tickets on the horse along the way, well, that's great, too, but the real gamble is a long-term one—that the colt he bought as a yearling at Saratoga will mature into an asset of immense value, perhaps returning millions in stud fees at the end of his glorious racing days.

Fillies also can be home run horses, particularly if they pass their talent on to their offspring, making those foals worth seven figures at an auction such as Fasig-Tipton Saratoga. But fillies are less likely to win the Kentucky Derby, which has only produced three female winners in its 130-year history. They are not syndicated, as stallions are, a fact that naturally reduces their total value. And their 11-month pregnancy means the payoff from their foals comes only after a long wait, making them a longer-term risk than a stallion, who starts reaping stud fees almost immediately. A mare produces one foal a year, while a stallion can sire well over 100 foals annually. For all those reasons, people like King generally will risk more on colts than fillies at auction.

King almost passed up the 2001 Saratoga horse sale and left professional buying agent Buzz Chace, a middle-aged connoisseur of cigars and bloodstock, to do his bidding instead.

"But I told him, 'Roger, why don't you get on your plane and come have some fun?'" Chace said. "This man loves action."

The price of King's fun so far, as he took a break from the auction and sat outside smoking, had been $1.85 million. That was what he had bid, about 20 minutes earlier, for one of the first yearlings through the ring, a price that sent an electric thrill through the spectators, and the sellers, that filled the round pavilion.

When Lot Number 3—a tall, muscular colt called simply Hip 3 in sales lingo, due to the number temporarily pasted on each satiny flank—stepped into the pavilion, he drew a crowd of appreciative spectators in with him. Buyers and sellers jammed the aisles, while tourists peered through the glass doors and ringed the upstairs gallery. The bidding arena's red-cushioned seats quickly filled as multimillionaires of both the old- and new-money varieties took their places. From his position on the auctioneer's high stand, Fasig-Tipton's Walt Robertson could see that all the money was there for Hip 3. The world's wealthiest racehorse owners and their regular bidding agents stood out like sparkling jewels in the crowd, a sight to cheer the auctioneer's heart.

Word had gotten around in the course of the week that this colt might bring a million or two. To the average citizen looking down from the gallery that night, it wasn't obvious why. The horse was pretty enough, but he was, after all, a completely blank slate. Hip 3 was just a year old, months away from seeing his first saddle, but the knowledgeable market-watchers around the sale grounds already were estimating his potential auction value as equivalent to the combined purses of the Kentucky Derby and the Preakness Stakes—which he might possibly run in at age 3, if he was much more talented and fortunate than about 33,000 other horses born in 2000. On the face of it, a couple of million seemed a ridiculous price to pay for such an unproven commodity, however beautiful.

"Here's why," said one experienced auction-goer watching the ring from the spectators' gallery above it. He folded his auction catalog's pages back to display Hip 3's pedigree description for his date, a blond woman holding a red cocktail in a plastic cup. The catalog page was essentially a list of horses' names and the races they had won. The man planted a manicured forefinger under one of the names, offset from most of the others by the fact that it was printed in all upper-case letters and bold type. "He's a half-brother to Graeme Hall and this horse." He slid his finger up one line on the page to point out the name Harmony Lodge.

The woman he was addressing looked at the names blankly.

Her informant tried again. "It's a big deal," he said. "They've won big races. All the names on this page that are printed in bold are this colt's best relatives. And his sire is Unbridled's Song. He was a 2-year-old champion, he won a Breeders' Cup race, and people think he's going to make a good sire."

His date was nonplussed. "People *think* he'll be a good sire."

The chocolate-colored colt stood glistening in the ring below, rolling a nervous, white-rimmed eye at the bidders seated in expanding semicircular rows around him. Someone cast an opening bid of $200,000, and within minutes the light bulbs on the price board above the colt indicated $1.5 million.

"My God," the woman said, shaking her head and peering over the railing at the colt slowly circling below in the dyed green shavings of the auction ring. "I mean, Jesus, it's a *horse*."

King bids like he dresses, which is to say with a theatrical carelessness that bucks the ancient discretion and formality of offering a million dollars to Fasig-Tipton Company's tuxedoed auctioneer. His $1.5 million bid finished off a couple of other gentlemen, who signaled they were closing their wallets with the traditional subtle frown and quick head-shake. That left one other rival, seated two rows behind King and Chace: Satish Sanan, a bespectacled 53-year-old native of the Punjab who got into Thoroughbreds after making about $44 million when part of his computer consulting company, IMR Global, went public in the summer of 1997—just in time for the select yearling sales.

Sanan hired Hall of Fame trainer D. Wayne Lukas, who had already won three Kentucky Derbies and was known for spending clients' money freely to acquire potential Derby candidates. He plunged into the market with a fervor that raised eyebrows and got people talking from Kentucky's breeding farms to California's race-tracks to England's hallowed training grounds. His goal, he said right from the beginning, was to "win classic races around the world," including the Kentucky Derby and England's famed Epsom Derby. Much of the Thoroughbred world was skeptical.

"He's a turkey fattened for plucking," one bloodstock agent said in 1997 as Sanan, with Lukas by his side, signed for the most expensive horse at the Keeneland September yearling sale that year, a $2.3 million colt by the great sire Mr. Prospector.

Four years later, Sanan had by his own estimation spent more than $100 million on bloodstock. Some things had changed. He had fired Lukas, whose habit of ignoring his business-minded client's bidding limits had been irksome. He had settled in to a palatial 760-acre farm and training center in central Florida, which he named Padua Stables. He had not won either Derby yet, but he was still in the game, even after the technology stock flame-out caused him to skip a few sales and auction some of his own horses in 1999. He had a team of expert advisers, including two of Lukas's former assistants, and his proven ability to pay a million or two for a horse they liked meant Sanan was still a major force in the elite Thoroughbred market.

Sanan, a short, plump man, had the air of a former high-school computer-club president. Next to his daughter, a stiletto-heeled twentysomething in a clingy summer dress with a cashmere wrap draped around her shoulders, Sanan, in his somber black jacket and drab gray shirt, looked like a quail roosting beside a peacock. He seemed an unlikely challenger to the steamrolling King. But

Sanan, a longtime gambler who had put himself through college with his winnings, had built a reputation as a fearless bidder who liked to bet on his own judgment, and not just at the races. When he wasn't bidding, he enjoyed placing over-under wagers with sellers on what their yearlings would bring. Sanan also liked action, but he was not flamboyant about it.

Four years after his flashy auction debut, the 2001-model Sanan was more selective and careful, bidding on just a few highly desirable yearlings at only a handful of sales a year. Sanan came to Saratoga looking for a few good horses, and the Unbridled's Song colt was one he was willing to pay a lot for.

Sanan and King, each now settling in against a serious challenge, hammered at each other, rapidly exchanging $50,000 raises in a series of silent, nearly invisible nods. As the price climbed to $1.75 million, many spectators still hadn't been able to spot the two bidders, and a rustle and murmur went through the pavilion as people craned to identify them.

King seemed to have won, though you wouldn't have known it by looking at him. Like everyone else, he and Chace sat motionless, eyes dull and faces blank, as if they happened to be sitting next to each other at a lunch counter. What they were doing was listening, waiting for Sanan to answer King's $1.75 million bid.

Robertson, sitting bolt upright in the auctioneer's stand with his left hand extended toward King and the gavel raised in his right, looked inquiringly at Sanan and kept up his patter. But Sanan was silent. Robertson fell silent, too, and gave his gavel a warning flick upward. Before he could bring it down again, Sanan suddenly nodded his head: $1.8 million.

The surprised crowd let out a gasp. Sanan beamed, but King was disgusted. He stood up quickly, shooed his bid-spotter away in exasperation, and stalked up the aisle, past Sanan's seat, and out of the pavilion.

"He'll be back," Fasig-Tipton announcer Terence Collier coolly informed the bemused crowd, who through the glass doors could see King unconcernedly lighting up a cigarette.

"Did you like that move with the cigarette?" King said later. "I was trying to slow them down. There was a lot of billionaires in that room."

King puffed and chatted with a few astonished spectators gathered outside, while inside the pavilion auctioneer Robertson kept up a meaningless gabble, a sort of verbal holding pattern, designed to let King know the bidding was still on.

Impulsively, King flicked the cigarette aside, strode purposefully back into the pavilion, and sat down, crossing his arms indignantly. "Five," he said loudly.

The price board immediately clicked to $1.85 million. There was another rustle as the crowd turned now to look at Sanan.

Sanan, unwilling to give in but reluctant to go much farther against King, decided to try a new tactic. He left his seat and approached King, asking him quietly if he would like to call it a draw and go in as partners on the colt.

"I don't need a fucking partner," King answered, theatrically waving Sanan away without looking at him. "I own *Wheel of Fortune*."

Sanan shook his head good-naturedly and returned to his seat, where he declined to bid again. As the crowd erupted into applause and cheers, the victorious King stood up, exultantly pumping both fists in the air like a heavyweight champ. Chace, meanwhile, handled the mundane business of signing the auction receipt, and a groom led Hip 3 out of the ring.

"Buzz, you got a tough man," Sanan said as Chace left the pavilion and headed out back, where the horses waited on deck and he could light up a cigar before his next round of bidding.

"I've got a tough man, all right," Chace said. "He was ready to go a little farther."

King sauntered out of the pavilion for a smoke, too. In effect, he had just placed a $1.85 million bet that the Unbridled's Song colt, by reason of inherent athleticism or propitious genetic balance, would become a superior racehorse. Even if he was right, he wouldn't see the payoff for a couple of years. Barring any mishaps and setbacks of the kind that often seem to plague young athletes, the colt would probably start his racing career in about a year. In the meantime he would learn everything from the feel of a rider to how to break from the starting gate. And once he started, it could be several more months, or possibly another year, before his real potential—if he had any—would become clear. If King and Chace were right, and if they were lucky, Hip 3 could become the next Secretariat, a champion that could win the Triple Crown and generate untold millions in breeding fees and syndication value.

All of that, if it was there at all, was years in the future. What mattered immediately to King, now slumped on the park bench outside and drawing on his cigarette with an almost postcoital air of contentment, was that he had already won. He had beaten a roomful of billionaires at the bidding game and had paid the night's highest price for a horse.

Sanan, meanwhile, had turned the catalog page. He'd lost that hand to King, but there would be more to play in the sale's remaining two days. The stakes would be higher for a son of 1977 Triple Crown winner Seattle Slew that Sanan liked even better than Hip 3.

Out back in Barn 8 West, one of a cluster of identical wooden rectangles that ranged behind the pavilion, the owner of Blackburn Farm had a special interest in the outcome of King versus Sanan. Whichever way the gavel eventually fell, the people who had bred and raised Hip 3 already knew this: They had struck it rich with this horse.

The Unbridled's Song colt was still a risky quantity, a young Thoroughbred whose running ability was entirely unknown and who, like all horses, was subject to any number of potential physical problems, mental distractions, and simple lack of talent. But that was now Mr. King's worry. The people who had been worrying about the colt for the last year—namely, his breeder, Joe Greeley, and his selling agent, Michael Barnett—were cashing out.

The biggest payoff went to Greeley, who would actually receive the check. But Greeley's happy position was evident only in the small smile he wore as he stood under the spreading branches of an elm tree outside Barn 8. As Hip 3 came back from the auction ring to the dimly lit shedrow, Greeley and Barnett were quietly accepting handshakes from other sellers who, behind their grinning congrats, had already mentally calculated the exact trajectory of their colleagues' home run.

Greeley would have paid a $30,000 stud fee to breed his mare Win Crafty Lady to Unbridled's Song in the first place, and it would have cost him, on average, $12,000 to feed and care for the resulting foal from birth to the yearling season. Greeley then would have paid Barnett, his consigning agent, a total of about $2,400, or $40 a day for two months, to get the yearling ready for sale, a process that includes special feeding programs to promote growth, daily grooming to bring a bloom to the coat, and frequent hand-walking to get the colt fit and muscular. Greeley would also pay both Barnett and the Fasig-Tipton auction house 5 percent of the final sale price. So, from a total outlay of about $44,400 over two years—from the colt's conception to his sale—Greeley theoretically had made a $1,620,600 profit, after paying Fasig-Tipton and Barnett their commissions.

The colt's seven-minute appearance in the auction ring had yielded far less for Barnett, but his $92,500 cut was ample. The publicity was also important. Barnett's Blackburn Farm consignment was making its debut at the Saratoga sale, and the colt's $1.85 million price undoubtedly would send inquiries burning down the telephone lines to Blackburn's office in tiny Spring Station, Kentucky. A price like that spoke for itself, and you got the idea that would be a relief to the quiet Barnett, a tall man with slightly graying dark hair and the bearing of a gentleman farmer rather than a slick marketer.

"We're small and we'd kind of like to stay small," he said.

But such a sale could help draw important clients with exceptionally well-bred stock. And buyers, too, who would sense from King's outlay that this Barnett fellow, new at Saratoga, had the goods to offer.

Despite the magnitude of their success, there was no high-fiving at the Blackburn Farm barn. Instead, Greeley and Barnett were musing about why this particular colt, whom Barnett described as "nice," should suddenly be worth almost $2 million.

"I really thought Unbridled's Song was one of the best horses I ever saw run," Greeley said by way of explaining why he had decided to breed his good mare to an unproven stallion.

"The thing I liked is that, if you go back through the generations and put it all on paper, there's a whole lot of inbreeding, especially from the In Reality family," Barnett added studiously, waggling his index finger over the catalog page, where abbreviated family trees for Win Crafty Lady and Unbridled's Song converged to a single point, the $1.85 million colt, now contentedly dozing in his dim, straw-bedded stall.

The In Reality family does have formidable appeal, because that famous stallion's relatives have provided one of the sport's most consistent sources of successful racehorses. Greeley's $1.85 million colt was indeed related to In Reality, though the legendary name appeared five generations back on his sire's side and—thanks to the artful inbreeding Barnett alluded to—four generations distant on his dam's side, as well. Too far back to fit on the catalog page, but, in the mystical processes of genetics that fuel countless horsemen's dreams, the In Reality influence undeniably was present, double-dosed, in Hip 3's chromosomes.

Barnett reeled off the famous equine names sprinkled through the colt's pedigree, counting back through the generations and explaining the esthetic appeal and genetic power of inbreeding to In Reality's female family and to another great sire, Raise a Native.

"It's all about quality horses," he said earnestly. "I think when you go back and look at the pedigree . . ."

Barnett's explanation trailed off into a pause, and then he looked up from the catalog page, lowering his voice apologetically. "Well, I don't know. Really, it's a crapshoot. You take a shot with a sire."

Back on his park bench, nearing the end of his cigarette, an experienced craps player concurred.

"Sure, it's a crapshoot," King said with a shrug. "It's *all* a crapshoot. Buzz picks out the horses for me, and he loved this one."

He ground his cigarette out on the end of the bench and stood up, turning toward the pool of light over an outdoor bar. A man at one of the white-clothed tables raised his arm to wave King over.

"But it's fun to do," King said, pushing his hands into the pockets of his khakis and turning to head for his drink. "It's a game."

Thoroughbred racing is a game, but for many it is also big business, as Enoch Tranter realized in 1917 when he packed the Fasig-Tipton trunks and first headed upstate in pursuit of sporting families like the Vanderbilts and Whitneys.

Such families did not make their fortunes in racing, and they generally kept stables as a hobby rather than a business; their

11

dreams were about historic victories in glorious races, not about maintaining a profitable bottom line at the barn. From the sport's earliest days in America, the nation's wealthy have been willing to gamble large sums of money in pursuit of what racetrackers call the big horse—a racehorse that can write his name in the sporting annals and in the history of the breed itself through his progeny.

The quest to identify and acquire such horses has created numerous spin-off businesses, feeding tens of thousands of other horsemen, agents, veterinarians, and advisers (some legitimate and some quacks), making a number of them millionaires in their own right. Within the last century, the search also has transformed Thoroughbred breeding from a gentleman's hobby to a global agricultural industry now worth nearly $1 billion annually. And it has changed the horse itself from a mere animal into a commercial product that is designed specifically for the marketplace and that is, under the right circumstances, potentially worth tens of millions of dollars.

"Potential" is the operative word at a yearling auction, where the horses are unbroken and the buyers, however expert they may be, can only judge each horse by his pedigree, looks, and walk. "Potential," with its whisper of potency and promise to be fulfilled on the racetrack and then through breeding, is the addictive element for a buyer at auction, the thing that makes him raise his hand to keep in the bidding game, even once he has passed his limit.

Potential is like the nicotine in a cigarette, but it's also like the smoke: ephemeral, hard to measure, and subject to change with the wind. Of course, no one knows for sure whether an individual horse will fulfill his potential or not, which is why even the breeders who create the horses have founded their catechism on a hopeful, rather than an authoritative, axiom: "Breed the best to the best and hope for the best."

But there are distinct patterns and predictors that can make one horse a better risk than another, and, just as bettors pore over past performances in the *Daily Racing Form* before placing their wagers, buyers like King and Sanan employ experts—trainers, veterinarians lugging X-ray machines and endoscopes, and pedigree analysts shuffling reams of computer-generated statistics—to help them assess which horse to buy. This team of experts and the infor-

12

mation they generate ideally improve a bidder's chances of picking a winner in the auction ring, just as you would expect to improve your poker game if you had five professional players sitting behind you at the table and telling you what to do.

The outcome of the Thoroughbred game, like any other gamble, can go either way. Racing's 300-year history in North America is littered with tales of fake jewels and hard luck, but it is also studded with "against the odds" stories of apparent duds or cheap horses that turned out to be champions. Those dreams keep many owners going, but the reality is much bleaker. About 33,000 Thoroughbred foals are born each year in North America; in 2001 there were 70,942 active runners of all ages at the racetrack, and they earned an average of just $16,159. Seventeen percent of them earned less than $1,000, and 9 percent earned nothing at all.

Only 3 percent of the horses that made it to the starting gate were good enough to win in stakes company, the upper echelon of racing, in 2001. Fewer than that are talented enough to win Grade 1 races, contests such as the Kentucky Derby, which are the pinnacle of achievement. Those elite horses, representing about 2 percent of all starters, are well worth having, not the least because those few bright talents will earn almost a quarter of the $1.2 billion available in North American purses each year.

The Derby is open only to 3-year-olds, and of course only one horse out of each year's crop of foals can win it. Three, at the most, can win the races that make up the Triple Crown: the Derby, the Preakness, and the Belmont Stakes. A horse that can sweep all three, a difficult feat that has not been achieved since 1978, when Affirmed did it, is among the rarest of all creatures. Only 11 have ever succeeded since Sir Barton in 1919, and there is more than historic glory awaiting the next Triple Crown winner: He will also receive a $5 million bonus sponsored by the Visa credit-card company.

The odds of making it to any winner's circle, let alone the one at Churchill Downs on the first Saturday in May, are daunting. But the impulse to try drives thousands of eager racehorse owners to horse sales every year, and it has yielded some spectacular individual stories of both success and failure.

The costly flops are legion. Norway—a $3 million son of the sport's current great sire, Storm Cat, and the famous mare

Weekend Surprise—was a half-brother to 1992 Horse of the Year A.P. Indy and 1990 Preakness Stakes winner Summer Squall. He never won a race and earned just $2,734 for his owners.

Another Storm Cat son, Tasmanian Tiger, fared even worse. Closely related to a champion filly named Storm Song, he brought $6.8 million at a yearling auction in 1999. Two years later, his owners gave up on him after he won just a single obscure race in his first few starts. They sold him to Hong Kong, an equine hinterland populated by outcasts from America and Europe. Tasmanian Tiger had made just three starts, and might have come around eventually, but he must have disappointed his owners, Coolmore Stud, very badly in his short time at the races: Despite his sparkling pedigree, they gelded him before putting him on the plane. Alongside Tasmanian Tiger for the flight was another well-bred and expensive disaster from the Coolmore stable, a $5.5 million colt named Diaghilev, who won twice but then tailed off badly and was beaten by 11 lengths in his final start in England.

Seattle Slew, on the other hand, cost just $17,500 and became racing's only undefeated Triple Crown winner when he won it in 1977. The financial rewards kept coming even after he stopped running. He became one of the Thoroughbred world's most influential sires, reaping millions in stud fees for his owners. In 1998, a $17,000 yearling, this one a colt named Real Quiet, won the Kentucky Derby, proving again that you don't have to pay a fortune to win the world's greatest horse race.

But that same summer, the Japanese entrepreneur Fusao Sekiguchi proved the opposite point was also true when he spent $4 million to buy what turned out to be the 2000 Kentucky Derby winner, Fusaichi Pegasus. After the Derby, Sekiguchi quickly sold Fusaichi Pegasus to Coolmore Stud for a record syndication value of $60 million. But so far, the matings of Mr. Prospector with Angel Fever, which have produced three yearlings and one weanling to sell at auction for an average price of $1.5 million, have only yielded one Fusaichi Pegasus; those other foals together have earned a total of $15,681 at the races.

What was the difference? Why did one of Angel Fever's foals become an equine gold mine, while her other offspring drifted from the auction ring straight into oblivion? They must all have looked promising, given their sale prices, but somewhere along the way Fusaichi Pegasus outpaced his siblings and wrote his name in lights.

The man who paid $4 million for Fusaichi Pegasus liked the horse from the moment he saw him. But even he couldn't fully explain why he had been willing to gamble such a sum on the colt, apparently following other buyers off the cliff in pursuit of winning Angel Fevers. But he did know for certain that he would have spent even more to get the colt, if necessary.

"I would have gone to $5 million," Fusao Sekiguchi told reporters after signing the auction receipt for Fusaichi Pegasus in 1998. "This was the only horse we were interested in. My first impression when I saw him was an inspiration."

Sekiguchi had listened to his adviser, the trainer John Ward, who liked the colt's straight legs and thought he was an unusually good example of a Mr. Prospector. But ultimately, if Sekiguchi is to be believed, it was a feeling that prompted him to reach into his pocket so deeply.

Satish Sanan, who had been one of the underbidders on Fusaichi Pegasus that hot afternoon in July 1998, knew that feeling well. If he had obeyed it to the exclusion of all good sense that day, he would already own a Derby winner. Instead, three years later, he was sitting in the Saratoga sale pavilion trying to buy another chance. Roger King had fought him off for the first horse on his short list, and now Sanan was waiting for his next candidate to come into the auction ring. In the plush seats around him, other owners were flipping through catalogs, leaning over to listen to the urgent whispers of their bloodstock advisers and trainers, or staring tensely ahead at the pale green tanbark behind the ropes where the next yearling would stand.

"When two people hook up, there is no logic, you know," Sanan said. "There is no logic at all. It's love. It's ego. I don't know why, but you just get stupid."

Sanan was determined not to get stupid at Saratoga, and that was one reason he had reined himself in when the bidding got hot for Hip 3. But there was another colt selling on the third and final night that represented an excellent opportunity for throwing caution to the wind.

And there was caution. The colt on Sanan's list was a popular selection due to his good looks and his breeding. He was an athletic-looking son of Seattle Slew, who at the age of 27 was becoming too frail to remain an active stud for much longer, a fact that would drive the price up on his few remaining foals—especially one that resembled him as clearly as this colt did. The colt's dam, Strawberry Reason, was a stakes winner herself, but she was only nine years old and had not yet proven that she would produce successful runners. This was her third foal, and the two born before him, though both winners, were still too young to give much indication of the colt's total genetic quality.

And, worryingly, there were some whispers on the sale ground that the colt was not quite as well made as he should be, that his ankles were suspect, that in fact he might not be sound enough to make it to the races at all.

One of those critics, Sanan knew, was his former trainer, D. Wayne Lukas. Lukas's snipes against a colt he knew Sanan liked were irritating, but they couldn't be discounted.

Before the sale's final session, Sanan met with his selection team, a group that included the two former Lukas assistants, a veterinarian, and Sanan's daughter, Nadia. The team members worked according to a rating system on which 10 was an exceptionally superior athlete, and the Seattle Slew colt scored consistently at seven or above on each team member's list.

Sanan knew that other buyers as wealthy as he was certainly had scored the colt high on their own systems, and it was possible that some of the chat about the ankles was designed to deflect other bidders. But if there really was something wrong with the colt's ankles, it was better to know it now. Sanan asked his vet, Dr. Bob Bloomer, to examine the colt's X-rays and the ankles themselves for a second time.

"He came back and said there was nothing wrong," Sanan said. "There was no dissension within the team, it was all just coming from the outside. Wayne and a couple of other people who weren't on the team were just taking shots at it."

• • •

By the time the auction's final session began at 7:30 P.M. on August 9, a sweltering heat wave had broken in violent thunderstorms. Bidders who normally lined the barn area and walking ring outside the pavilion crammed inside to escape the blustery weather, and power was out all over town, leaving Saratoga's restaurants, bars, and houses in the dark for the rest of the night. Fasig-Tipton's arena also was buffeted by the storm. Its lights flickered on and off, then died entirely just as the first horse walked in. The hushed crowd waited in the dark for two minutes until Fasig-Tipton's staff could switch to a generator, and when the lights came on again the sale got under way, the auctioneer's patter competing with the wind and rain that lashed against the pavilion windows.

But the weather didn't dampen the auction, even though a few major buyers—King and Sanan among them—had already headed out of Saratoga, leaving their bidding in the capable hands of their agents.

Sanan's Padua Stables team, headed by Nadia Sanan on the phone to her father, warmed up with a few easy purchases, buying two colts and two fillies for a total of $750,000, far less than several of their rivals were paying for single horses. The ruthless bidders from Coolmore Stud, who had lost out the night before on a $3.6 million Storm Cat colt that went to Dubai's crown prince, Sheikh Mohammed al-Maktoum, came back on the last night to win a $3 million colt by the fashionable young sire Kingmambo. This time, Sheikh Mohammed's man, John Ferguson, was the loser after a long bidding duel. Ferguson surrendered only after taking a long, final look at the Kingmambo colt from over the pavilion's balcony rail, and then he shook his head grimly, frowned, and let Coolmore have him. That was one less potential Derby runner for Maktoum, one of four sporting brothers from Dubai who had dominated European racing but had never won the Kentucky Derby. Like Sanan, Sheikh Mohammed had made the Kentucky Derby his primary target, and it would be painful if the Kingmambo colt turned out to be the one that got away.

Nadia Sanan, meanwhile, had a problem. Now that their top choice was nearing his entrance into the ring, her cell phone wasn't working. The storm, the multiplicity of competing cell-phone signals on the grounds—it didn't matter why, but with the Seattle Slew colt's sale imminent, Nadia couldn't contact her father as planned.

The sale rocketed on. Bob Baffert, a two-time Derby-winning trainer, signed for another $3 million colt by Mr. Prospector but coyly declined to admit that the purchase was for his major client, Saudi Arabian prince Ahmed bin Salman, the son of Riyadh's governor. The photographers and notebook-wielding reporters were still trying to tease that information out of Baffert when another colt stepped into the ring and promptly shot up to $600,000, with $100,000 bids still coming as regularly as the ticks of a clock.

It was the Seattle Slew colt, but Nadia Sanan was nowhere to be seen. The Sanan family's seats in the pavilion's lower level were empty.

In the company's administrative offices behind the pavilion, Fasig-Tipton executive Boyd Browning interrupted his conversation with one of Prince Ahmed's agents and turned to look at a closed-circuit television set. Seeing the Seattle Slew colt turning calmly in the ring as the bids escalated, Browning excused himself and, dodging tourists and idle bidders running through the rain, dashed across to the pavilion and up the stairs to its balcony. Browning had arranged a contingency plan for Nadia and wanted to make sure she had gotten there in time.

The Seattle Slew colt's price reached $1.4 million. One of the players appeared to be bidding invisibly from somewhere upstairs, where a spotter could relay the raises but the general public, searching the gallery faces for a telltale nod or mouthed word, couldn't pinpoint their origin. The invisible bidder offered $1.5 million.

Browning smiled to himself. It was Nadia, bidding from a phone very few people even knew about, located in the price-board operator's booth in the back of the balcony. Crouched behind the operator's chair, her handbag perched atop the sound board, Nadia was on his telephone line to her father, and she had just bid up to their agreed limit. Her brief now was to do the thing her father couldn't do: stop.

"We're out," she told him as someone braving the rain outside the pavilion countered with $1.6 million.

"Bid fifty," Sanan told her. "Don't stop or I'll call someone from Fasig-Tipton and get them to do it for me."

The price climbed. John Ferguson, inside the pavilion, offered $2 million, and auctioneer Robertson promptly asked for $2.1 million. There were no takers. Robertson asked for $2,050,000, sliding his eyes in the direction of the booth. Nadia gave it.

Suddenly, the anonymous bidder outside the pavilion jumped back in, bidding $2.1 million. It appeared to be a final offer on his part, coming after a moment's reconsideration.

Nadia, resting her right elbow on the operator's chair and pressing the telephone receiver into her left ear, bid $2.15 million on her father's instruction.

The Seattle Slew colt flicked his ears back and forth from Robertson's rapid-fire chanting behind him to the bid-spotter's yelps in front of him. Like his father, he was a plain, dark brown color with no visible white, but his shoulders, back, and hips sparkled here and there with the raindrops he had walked through on the way from his barn. His elegant head was refined, with a bright, intelligent eye that was eerily reminiscent of his powerful sire's. But there was no answering bid from the party outside.

The hammer came down with a sharp crack, and Satish Sanan had his horse, the last million-dollar horse sold at Saratoga in 2001. Nadia's slender, olive-skinned arm emerged from the booth to collect the receipt.

The session was almost over, and buyers were beginning to leave the pavilion. The last few sale yearlings, soaked with the torrential rain, passed through the ring, and many of the horsey set huddled miserably under the building's eaves as valets wheeled a line of glistening Cadillac SUV's and Jaguars up to the entrance. Thunder rattled the pavilion windows again, and Fasig-Tipton announcer Terence Collier told the crowd that, sadly, Siro's restaurant, the traditional post-sale nightspot, was out of power like the rest of Saratoga.

It was the only bad news of the night. The explosive final session had made the 2001 Fasig-Tipton Saratoga select yearling sale the most profitable auction in the company's 103-year history. Of the 162 unbroken young horses that rang up $62 million in the three nights from August 7-9, nine brought final bids of $1 million or more from their hopeful new owners.

A year and a half later, most of those owners would still be awaiting a payoff, any payoff, in their expensive horses' careers. The nine millionaire yearlings—eight colts and one filly—overwhelmingly would illustrate the various setbacks, disappointments, and bafflements that are typical in the racing game. If they had the kind of talent, endurance, and luck it would take to become home run horses, the vast majority had not yet shown it after their first year at the track.

By the end of 2002 one of the millionaire colts was laid up at a California training center with a cracked knee, never having even run in a workout, let alone a race. One had been sent to England, where he earned a little more than $13,000 on a $3 million initial investment. A third was also in England, winless, and had earned just $1,275. The fourth was in America, where he finished fourth in his only race, picking up a check for $1,000. Number five, named Athlete, had yet to enter a race. Another, given the more realistic name Strong Hope, also was unraced. And yet another had been plagued by hoof trouble and was sidelined at a farm, with no starts or workouts to his credit. The sole filly on the list, a $2 million yearling sent to race in Canada, had done considerably better, winning a stakes race, placing in a Grade 1 contest, and bringing in $174,270.

But only one of the nine horses would emerge as a true home run horse in 2002. As the others struggled, he would be named a champion. He would be celebrated as the early favorite for the 2003 Kentucky Derby. Months before he turned 3, his breeding rights already would be valued at $24 million—more than 10 times what his owner paid for him.

Bidding rivals Roger King and Satish Sanan would be on opposite sides of this equation, one a loser and one a winner by the end of 2002.

But that was more than a year away. On August 9, 2001, a few of Saratoga's buyers, animated by the night's events, lingered in Fasig-Tipton's covered bar behind the pavilion, then gradually filtered home through the dark streets. Behind them, humming along on a generator and the electrifying bids of gambling billionaires, the lights still blazed at Fasig-Tipton.

Roger King was long gone, having flown out the day before on another expedition to Las Vegas. Satish Sanan hung up the phone with Nadia and idly ran possible names for his new horses through his mind. He hit upon a good one for his Seattle Slew colt with the "suspect" ankles that, it appeared, someone else had wanted badly enough to bid the price up to $2.15 million. Sanan decided that if the colt showed promise, he would name him Vindication.

2 The Payoff

FOURTEEN MONTHS AFTER the 2001 Saratoga yearling sale, Satish Sanan was exactly where he had hoped he would be: standing by the rail at Arlington International Racecourse near Chicago, awaiting Vindication.

Sanan's $2.15 million purchase had indeed vindicated his owner's judgment, even if he hadn't quite paid for himself. The Seattle Slew colt had won all three of his 2-year-old races, and had done it with ease, motoring past his rivals with the assurance that warms an owner's heart. Those victories had earned Vindication $124,550 and a ticket to the $1 million Breeders' Cup Juvenile, the season-ending showdown for the best horses of his age group. It was the kind of thing that made the hair stand up on the back of an owner's neck. How good was this colt? If Vindication won the Juvenile, he would be the obvious choice to be named the year's 2-year-old champion, and that title, plus a Breeders' Cup victory, would certify him as a home run horse already, even before he got to the Kentucky Derby. Which would, of course, be the target in 2003.

The Breeders' Cup Juvenile would almost automatically identify the early favorite for the Derby, despite the fact that in the relatively brief history of the Breeders' Cup, no Juvenile winner had gone on to win the roses. Open only to 2-year-old males, it was just one of eight races worth a total of $13 million at the Breeders' Cup World Thoroughbred Championships, and it wasn't even considered the highlight. The featured event was the Classic, whose $4 million purse made it one of the world's richest races. The Classic, open to 3-year-olds and up, and contested over the Kentucky Derby distance of 1 ¼ miles, had been designed as an opportunity to test racing's top horses—including, organizers always hoped, the current Derby winner—against each other. The Juvenile, by contrast, was designed to identify rising stars. It did so from its first running in 1984, when third-place finisher Spend a Buck won the following season's Derby, and Juvenile runner-up Tank's Prospect took the Preakness.

The Breeders' Cup Juvenile is well worth winning. The winner's share of the purse in 2002 exceeded $556,000. More importantly, a colt who wins the race also jumps substantially in value. The victory goes, as it were, on his permanent record, where it serves as priceless advertising to breeders that this horse was good enough to beat the best in the world in his first racing season, a fact that does not change even if he never runs another step. Winning the Breeders' Cup Juvenile gives proof of combined precocity and class, a blend that is highly prized in today's commercial Thoroughbred world.

Vindication was good enough, sound enough, and fortunate enough to make it to Chicago for the Breeders' Cup Juvenile late in October. There he faced 13 rivals, a mixed bag of runners who reflected the vagaries of racing and breeding. Four of the entrants were bred by their owners and never went to auction, but the rest represented a great economic swath. The millionaire horses were there in force, thanks mostly to Coolmore Stud and its associate, Michael Tabor, who owned three million-dollar entrants in the race: $6.4 million Van Nistelrooy, a Storm Cat colt who had been the most expensive yearling of 2001; Hold That Tiger, another Storm Cat colt that they had bought for $1.1 million as a weanling; and a Seattle Slew colt named Tomahawk that cost $2.5 million. Tabor also owned Zavata, a relative bargain he had bought for $575,000 at a 2-year-old sale early in the year.

But there were other, far less expensive runners. There was Whywhywhy, who brought $27,000 as a yearling, failed to reach his reserve price, and finally was sold privately. Most Feared, almost 30-1 for the race, was the product of a nearly unknown Texas stallion named Commanchero and a mare that had once sold for $3,900 in New Mexico. And there was Vindication, about whom Satish Sanan cherished a deep conviction: Finally, this one—surely—would be the horse.

But Vindication was not the horse to beat in the Breeders' Cup Juvenile. The favorite was another colt who was undefeated in three races and whose bloodlines were impeccable. His sire was the young stallion Pulpit, a son of the highly successful sire and 1992 Horse of the Year A.P. Indy and once a leading contender for the Derby himself. His dam was the Storm Cat mare Caress, who earned almost $700,000 and had sold recently for $3.1 million. The colt's name also made him sound like the star of a Western epic: Sky Mesa.

Sky Mesa's three wins had come against much tougher competition than Vindication's had. He already had won a Grade 1 stakes, and his earnings when he arrived at Arlington were $416,576, about four times higher than Vindication's. Like Satish Sanan's colt, Sky Mesa was gunning for a championship title in the Breeders' Cup. If he won, the valuable 2-year-old crown would certainly be his. And Sky Mesa's owner, Oklahoma oilman John Oxley, was every bit as eager to point for the Derby as Sanan was. Oxley knew what it was like to win America's greatest horse race, the numbing rush that made you feel as if you were levitating from your box seat to the winner's circle, the surprising heft of the blanket of roses that you held when your winner retired to the barn, the deep sense of historic moment and dignity when Kentucky's governor raised a champagne toast to you, the winner of the Kentucky Derby. Oxley had won the race in 2001 with Monarchos, a gray colt who was now standing at stud at Claiborne Farm, which was also home to Pulpit.

The man who had trained Oxley's Derby winner was John Ward, a weatherbeaten Kentuckian who was also handling Sky Mesa's campaign. Ward, the same man who had advised Fusao Sekiguchi to purchase 2000 Derby winner Fusaichi Pegasus, had helped Oxley select Sky Mesa from the Keeneland September yearling sale. Oxley had paid $750,000 for Sky Mesa, and, as the horses spun around Arlington's racetrack in the last few days of training for the

Breeders' Cup Juvenile, it looked as if he had gotten a better deal than Sanan had on Vindication.

But near dawn on the morning before the race, as Ward was starting his day in the barn, he noticed that his stable star looked a little light on his right front leg. It wasn't exactly lameness, more a shift of balance. But it was the kind of change that sends a shudder down a trainer's spine. Ward unwrapped the protective bandages that Sky Mesa regularly wore in his stall, and, sure enough, the leg was slightly swollen on both sides just above the ankle. With the race just one day away, Ward knew what he had to do.

At 7:00 A.M., he called Oxley's room at the Four Seasons Hotel in Chicago and recommended they scratch the favorite from the Breeders' Cup Juvenile. It was a bitter pill, but the decision was in many ways an easy one. In the first place, they couldn't risk ruining the colt by running him. Second, Sky Mesa already had proven himself to be championship caliber. And, after all, the big prize was the Kentucky Derby. It was as much a business decision as a sporting one.

"Sky Mesa is definitely a 'big horse' already," Ward said later that morning. "Missing this race is a blip in his career. He's already established himself as a major candidate for breeding. He's already won his Grade 1. In the eyes of the economic side of our business, he has cleared all the major hurdles. People who breed horses and pay money for these horses, if a horse misses the championship series, so what? That happens to all of them down the line. It doesn't diminish their ability. If he turns out to never race again, then it would be a problem. But, right now, this horse goes into next year as one of the co-favorites for the classics on the basis of what he's already done. Our main consideration is getting him back on the Derby trail in the spring.

"He's a big horse because opportunities still remain with him and he's cleared all the financial hurdles. When you're racing, unless you are just the truest of true sportsmen—and I'm not sure there are many of those left in the world—winning and economics are hand in hand. When you lose, economics go to a negative indicator. There's a double reward in racing now for winning. At this point, we're playing in the Thoroughbred game to invest for development and either resale or future stud value.

"But anybody new in the business, we are very frank with them," he added. "We tell them exactly what can happen. We tell them that tragedies do happen and this is a business of ups and downs. We try to lay it out to them as hard and as cold as we can, so they're not surprised. We make hard phone calls all the time. It can be, 'Your horse pulled up bad this morning,' or 'Your horse got a cut,' or 'This horse doesn't have any talent.' If they moan and groan and don't like it, they're not going to be around long in this business."

Now, Ward and Oxley were just interested onlookers for the Juvenile. The race's outcome might affect Sky Mesa's shot at the season's 2-year-old championship, but it wouldn't alter much else for him. On the other hand, Sky Mesa's late scratch from the race opened up a new opportunity for everyone else in the Juvenile. And that opportunity was tangible in financial terms, as every owner and trainer knew very well.

"If you look at all the Breeders' Cup races, the Juvenile creates the biggest financial swing of any of the races," Ward said. "In other words, if you win the Classic, you win a big purse, but it's not going to affect the value of the animal that much, because their value is pretty much set by then. The winner of the Juvenile Fillies doesn't usually go up that much in value off that race, because how many winners of the Juvenile Fillies have gone on to be syndicated for $25 million? In all the other races, the winners will increase some in value if you appraise them. But the biggest increase by far will be the winner of the juvenile colts' race. Because it's a one-race championship. A horse can go from being a horse that has just won his first race to being the champion, in one race."

While John Ward was rewrapping Sky Mesa's legs and putting his 2003 Kentucky Derby contender on the shelf for the rest of the season, trainer Bob Baffert was sending Vindication around the track for his final pre-Juvenile exercise. It was a cold, raw morning. Overnight rains had beaten the track into sludge, and red-faced trainers huddled along the rails, hands deep in their coat pockets and hats pulled low.

"I'm colder than a well-digger's ass," Baffert complained, hunching into his leather jacket. His cowboy boots left damp impressions in the path as he followed Vindication from the barn to the race-track.

But the dark bay colt seemed to be thriving in the damp chill. He bounced along, head up and ears alert. His back legs were wrapped in royal-blue racing bandages secured with a couple of bands of light blue tape, which gave him a sporty, race-car look. His groom had carefully braided Vindication's tail and wrapped it up tightly in a "mud knot," to keep it out of the gritty slop of the race-track, and that emphasized the hard, round muscles of the colt's hindquarters. His coat was a deep, glossy brown and gleamed with good health even in the dull weather. Vindication splashed merrily along through the puddles on the horse path, then, with his rider standing up in the irons, he trotted onto the racetrack.

Watching his colt from the paved apron by the grandstand rail, Satish Sanan was impervious to the piercing breeze. Standing in an excited crowd of a half-dozen friends and family members, Sanan beamed as he and Baffert watched Vindication go by.

"This guy looks like Seattle Slew," Baffert said. "He's like a clone of his dad."

Sanan's smile widened. "He *does* look remarkably like Seattle Slew," he agreed.

The group grew hushed as Vindication became smaller and smaller, jogging away from them. He eventually picked up a gallop, gliding smoothly across the muddy racing strip, just stretching his legs. When the colt finally pulled up, a passerby who also had stopped to watch shook hands with Sanan and wished him luck.

"Thank you, we'll need it," Sanan said, giving the man's hand a vigorous pump. "You always need it."

That was true, Baffert agreed. Look at Sky Mesa. He shook his head. "That's why you can't get excited about them until you lead them over there to run," he said. "You can't brag on them. You've got to get them there."

Another of Baffert's clients, had he been there to hear the remark, would have known exactly what Baffert meant. Roger King, who had outbid Sanan to buy Saratoga's Hip Number 3 for $1.85 million, did not have a horse in the Breeders' Cup Juvenile. Hip 3, the Unbridled's Song-Win Crafty Lady colt, was now known as Mister C's Song. But he was not yet known as a racehorse.

"He came in from the training farm, and something just wasn't right with him," Baffert said of King's colt. "So we backed off on him. At first, we couldn't find anything wrong with him, and sure enough, he finally blew out a huge abscess. He's just coming back now. I don't know what to think about him. We barely got to work him, and then I had to give him the summer off, so he's barely back to galloping now. But he should be a nice horse.

"He's a *beautiful* horse," he added. "You know, these 2-year-olds, they just get little things. You know, some horses are lucky and some aren't lucky. Some take a little bit longer, and some it seems like they just come around quick. Some horses never get sick, they never get sore shins, there's just something about the way they're made that things like that don't happen to them."

Vindication pranced off the track again on his way home. His easy gallop seemed to have made him feel stronger. Baffert liked what he saw.

"So far, this one's never missed a day at work," he said, nodding his head toward Vindication. "He's been a really good horse, and I've been fortunate with him. I think he's slowly becoming a paparazzi horse. He's getting some followers. But he has to prove himself, come Saturday."

Breeders' Cup Day dawned bleak, wet, and cold. Tour buses lumbered by industrial buildings that bordered Arlington International Racecourse's stable area, passing stolid brick-fronted storehouses and factories that bore names like Vonberg Valve and Midwest Insert Composite Molding and Assembly Company.

The track's grandstand rose like a monument over the neighborhood, modern and glassy, decorated on Breeders' Cup Day with the snapping flags of many nations, meant to symbolize the international competition on the race card. Arlington, too, was part of an industry, just of a flashier kind. The Breeders' Cup would generate more than $115,500,000 in wagers, both on track and around the country through simulcast outlets. Breeders' Cup Ltd., which put on the event each year at a different North American racetrack, would give out $13 million in purses to the runners in 2002. The horses, their owners and trainers, racing fans, jockeys—all were cogs in the system that made the hefty yearling-sale prices and stud fees possible. As hard as it was to imagine in the bleak light of that morning, Breeders' Cup 2002 really would be a crowning moment for the winners.

On the backstretch at 10:30 A.M., all was quiet, except for the splash of hose water on horses' legs and the scrape of rakes around shedrows. Veterinarians made their rounds, giving injections of two legal medications: phenylbutazone, an anti-inflammatory used to relieve minor soreness in joints and muscles, and furosemide, a diuretic thought to prevent small blood vessels in the respiratory system from rupturing when a horse runs. An old groom with a drooping gray handlebar mustache grunted and heaved a sweet-smelling forkful of straw and muck into a green metal Dumpster between two barns. In a stall nearby, a young Hispanic groom knelt down by a horse's right knee, holding three large safety pins between his teeth as he wrapped a bandage. A sharp tapping noise came from a farrier somewhere, and exercise riders, still wearing their helmets, were soaping saddles and bridles, their hands bare and wet in the cold morning air.

It was business as usual in the barns, but there was a hum of excitement about the upcoming Breeders' Cup races. Band music wafted out of the clubhouse and a white limousine cruised past the stable gate on its way to the track's entrance.

"It's all over now but the running," one trainer said, rubbing his hands together. "Here we go."

An owner wearing Gucci loafers and a black cashmere coat picked his way along the sticky mud of the horse path, heading from the barns to the clubhouse. The horse paths were scarred with a thousand hoofprints heading in every direction. He delicately sidestepped a pile of fresh manure, then looked up and smiled at a passerby.

"You have to walk through a lot of horse shit to get to the winner's circle," he said.

No one knew this better than Satish Sanan, the man who had spent $100 million to come up with a handful of good horses. The reason he got into racing in the first place, back when he was a student living in the YMCA in Liverpool, England, was because he loved to gamble. Now that he was an immensely wealthy man, he could gamble on a higher level, and the rewards were greater.

"I own horses because I love this game, I really do," he said. "I love to go to the track. This is the only place where I forget everything. When I'm at the track, it's the only time I forget business. It's escapism.

"Thoroughbred racing, when you win a race, the high you get from that, you won't get that anywhere else. You can go to a casino and sit all night and gamble, and I do those things, too, but nothing compares to racing. It's a thrill. It's the best two minutes of adrenaline that I've ever found. I've sat all night at a casino and gambled away hundreds of thousands of dollars, and you just don't get the same thrill. I think it's the horses, and it's just the competitive nature of the game. It's not like poker, it's not like baccarat, you're not just sitting at a table. You have different variables come into it: different trainers, different horses, conditions, and so on. There are so many variables, so to go out there and win one is something, especially a big one."

Sanan had one Breeders' Cup winner back in 1999, when one of his first horses, Cash Run, won the Juvenile Fillies. He'd had six others run in Breeders' Cup races, including three in the Juvenile, but to no avail. Sanan said that his early success with Cash Run and a handful of other stakes-winning 2-year-olds lulled him into thinking, as he put it, "Shit, this game is easy."

It wasn't just hubris that made him hit a dry spell soon afterward, Sanan thought. He felt he had gotten dragged off his original business plan for the Thoroughbred operation, mainly by spending far too much money for horses that didn't suit his ultimate strategy, to develop a broodmare band.

"And an awful lot of it had to do with Wayne," he said, referring to trainer D. Wayne Lukas. "He is just an eternal optimist, and, Jesus, you sit with him, he'll sell you anything. Every year, you buy horses, and every year he'll tell you you've got the Triple Crown winner, you're going to hit home runs. We did hit some, but it was at great cost.

"We learned our lesson," Sanan continued. "We thought you could just go spend a lot of money and buy the best horses. If that was true, then the Maktoum brothers would own racing worldwide. They would have won the Triple Crown, but they still haven't won the Derby. You simply can't do that, and that's why you love this game: It's so unpredictable. You can win whether you buy a horse for $20,000 or $2,000,000. But we got a little bit cocky and thought that we could do that."

Vindication was well past the high end of that range, but, on the other hand, here he was. One of the favorites for the Breeders' Cup Juvenile. On the brink of a championship. A stallion prospect potentially worth tens of millions.

"We wanted this horse," Sanan said. "I do have a feeling about this horse. I don't want to jinx it, but we've paid our dues in this game, and I think this probably is our time. But we'll need a little racing luck. The odds are against you. But it's unlike any other business, even though we're running it as a business. In business, if you want to spend $5 million, I have seven VP's go through the deal and I put them through the wringer. At the sales, we spend $20 million in two days and I don't blink an eyelid. It's about passion and love, and that's the reason you do it."

The race went exactly as Sanan had hoped. Vindication shot out of the gate and onto the lead, winging through the first quarter-mile in 23.29 seconds, the half-mile in 46.11, three-quarters in 1:09.98. His stablemate Bull Market briefly headed him as they rolled into the homestretch, but jockey Mike Smith let Vindication out another notch, and they glided past Bull Market. Vindication's stride was as fluid and graceful as wind rippling across silk, and he seemed to be running almost without effort. When he reached the finish line, he had easily put nearly three lengths of daylight between himself and runner-up Kafwain, another Baffert trainee. Of the other million-dollar yearlings in the race, Hold That Tiger, the least expensive at $1.1 million, finished third; Van Nistelrooy, the $6.4 million colt, was fifth, while $2.5 million Tomahawk was eighth.

A month later, Satish Sanan closed a deal with Hill 'n' Dale Farm in Lexington, Kentucky, to syndicate Vindication upon his eventual retirement from racing. The Sanan family kept what they termed "a majority interest" in the colt's breeding rights with an eye toward mating some of their growing broodmare band with him. The deal, according to bloodstock agents in the know, put 2-year-old Vindication's total value at $24 million.

The stud deal for Vindication was sizable but not startling. Twenty years earlier, when a bidding war over 1982 Belmont Stakes winner Conquistador Cielo resulted in a record $36.4 million syndication—almost $1 million per share—*that* had been startling. But by the time Vindication came along, such prices were almost commonplace. Underpinning the swollen price tags were business practices that could nearly guarantee shareholders a quick out on almost any horse, within several years of his purchase for stud duty, sometimes even before his actual talent as a sire was fully revealed.

In 1982, stallions rarely covered more than 60 broodmares during the annual breeding season, which lasted approximately from mid-February until the first week of July. But in Vindication's era, farms and their veterinarians had come close to perfecting the business and science of stallion management. In the late 1980's and early 1990's, a few daring stud farms had begun pushing the accepted bounds of their trade, starting with the number of mares they booked to their stallions. That number crept upward to 70, then 80, and—shockingly, to some breeders' minds—past the 100 mark. By 2003, it had expanded beyond 175.

Some commercial mare owners were nervous about the big-book trend, fearing that stallion owners were going to flood the yearling market with their sires' get, thus devaluing the product and making it harder for individual sellers to make a profit. But from the shareholders' point of view, the more mares a stallion got, the better the bottom line. First, more mares meant more live foals, and—because most stud fees were paid only when mares gave birth to live foals who were able to stand and nurse—that meant more income. Second, the more foals a stallion had running for him at the racetrack, the better the chances of their racking up wins and earnings. Since the all-important stallion rankings were tallied according to total progeny earnings, horses that had large crops of runners owned a distinct advantage over those that didn't. Under this numbers game, a stallion with 50 average runners could still fare well against a horse that had sired a smaller crop and one top-notch winner.

To the new M.B.A.'s of stallion management, a major obstacle to increasing profits was the Thoroughbred business's traditional breeding season. The longstanding span from mid-February to early July was designed mainly to keep the production of race-horses orderly and eliminate age-related confusion once a runner got to the track. The Jockey Club, the breed registry for Thoroughbreds, mandates that all Thoroughbreds turn a year older on January 1, regardless of their actual birthdays. Equine gestation takes 11 months. So by operating on the mid-February to early July schedule, breeders ensure that foals are born between January and June, with ample time before they officially become yearlings on January 1 the following year. But under this seasonal system, stallion owners' main source of income was idle for half the year. It was as if a manufacturer hurriedly produced goods for six months, then shuttered his factory and twiddled his thumbs the rest of the year.

Two of the farms that blazed the way in mass production of foals, the Irish-owned Coolmore Stud (which has a branch called Ashford Stud in Kentucky) and a farm called Vinery, soon found a way around this. They reasoned that while stallions were growing fat and dappled in Kentucky's summertime paddocks, the horses in the Southern Hemisphere were gearing up to start their breeding season, and vice versa. And given the increase in international cargo shipment, there was no reason that Thoroughbred stallions couldn't start commuting to work for part of the year. This innovation, which carried racehorse breeding another step away from agriculture and toward industry, was met with some skepticism, and even outrage, by the more tradition-minded breeders. What about a stallion's health? Surely year-round breeding and the hardship of airline travel to Australia or South America and back would take a toll on fertility. But the trend was underway, and the fertility questions seemed to be answered by stallions' expanding books in each hemisphere.

Some breeders still refuse to shuttle stallions from one hemisphere to another, either because they disagree with the practice or because, at about $10,000 per horse, it is too costly for stallions with less marketability. But others have jumped into the global market, setting up profitable lease deals to send their stallions to the Southern Hemisphere. Coolmore now dominates the global shuttling market and has added an Australian stud farm—so has Vinery—effectively allowing stallions to travel a highly profitable circuit, all under a single brand name.

In 1984, when his first foals were born, Conquistador Cielo had 34 horses on the ground after being bred to between 45 and 55 mares the previous season. Two decades later, the busiest stallion in the world was the Coolmore sire Giant's Causeway. In 2002, he was bred to 213 mares in America and 108 in Australia for a grand total of 321. Such a number had never even seemed physically possible before, especially considering that the ruling bodies in both North America and Australia do not allow artificial insemination.

In strictly financial terms, Giant's Causeway's 321-mare season had been hugely profitable. His American stud fee was $135,000, for potential gross income of $28,755,000 in the Northern Hemisphere alone. He stood in Australia for a record stud fee of 137,500 Australian dollars, or about $104,000. For the full year of breeding, if all his mares produced live foals, Giant's Causeway could rake in nearly $39,987,000 for Coolmore. And they have 40 other stallions standing at farms in Ireland, Kentucky, and Australia.

As of 2004, Coolmore owned the world record for a total syndication value. When Japanese businessman Fusao Sekiguchi decided to put his Kentucky Derby winner, Fusaichi Pegasus, on the stallion market, Coolmore joined the bidding and quickly hammered its rivals under its crushing financial power. The Irish-based conglomerate bought a controlling interest in the 3-year-old Mr. Prospector colt, and though it did not disclose either its percentage or the price, insiders close to the deal confirmed that, under it, the horse's total syndication value was hovering around $60 million.

To professionals in other businesses who read that headline over breakfast the next day, the deal seemed outrageous, built to collapse under its own expense. How could any horse be worth $60 million? But in 2001, his first year at stud, Fusaichi Pegasus covered 274 mares in the Northern and Southern Hemispheres for total potential income of $32,859,000, assuming that all mare owners paid the full stud fee and that all the foals were born alive. Under the industrial economics of the modern stallion business, a horse could indeed be worth $60 million, based as always on that ephemeral notion of potential. And potential is an especially strong aphrodisiac for stallion investors during a yearling-market boom. When prices soar for elite yearlings, owners of elite stallions happily bump up their stud fees, and income grows. All of which makes it more expensive to buy a hot young stallion prospect, leading to bigger syndication values. The cycle rolls on, spilling money as it goes—unless the stallion's foals don't sell or can't run, or the stallion dies an untimely death early in his career.

With its stallion shuttles and mare books the size of the Manhattan phone directory, the new world of international Thoroughbred breeding has made it easier for investors to make money faster from their stallions. Before, stallion owners had to sell their first-year studs hard, then wait and worry during the three years it took the horse's first crop of foals to be conceived, born, and eventually put in the starting gate as 2-year-olds. Stallion owners still have to sell their unproven first-year stallions aggressively. But with the new business practices, many can recoup their initial investment in a stallion even before his first runners make a name for themselves, or soon afterward. If a horse's first runners do not appear to be good enough to keep him among the nation's top sires for the next few years, a syndicate can opt to sell the stallion quickly, before his value drops further, to a smaller or foreign market.

Vindication would arrive on the market at an opportune time, from the moneymaking point of view. But Sanan and Hill 'n' Dale Farm would not set the colt's stud fee until he retired from the racetrack, and his first-year fee would be influenced by the issue foremost in their minds: how Vindication would perform on the Triple Crown trail.

Trainer Bob Baffert knew how to get to the Derby. Better yet, he knew how to get to the winner's circle. In late December, people started pestering him about Vindication's next start, but Baffert was coy.

"When he's ready, I'll put him in a race," he told a *Daily Racing Form* reporter who stopped by the barn. "I just want to gradually get him ready. I want to keep his mind level."

Baffert had good reason to worry about Vindication's state of mind. The colt's sire, Seattle Slew, had been notoriously temperamental, a characteristic that made gearing a racehorse up for a high-stakes campaign like the Triple Crown that much harder. Baffert, like any trainer with a potential Triple Crown candidate, needed his horse to stay tranquil and unpressured. From his vantage point at California's Santa Anita Park in December, the path to the Derby loomed ahead like a treacherous stretch of whitewater that could buffet Vindication physically and mentally. It was Baffert's job to keep him in the calm shallows as much as possible while preparing the colt to run, and, as Baffert put it, "I don't want to jinx myself by bragging on him."

On New Year's Eve, Baffert gave the colt a three-furlong workout at Santa Anita, more or less to blow the dust off him and start his 2003 campaign. Vindication worked four more times over the next few weeks, and then on January 25 he fired off a work so sharp—five furlongs in 58.40—that Baffert was inclined to give him more than his usual seven days off between fast workouts. Baffert also rearranged the colt's daily exercise schedule. He started sending his champion out at 6:30 in the morning instead of 9:00. The alterations were small but significant, and they made people suspect that something might be wrong with Vindication. This suggestion got Baffert's hackles up, but he said little about Vindication's plans, except to reveal that the colt would probably make only two starts before the Derby.

"Vindication is a light horse, and he gets wound up," Baffert said. "I don't want to wind him up too early. I can train one up to a race. I don't have to run him into shape. Believe me, I know what I'm doing."

No one doubted Baffert's ability to get a horse to Churchill Downs on the first Saturday in May. But the Derby campaign is on an infamously tight schedule. Even small problems can bump a horse hopelessly off the path. And by early February, Vindication had run into trouble. He had, it turned out, bruised a hoof shortly after his blazing January 25 workout and missed a few days of training. He returned to the racetrack for a couple of mornings in the first week of February, and then he turned up with swelling in his left foreleg that proved to be a suspensory-ligament injury.

It was not a life-threatening problem, and to anyone standing around in Baffert's shedrow it probably wouldn't have seemed that anything was out of the ordinary. But the complicated and delicate mechanism that is a young racehorse had, in fact, gone badly awry. When Baffert heard the diagnosis from his vet—that Vindication had injured a suspensory ligament, part of the lower leg's crucial apparatus—he knew that the colt now had no chance at making the Kentucky Derby or indeed any of the Triple Crown races. The veterinarian confirmed Baffert's suspicion: Vindication would need two months out of training, then a reassessment of the ligament by ultrasound.

Vindication, an undefeated champion rippling with muscular good health, a colt who had been breezing powerfully toward his eagerly anticipated Derby bid, went back into his stall for 60 days of rest.

The Derby was only three months away. The timing was not just terrible. It was irreparable.

The injury, fortunately, was not irreparable, though it would keep Vindication off the track through the full Triple Crown season. The Sanans, hoping to salvage an autumn campaign that would culminate in the $4 million Breeders' Cup Classic, immediately set to work on Vindication's recuperation.

Between February and June, the colt underwent extraordinary treatments, including stem-cell therapy. He stood for prescribed periods in the enormous enclosed capsule of a hyperbaric oxygen chamber that research had shown might speed healing. Finally, he returned to Padua's training center in Summerfield, Florida, where he started light training again. On June 5—two days before Vindication would have been running in the Belmont Stakes, had he stayed sound—the Sanans issued a cheerful press release noting that their champion was "training forwardly" for his ultimate goal in the Breeders' Cup. The leg looked "perfect," the colt had "never looked better in his life," and "we couldn't be more pleased with him right now."

Vindication never ran again. He returned briefly to Baffert's barn in the summer, but by August both Baffert and Sanan knew that they had run out of time to make the Breeders' Cup. Besides, the colt's stud plans were already set. Realistically, no one wanted to risk losing a race now, because that likely would tarnish breeders' perceptions of Vindication, a problem that would affect the stud fee Sanan and Hill 'n' Dale could ask.

Missing the Classic was a hard blow for Sanan, who had already seen his Derby hopes derailed.

The next phase of Vindication's career would be less glamorous than a run for the roses would have been, but, on the other hand, it would be far more profitable. Hill 'n' Dale set the colt's 2004 stud fee at $50,000. Their advertising emphasized that though Vindication's career had been brief, he had never been beaten and had won one of the world's toughest races, the Breeders' Cup Juvenile, in crushing style.

Vindication had a lot going for him. His conformation was good, he was a son of a highly successful stallion, and he did have a sparkling, if short, resume. There was every reason to think the colt would have a big start at stud—especially when you considered that horses who had stirred far less interest had gone on to do great things as stallions. Storm Cat, North America's most expensive stud, was one of those, and Sanan, like countless other hopeful stallion owners, could take inspiration from his story.

Storm Cat is indisputably the current king of Thoroughbred stallions. At age 21, he commands a $500,000 fee for every breeding session, more than most people pay for their houses. In 2003, Storm Cat—who is too valuable to risk on a shuttle and stays at Overbrook Farm in Lexington all year—bred 116 mares, which would have resulted in a total income of $58 million for the year, if all of those breeders had paid his stud fee. Not all of them did. In 1999, when the stallion was 16 years old, his owner, W. T. Young, a shrewd Kentucky businessman and self-made multimillionaire, wisely sold Coolmore an undisclosed number of lifetime breeding rights to Storm Cat.

"It made good economic sense with this stallion," explained Ric Waldman, the bloodstock adviser who has managed Storm Cat throughout the horse's stud career. "It minimizes the exposure one has when owning 100 percent of a stallion. As he ages, the insurance on him becomes more and more costly and eventually becomes unaffordable."

The price of Coolmore's lifetime breeding rights was not disclosed, but lifetime breeding rights for the stallion's remaining days would obviously have been worth millions, given his stud fee and fabulous progeny record, both in the sale ring—where Coolmore's principals themselves continue to drive Storm Cat's average up by bidding exorbitant amounts on his yearlings—and on the racetrack.

It wasn't always this way. Young, who died in early 2004, had had the satisfaction of watching Storm Cat go from an unpopular stud prospect to one of the world's leading sires.

Storm Cat was a colt by Storm Bird, whose sire, Northern Dancer, was one of the era's most influential stallions. His dam was the Secretariat mare Terlingua, one of the first important horses that helped make trainer D. Wayne Lukas's name in the late 1970's. His breeding was quite good, and he wasn't a bad runner, either. At age 2, he was second in the 1985 Breeders' Cup Juvenile in a finish so close that Young went down to the winner's circle, only to discover there that Tasso had been declared the winner. Storm Cat won a Grade 1 race at 2, an important achievement for a future stallion in a modern market that prefers early-developing horses. He won half his eight lifetime starts and finished worse than third only once.

But Storm Cat's career stalled after an injury, and Young eventually retired him to Overbrook with little fanfare. By the time Storm Cat's first foals were born, he had been overshadowed by a brighter light in Young's racing stable. That was Grand Canyon, a 2-year-old colt in training with Lukas, and he appeared to be the real thing. In his first racing season, Grand Canyon won four races, including a pair of Grade 1 events, by a combined margin of more than 20 lengths. He looked like the second coming of Secretariat, and he was by the fashionable and lightning-fast stallion Fappiano, a perfect alignment for a future stallion career.

"Grand Canyon was one of the most exciting 2-year-olds in my memory, and the farm was trying to set up and prepare for his eventual retirement," Waldman remembered. "Little did we know, a few months later, he'd be dead."

At the end of his juvenile season, Grand Canyon developed laminitis, an intensely painful hoof disease. Overbrook had to have the colt put down. The farm, which had only just opened its stallion business, now looked to Storm Cat as its flagship stud. But breeders were wary of the horse. His 2-year-old record was good, but he had raced only twice at 3 due to injury, and then he never ran again. Breeders who came to look at Storm Cat in Lexington after his retirement saw something they thought might explain the brevity of his career. His legs were crooked, a flaw generally seen as contributing to unsoundness. If he passed that conformation on to his progeny, the foals would, breeders believed, be hard to sell.

"His conformation didn't leave the most favorable impression," Waldman acknowledged. "Now, we're more forgiving of that, because we see that those conformation traits we were so critical of have gone on to get good racehorses. No one knew then that they were looking at the prototype that would end up with those runners. Also, he had been injured, and then they attempted to run him at 3 and 4, so he didn't stand at stud until he was 5. So there was a long time between his top performances and when he retired. He was a difficult horse to create a following for."

Young called breeders with mares he thought would match his stallion well and offered them free seasons to Storm Cat, who was advertised with a $30,000 stud fee. He told others he would put up the stud fee in exchange for a half-interest in the resulting foal. He eventually dropped the stallion's fee to $20,000—still expensive by many standards, but well below what Storm Cat came to be worth.

"We did everything short of begging," said Waldman. "We had to be fairly creative in trying to get Storm Cat past his first four years, when his progeny could finally do the talking."

They didn't just talk, they shouted. His first crop went to the races in 1991. There were only 39 Storm Cat runners in that first crop, but two of them—the colt Harlan and the filly November Snow—turned out to be Grade 1 winners. People started to take notice of this crooked-legged beast at Overbrook. Storm Cat's annual crop of foals almost doubled in size, from 46 foals conceived in 1991 to 76 conceived in 1992. He was off and running, because his foals were.

Storm Cat went on to sire eight champions, more than 100 stakes winners, and more than 25 Grade 1 winners. Many of those runners, including most of his champions, were most successful overseas and served as good advertising to buyers such as Coolmore, who had large British or European racing stables. Through 2003, Storm Cat's lifetime progeny earnings were above

$77,000,000. His average yearling price in 2003 was $945,333. One of his sons, incidentally, was Coolmore's immensely profitable stallion Giant's Causeway, an asset that encouraged stud farms to pursue Storm Cat sons with increased zeal. Storm Cat was an unqualified success story, the kind of enormous profit-churner that every owner hopes to get when he sends his horse to stud.

But there is another side of the Storm Cat example, and it is illustrated by Tasso. The colt that nosed out Storm Cat in the 1985 Breeders' Cup Juvenile was a son of the talented stallion Fappiano, the sire of Young's highly promising and much lamented Grand Canyon. After the Breeders' Cup, Tasso was named the year's 2-year-old champion. He raced again at 3, then retired, with more than $1.2 million in winnings, to the prestigious Lane's End Farm in Kentucky. His future seemed assured.

Tasso, the first important horse sired by Fappiano, was expected to carry the bloodline on successfully. But nothing about horses is entirely assured, and Tasso never did sire the big winner he needed to stay afloat as a stallion. He gradually slipped down the ladder and into oblivion. He got a small flock of stakes winners, but most of them were in racing's minor events. His best success came in Italy, where he sired two champions. And in a brief, glowing year, he got an English runner that performed well in some of that country's best races. But his winners in America were sparse and not highly regarded, and Lane's End jettisoned him. Tasso stood for a time in Florida, where it was hoped he might fare better in a smaller stallion pool. He didn't, and was sold on to Saudi Arabia, then to India, and then back to Saudi Arabia again.

An even more illustrious horse from the 1985 season did only slightly better. Spend a Buck, winner of the 1985 Kentucky Derby and that year's Horse of the Year, also retired to Lane's End. His owner, Dennis Diaz, had bought the Buckaroo colt for just $12,000 as a yearling, and Spend a Buck had paid him back with huge interest: He not only won the Derby, but also an additional $2.6 million by skipping the Preakness to run in the Jersey Derby, where his victory earned him a huge bonus. But Spend a Buck could not complete the full circle. As a sire, he too failed to come up with enough good runners to keep his name on the marquee and finally ended up in Brazil. There he was regarded as the best sire to come along in 30 years.

And so Vindication once again went back to his stall, but this time the stall was in Lexington, Kentucky, at Hill 'n' Dale Farm. A 1,600-page local stallion directory, a cross between a phone book and little black book for mares, arrived in Thoroughbred breeders' mailboxes at the end of 2003. In it, they found an advertisement for Vindication, featuring a five-by-seven color picture of the precocious champion, carefully groomed, his dark coat gleaming like polished ebony. The caption, written in large, boldface type, strove to remind people that during his glorious exploits on the racetrack, however brief, the colt had never been pressed by any rival.

"VINDICATION," it proclaimed, "Unbeaten and Untested." Given that the colt made so few starts at 2 and none at 3, breeders might have read "untested" as "unproven." But those who sent their mares to Vindication would gamble that he had proven just enough to tempt future yearling buyers.

3 A Kingdom in a Horse

FROM ITS BEGINNING three centuries ago, the Thoroughbred breed has always been about the stallion. Three sires, all of Arabian origin and imported to England, are the very bedrock of the breed. Every modern Thoroughbred's family tree, including Vindication's, arrives eventually at one or more of those names: the Byerley Turk, the Darley Arabian, and the Godolphin Barb.

Vindication, like most Thoroughbreds today, has all three names embedded in the roots of his family tree, and the oldest branches of his pedigree wind through some of racing's greatest names and most vivid stories, dating back to an era when there was no Stud Book and the Thoroughbred, as a distinct breed, had yet to be developed. The circumstances of the Byerley, Darley, and Godolphin stallions' arrival in England are varied and picturesque by today's standards: One was a warhorse, another an exotic item collected by a merchant, and the third a discarded diplomatic gift. But running through even their old tales is a note of commercial enterprise that has its echoes in the modern Thoroughbred marketplace. The Thoroughbred, the result of combining Arabian stallions' bloodlines with those of the heavier English mares, was something of a manufactured product from the start. And then, as now, the right horse could bring riches, glory, and social status to the people who controlled him.

Princes, sheikhs, and wealthy merchants always have paid outrageous sums for horses they think will be exceptionally fast and sound. Three hundred years before Saratoga appeared on a map, horse-trading already was a thriving international business, thanks largely to the wars and imperial explorations that brought far-flung cultures together, sometimes violently. It is not surprising, given their vast wanderings and conquests, that the English were the ones who would develop the Thoroughbred, combining bloodlines from the Eastern and Western Hemispheres. Their goals in breeding horses then were much the same as they are today: to get a fast, sound horse that could win. But "win" in 14th- and 15th-century England referred to battles as well as races.

In the 1500's and 1600's, the place to buy the world's most fashionable horseflesh was the Levant, the countries that ringed the eastern half of the Mediterranean from Greece to Egypt. Of those, the prime source for horses was Turkey, which had established the Ottoman Empire from the backs of speedy, light-boned cavalry horses. In the 1600's and 1700's, Turkish horses—and those from places like the North African Barbary States and Arabia, which were under strong Ottoman influence—were famous for their physical beauty, swiftness, agility, and fiery temperament, all of which made them useful for both sporting and military endeavors.

England's hefty, rough-hewn horses of the time had been bred mainly for pulling four-wheeled carriages and heaving the staggering weight of men and their armor into battle. But as gunpowder proliferated in warfare, armor became less important than speed and quick handling, and this put lighter, faster horses in demand.

By the early 1600's England's King James I was sufficiently intrigued to buy an imported stallion from a London merchant named Markham for the fabulous sum of 500 pounds. Englishmen who could afford these luxurious imports, or who received them as gifts from foreigners, crossed them with the stout native breeds and gradually developed something highly appealing for both battlefields and racing fields: a breed of horse that combined speed and stamina.

The Thoroughbred's exact origins are lost in the murk of time and haphazard matings. In the 1600's and 1700's, the military and sporting noblemen who bred horses were simply experimenting, and the ingredients of their stud-farm laboratories consisted of animals such as Alcock's Arab, the Morocco Barb, D'Arcy's Yellow Turk, and the Old Bald Peg Arab. The names were colorful and descriptive in a general way, but they were also inclined to shift like sand when the horses were sold and other owners appended their names to them; one prominent import of the late 1600's, for example, was known alternately as Lister's Turk and the Stradling Turk, and many similar horses would have been bred to mares with vague names such as Mr. Jasper's Brown Mare. With no formal registry to demand clarity, record-keeping was scanty, and it is often impossible to tell when horses were imported, when their foals were born, and what exactly a particular foal's parentage might have been. At the time, it didn't seem to matter much. Breeding horses was a pastime and a sideline, not a formal profession.

What is certain is that these mixed-blood horses became increasingly popular. By the late 1600's, the desert horses were being imported at a brisk pace—as brisk, that is, as tall-mast shipping from the Levant to Britain would allow. In less than 100 years, that key trio of Levantine stallions—the Byerley Turk, Darley Arabian, and Godolphin Barb—would arrive on English shores.

Captain Robert Byerley, a 28-year-old English cavalry officer serving under King William III, didn't go looking for a foreign stallion to breed. Instead, he came by his Turk in an expedient but bloody manner: He took him from a Turkish officer captured in the siege of Buda, Hungary, in 1688. The horse was, according to paintings later made of him, a plain bay with no apparent white. But he was uncommonly elegant, with the graceful head, slightly concave in profile, that is typical of Arabian horses, as well as long, slender legs, and a full, flowing tail. More importantly, from Byerley's point of view, the Turk was a stout performer in battle.

Byerley took the horse with him when he was sent to Ireland in 1690, where wars were raging between the Irish and English. By then Byerley apparently had discovered the twofold advantages to having a fast and handy mount, because on his way to meet his troops at the Battle of the Boyne, Byerley—now a colonel—stopped to enter his horse in a race at Downpatrick, a horseshoe-shaped Irish turf course that ran for three miles over gently rolling land. The horse won his race, and Byerley got a silver bell as a trophy. The pair went from there straight to battle, where, it is said, Byerley's Turk proved most valuable in reconnaissance work, because he was so fast.

Byerley eventually retired from the military and returned to his family home in Durham, England, where his Turk stallion was a popular sire with local breeders. The Turk's foals ended up in the hands of such aristocrats as the Duke of Kingston and Lord Bristol, who raced them with good success, then bred from them, and got more speedy racehorses. When Byerley moved late in his life to the picturesque town of Knaresborough, in Yorkshire, his Turk moved with him, dying there at Byerley's Goldsborough Hall.

Byerley represented military procurement of the fashionable Turkish blood. But one of his neighbors down the road from Goldsborough had more commercial interests in mind. Around the time that Byerley's Turk was ending his stud career, just 25 miles away at Richard Darley's Aldby Park a new stallion from the Levantine herds was about to become the next big thing.

Darley, who inherited Aldby from his wealthy farming and trading family, also inherited their interest in sports and gaming (a visiting clergyman once noted with distaste that the family hosted enthusiastic card and dice games). Around 1700, Darley sent a letter overseas to his son, Thomas, and asked him to find a good stallion from the Ottoman bloodlines that had come so much into fashion. Thomas was in an ideal position to acquire such a horse. Based in the Syrian city of Aleppo, Thomas was a merchant with the exclusive trading firm Levant Company and, just as important, was also British Consul to the Levant on behalf of Queen Anne (who was, as it happens, a great racing patron, founder of Ascot racecourse, and an influential force in improving English racing stock).

Thomas saw a suitable colt for his father in a Bedouin herd owned by one Sheikh Mirza II, and he apparently agreed to buy the horse for 300 gold sovereigns. The colt he selected was a bright bay 3-year-old with three white socks and a white blaze that ran from the middle of his forehead to the tip of his nose. Darley felt his father would like the horse, who seemed to be the best of the herd. But Mirza, as the story goes, had second thoughts about letting the young horse go. When his promised colt did not arrive in a timely manner, the younger Darley is reputed to have hired British sailors to take possession of the horse. They did, prompting the aggrieved sheikh to write Queen Anne in 1704 with the complaint that Darley and the sailors had "foully stolen" one of his finest animals.

By the time Sheikh Mirza's protest reached England, the colt had, too. Thomas Darley believed that the horse's name was Mannika, but from the moment the colt arrived at Aldby he would be known as the Darley Arabian. He never raced, but this did not prevent the Darley family from breeding its own mares to him, and it clearly did not stop him from becoming a successful sire. Mated primarily with the middling Darley broodmares, the Arabian initially did not seem to be headed for stardom. But when another Yorkshireman, Leonard Childers, decided to breed an inexpensive mare named Betty Leedes to the Darley Arabian, he beat the odds and got an eye-popping runner that immediately cemented the stallion's reputation.

The horse in question was known variously as Bay Childers for his color, Devonshire Childers for his eventual purchase by the Duke of Devonshire, and, most lastingly, Flying Childers for his blazing speed. Leonard Childers, not surprisingly, went back to the well. When Flying Childers was 2 and just beginning to show his talent, Childers again bred his Betty Leedes to the Darley Arabian, getting another colt now known as Bartlett's Childers. That horse, like his father, never raced but went on to become an excellent sire.

Despite limited breeding opportunities, the Darley Arabian had established a flourishing bloodline so prolific it can still be found today in about 90 percent of the modern Thoroughbred population.

An even more improbable stallion emerged from the East in the 1720's. He was probably foaled in the Barbary States, where the Emperor of Morocco selected him as a gift for France's King Louis XIV. The gesture apparently did not impress the king, who sold the horse. There is little documentation as to exactly what happened next, but legend has it that the colt, a muscular bay with an unusually high-crested neck, ended up pulling a water cart around Paris, where a visiting Englishman noticed him and bought him. He ultimately ended up at the Earl of Godolphin's stud farm near Newmarket, England, where he landed the breeding game's most inglorious job: He was a teaser, used to test mares' receptiveness for breeding before they were sent to the earl's famous racehorse and stallion, Hobgoblin, a grandson of the Darley Arabian. The job did, at least, keep him in oats.

Then, in 1731, a chance occurrence gave the former cart-horse his big break. Hobgoblin, inexplicably, refused to cover one of the earl's mares. The mare, named Roxana, was sent to the long-suffering teaser instead, and the match produced a colt named Lath, who turned out to be one of the best runners of the mid-1730's. The cart-horse, now better known as the Godolphin Barb or Godolphin Arabian, was suddenly in fashion and getting mares as good as those who had always gone to Hobgoblin. The matches paid off with a herd of superior runners, several of whom went on to be potent sires and productive dams in their own right.

Three seemingly mundane and random events—a prisoner's capture in battle, a son's errand for his father, and a teaser's lucky promotion—introduced the bloodlines that would mingle to create the English Thoroughbred and, in 1764, the first home run horse in the breed's history.

Eclipse was foaled in England in the year of a solar eclipse that gave him his name. A chestnut colt with flashy white markings on his face and right hind leg, he seemed to have little else going for him. Legend has it that he was so spindly at birth, his breeder threatened to send him to a neighboring kennel as dog meat. The colt's looks improved somewhat, but he was violently ill-tempered and did not appear, at the time, to have much pedigree: He was out of a mare named Spiletta, who was famous for her Arabian beauty, but his sire, Marske, though a stakes winner, was small and plain.

None of that mattered much once Eclipse set foot on a race-course. Raced for just two seasons, he became so dominant that rival owners began scratching their horses rather than face the humiliation of running so far behind him. He is considered by many to be one of the greatest racehorses and sires of all time, a horse whose influence on the breed is still felt strongly today. And, like his modern counterparts, he showered wealth and standing on almost everyone who came into contact with him.

The man whose life he would most enrich was Dennis O'Kelly,

whose humble origins and scandalous career made him a very unlikely hero in the Sport of Kings.

O'Kelly was born around 1720, which meant he came of age at an opportune moment, just as England's Thoroughbred breed was beginning to flourish. O'Kelly flourished with it, happily reveling in the gambling society that wafted around England's racecourses.

49

As the second son of a poor Irish landowner in tiny County Carlow, O'Kelly had few prospects at home. Instead, at age 25, he bolted across the Irish Sea to London in search of work and adventure, preferably combined. Once in London, he hired himself out as a sedan-chair carrier, trundling ladies of means and titles through the city's narrow cobbled streets.

It hardly seemed an auspicious start, but the enterprising O'Kelly quickly found that a sedan-chair carrier could hire himself out to ladies for more pleasurable and profitable jobs, too. He became a gigolo to one particular aristocratic sponsor, whose name has been decorously blotted out in the histories. She paid him a full-time salary as a liveried sedan man as well as 25 guineas a tryst, but the deal ended with a crash when her husband discovered the arrangement. He divorced her, leaving O'Kelly with no income and a residual taste for the high life. He took up gambling in London's billiard halls but gradually sank into debt and finally was thrown into debtor's prison in the late 1750's.

And that was where his good luck began. He met Charlotte Hayes, a famed London madam who also was imprisoned for debt. Like O'Kelly, Hayes had luxurious tastes. She had shrewdly located her lavishly appointed brothel, ironically named The Cloisters, within easy reach of St. James's Palace, where it could cater discreetly to upper-class customers of both sexes at fantastic prices. She imported young women (and occasionally men) the way the aristocrats imported horses, procuring her human stock from overseas to fit her customers' fantasies. An anonymously written publication of the era, *Nocturnal Revels*, revealed that The Cloisters charged as much as 50 guineas for a night's entertainment—an exorbitant sum, considering the average monthly wage at the time was less than 20 guineas. Hayes also staged elaborately theatrical, invitation-only orgies that probably, in their production, helped bankrupt her.

O'Kelly and Hayes were put back on the streets in an amnesty following the death of King George II. They married, and Hayes immediately reopened her popular shop. The income poured in again, and O'Kelly got busy investing the proceeds with bookmakers at race meetings around London. Hobnobbing with the honorables, he discovered that he had a better eye for a horse than many of them, a fact that was helpful in the betting ring.

The wages of sin presented an excellent opportunity for O'Kelly to indulge his growing interest in the Turf and compete directly with the aristocrats: He bought a small string of racehorses and stabled them at the country house his wife purchased for them in Epsom. Their neighbors there included the Earl of Derby, who in 1780 would give his name to England's greatest race, the Epsom Derby.

By now, O'Kelly's wife and his own betting acumen had made him rich. He used some of the money to buy himself a military title, a bit of stick-on status that worked; his name generally appears in racing histories today as Colonel O'Kelly. But the fact that the roguish O'Kelly's name appears in the annals of the Turf at all is due entirely to Eclipse.

Eclipse was bred by the Duke of Cumberland, who conjured Eclipse by mingling the bloodlines of all three successful Arab sires. He mated his stallion Marske, a great-grandson of the Darley Arabian and a descendant of one of the Byerley Turk's daughters, with the mare Spiletta, one of the Godolphin Barb's granddaughters. The duke bred his own mares to Marske, and at the time of Eclipse's birth it appeared that, despite the advantage of that high-quality bloodstock, Marske was not much of a sire. The duke never found out otherwise, because he died of a blood clot in the brain when Eclipse was just a yearling in 1765.

The duke's Cranbourne Stud bloodstock went on the auction block, and the yearling Eclipse was sold to a Yorkshire mutton dealer named William Wildman for 75 guineas. Marske, who was thought to be small and unimpressive, went to a Dorsetshire farmer for a price so small it has been described merely as "a trifle."

Wildman quickly found that he had an exceptional runner on his hands. The colt had a nasty disposition and was difficult to train, and he had a habit of carrying his head excessively low when he ran, which made life hard for his riders. In portraits from the time,

Eclipse is habitually shown in a bad temper, with his ears pinned evilly. But Eclipse could run astonishingly fast. Whether because of his difficult personality or his owner's conservatism, Eclipse was not put in a race until 1769, when he was 5. Wildman, in the meantime, had had plenty of time to discover what he had, and that convinced him to track down the stallion Marske in Dorsetshire. The farmer who had bought him for a pittance had been breeding him to the local New Forest ponies for half a guinea each. Not yet having heard of Eclipse, he considered himself very lucky to sell the stallion to Wildman for 20 guineas.

Eclipse's first race was at Epsom, in a contest consisting of two four-mile heats. Wildman's chestnut flew away from his rivals in the first heat, leaving spectators and gamblers agog. One of the men in the crowd was O'Kelly, who had, as usual, ridden over for the meet. He made his way to the betting ring and placed his wager on the second heat, uttering a line that is immortal in racing circles: "Eclipse first, and the rest nowhere."

The second heat went much as O'Kelly had predicted. Eclipse outdistanced his four rivals without ever feeling his jockey's whip. O'Kelly promptly bought a half-interest in the great runner for 650 guineas. Later, as Eclipse piled victory upon victory, O'Kelly bought Wildman out entirely for another 1,100 guineas. In the true sign of the home run horse, Eclipse was shedding wealth on all connected with him. His 20-guinea sire, once exiled to the New Forest pony herds, became a hot property, and Wildman sold him, too, getting 1,000 guineas from the Earl of Abingdon.

O'Kelly, who also had taken over Eclipse's training, had bought Eclipse with his stud value in mind. The horse's talents were so prodigious they could not be hidden to effect a betting coup, so they might as well be publicized for his stud career. Eclipse retired to O'Kelly's Epsom farm, Clay Hill, in 1770 after two seasons. He had won all 18 of his races without ever being seriously challenged. His stud fee of 50 guineas rivaled the extravagant prices of The Cloisters brothel and brought in even more income. Madam Charlotte Hayes, on her retirement, was said to be worth 20,000 pounds, whereas O'Kelly estimated that Eclipse's breeding rights had brought in 25,000 pounds for the couple. More importantly, from the breed's perspective, the brilliant chestnut flash went on to sire 335 winners. Two of his sons, Young Eclipse and Serjeant, put Dennis O'Kelly—former gigolo and debtor turned aristocratic poseur—permanently among the noblemen in Turf history by winning the Epsom Derby in 1781 and 1784. Eclipse sired a third Derby winner, Saltram, for another owner.

Eclipse stood in Epsom for most of his years at stud. But in 1788, O'Kelly, now an old man suffering from gout, bought a Middlesex estate called Cannons Park and relocated his aging stallion there. The 24-year-old horse likely would not have stood the travel on foot, and so O'Kelly arranged to have his priceless stallion hauled to Cannons Park in a horse-drawn box, in what is believed to be the first incidence of shipping a horse by van.

Eclipse enriched O'Kelly financially and socially, giving him an improbably high, if sometimes grudging, status among England's gentry. The Jockey Club, a strictly exclusive organization that had been formed in 1750 and administered the racing game, never extended membership to the scandalous O'Kelly, but they let in his son Andrew. In its offices today, the club still has a 1770 portrait of Eclipse, and O'Kelly's name remains forever in the record books beside the great horse's.

Eclipse died of colic at Cannons Park on February 25, 1789, a little more than a year after his owner's death. When Eclipse died, O'Kelly's son arranged to have the horse's skin stuffed. The taxidermic Eclipse remained in a hayloft at Cannons until it finally disintegrated. A lone rectangular patch of skin and glossy copper hair, about three inches long and one inch across, survived when Andrew O'Kelly gave it to a neighbor. Preserved in a frame with a letter explaining its provenance, it, too, is now owned by The Jockey Club. Eclipse's skeleton has also been preserved and stands at the National Horseracing Museum in Newmarket.

But by far the most enduring part of Eclipse is his blood. The Eclipse line, carried on by a succession of champions and leading sires, was so potent that today, some 90 percent of all Thoroughbreds, including Vindication, trace back to him and thus back even farther to the Darley Arabian. Eclipse's bloodlines, re-invigorated by such great descendants as champion sires Phalaris and Northern Dancer, were still exerting influence in Thoroughbred auctions and races around the world more than two centuries after Eclipse first took up stud duty. And, like Eclipse, those horses also brought wealth to those who controlled them.

Two years after Eclipse's death, a Jockey Club official named James Weatherby published the Thoroughbred breed's first General Stud Book, effectively ending the era of mixed-blood experimentation. Thoroughbreds now would have to be registered to compete. To be eligible for registration, they would have to have pedigrees tracing through horses in the General Stud Book, all the way back to the Darley Arabian, the Byerley Turk, or the Godolphin Barb. The Thoroughbred was now a formal and definable breed of horse.

English Thoroughbred bloodstock inevitably found its way to the American colonies, starting in 1747 when Governor Samuel Ogle of Maryland imported a pair of Thoroughbreds named Spark and Queen Mab. Over the next two centuries, the Thoroughbred became the subject of a vast and highly regulated business that combined sport and commerce. Its heart remained in England, the cradle of the breed, but its business-minded head was located in America's former Indian territory of Kentucky. Even there in the colonial wilds, the English Jockey Club's breeding rules would finally take hold, so that in the year 2000 a buyer could rest assured that his registered Kentucky Thoroughbred also traced back to the Byerley Turk, Darley Arabian, or Godolphin Barb.

Robert Byerley, Richard Darley, and the Earl of Godolphin had a definite goal in mind when they began breeding their stallions: production of a light, strong, fast horse. That goal has changed little in the succeeding centuries, and there is much about Thoroughbred breeding today that Byerley, Darley, and Godolphin undoubtedly would recognize: its internationalism, its quest for speed and soundness, the willingness of wealthy people to pay large sums for horses they like, and the ability of a great horse to confer wealth and status on his human connections. But the three men whose names are synonymous with the Thoroughbred's origins could never have imagined how industrialized their pastime gradually would become once it crossed the Atlantic to America.

In the American colonies, as in England, Thoroughbred breeding and racing began as the aristocracy's privilege. As America matured and gained independence, its definition of "aristocracy" changed to include self-made men, but the effect was much the same: The wealthiest families still owned the horses and controlled the bloodlines, and that put them firmly in charge of the Thoroughbred sport. The rise of industrialism begot capitalist robber barons whose families, having arrived at the pinnacle of wealth, naturally turned to the sporting life. Those families—Wideners, Vanderbilts, Whitneys, Phippses, and others—built racing dynasties that eventually rivaled those of England.

But they had to get their horses from somewhere. The American demand for racehorses filled the pockets of already wealthy landowners who discovered they could sell the animals they once bred for fun, but it also presented an opportunity for bloodstock entrepreneurs. Foremost among those was John Madden, who began his adult life running in foot-race exhibitions at county fairs and ended it with $9 million, six Kentucky Derby winners, and the nation's first Triple Crown winner to his credit.

Madden came along at exactly the right time, and was exactly the right kind of man, to make a living from the new American business of Thoroughbreds. Born in 1856, he was the son of Irish immigrants in Bethlehem, Pennsylvania. His father, who was employed in the town's zinc works, died when John was 3 and left essentially no estate. John would have to make his own way in the world, and he did.

Madden's most obvious asset was his own athleticism. He was a big man, almost six feet tall, with a chest like a beer barrel and a square jaw that made him look pugnacious, which, in fact, he was. As a teenager, he went from county fair to county fair, running in foot races and challenging local boxing heroes to matches. He got paid, in part, by making bets on himself.

Madden's regular visits to the rollicking county fairs brought something else to his attention: horses. He found he liked them, and he gravitated toward the fierce and thundering competition of the trotting races. He learned to drive racing sulkies, plunged into the fray, and discovered he was as good at that as he was at boxing.

When he had accumulated enough in driving fees and winnings, Madden bought his own Standardbred trotting horse. By the time he was 30, Madden was horse-trading in earnest, and he had gained some notice as a man who knew a good horse and often had one to sell. At the age of 33, he did something daring. A particular pedigree cross, the stallion Belmont with the mare Waterwitch, was starting to show up here and there in trotting winner's circles, and people had begun to take note of it. Madden happened to know of a stallion with exactly that breeding who had been sold to England before the cross had started producing winners. He sailed for England, bought the stallion for 800 guineas, and shipped him back to the States. Within six months, he had sold him for $15,000.

By the time Madden moved to Lexington, Kentucky, around 1886, he had a personal worth of about $150,000, and he was ready to play in the big leagues of horse-trading, buying better-bred horses that could result in larger profits. The longer he stayed in the company of Lexington's farming class, the more evident it became that the big leagues in Kentucky did not mean Standardbred trotters. It meant horses of the running kind, the Thoroughbreds. That, Madden shrewdly discerned, was where the real commercial promise lay.

The first Thoroughbred Madden bought was a $1,500 foal named Castaway II; he sold him 10 days later for $1,600. Then he bought a yearling named Harry Reed for $400, trained him, and sent him out to win his first race by three lengths; two weeks after the race, Madden sold him, too, for $10,000. And so it went. Men who wanted to own racehorses flocked to Madden's stables and found an open and receptive shop. No matter how elegant the head looking over a stall door, no matter how purple the pedigree, Madden was always prepared to name a price. "Better to sell and repent than to keep and repent," he said.

In 1895, inspired by the good performances of a filly named Amanda V., Madden bought her weanling half-brother from the breeder for $1,200. Once in training with Madden, the colt, named Hamburg, turned into a 2-year-old champion. Madden eventually sold him, too, for a little over $40,000, a new record for a horse in training. Two months later, Madden used most of the money to buy a farm in Lexington that he called Hamburg Place, from which would flow a stream of stakes winners and profit-turners for Madden and his family, right up to the current generation: Madden's grandson Preston, with his wife, Anita, bred 1987 Kentucky Derby winner Alysheba.

The season after he bought the farm, Madden won his first Derby with a colt called Plaudit—and sold him shortly thereafter for $25,000. The buyer was William Collins Whitney, who had been doing with railroads what Madden had been doing with horses, buying cheap and reselling at enormous profit. Whitney soon put Madden on his payroll as a consultant to help him build a great racing dynasty. In helping men like Whitney establish their own racing and breeding empires, Madden had himself become very wealthy. He had also cut a path for a new professional class of horsemen who could start with little but a decent eye for bloodstock and use it to turn horses into a respectable income.

In the Thoroughbred profession, then as now, the best way to make money was to own the critical element that everyone needed to produce racehorses: the seed. A successful stallion could be active and earn stud fees for 20 years. The fees could go up, depending on his popularity and success. And his lucky owner, possessed of the racing game's most valuable commodity, could strictly limit other breeders' access to the stallion, forcing the price of a breeding session, or "season," up even more on the open market. And, of course, there was even more money to be made if the owner also sold the sire's foals at auction. A good stallion, over the long haul, really could be worth his weight in gold, providing the steady income that was otherwise so elusive in the Thoroughbred world.

Even Madden, who focused most of his attention on developing young horses to sell, made sure to stand a number of stallions, including one named Star Shoot that was a five-time leading sire.

"The sire is the most important factor on a farm," Madden once said. "He plants the seed and gives the form to the foal just as the grain is deposited in the soil and produces itself. A great racehorse that breeds true cannot fail. If he does not breed true, the quicker he is discarded, the better."

Despite its upside, stallion ownership was not for the fainthearted. First, it was expensive to acquire the horses that were most likely to become important sires. Those horses tended to be obvious to everyone, and the bidding ran high. If you did get such a top prospect, you were holding a hundred lottery tickets compared to someone else's single chance, but you were still gambling. No one could predict for sure which horses would make great sires and which would not. Even ones that seemed to have all the ammunition—blue-blooded pedigrees, accomplished race records, Atlas physiques—might turn out to be underachievers or, worse, completely infertile.

But the stallion, indisputably, was king of the game.

In the first half of the 20th century, the natural heirs to John Madden's successful commercialization of the Thoroughbred were men who understood very well that good stallions were the game's most valuable commodity. The Kentuckian who took the next logical step—selling shares in studs—was already wealthy when he started breeding Thoroughbreds. But his approach to that pursuit eventually opened Thoroughbred breeding to a wide array of people, turned horsemen into "investors," and helped transform the quaint Thoroughbred agriculture into a full-fledged, billion-dollar industry. The fulcrum on which that economic revolution turned was the stallion.

57

Leslie Combs II was a former West Virginia insurance executive who had returned to his roots in Kentucky and the horse business in 1937. His own pedigree was sprinkled with illustrious names in racing and breeding, most notably that of his great-grandfather Daniel Swigert. Swigert had raced the 1877 Derby winner, Baden-Baden, and founded the landmark Elmendorf Farm in Lexington, where he bred three more Derby winners: Hindoo in 1881, Apollo in 1882, and Ben Ali in 1886. When Combs put up his own sign on a breeding farm, he hammered it into a rich plot of land that had once been part of Elmendorf, and he named it Spendthrift Farm, after the 1879 Belmont Stakes winner his ancestors had bred.

Combs started with 127 acres that gradually expanded to 5,000 acres of rolling, fertile Bluegrass pastureland. The engine for Spendthrift Farm's physical growth was Combs's sophisticated breeding and sales operation, which started with his careful acquisition of wealthy clients who could and did spend money for the best available bloodstock. His stable of customers included cosmetics-company founder Elizabeth Arden, for whom he was a racing and breeding adviser, and textile millionaire John Hanes.

Combs, a balding man with a ruddy face and a broad smile, put a lot of effort into keeping his customers entertained. He referred to himself as Cousin Leslie, a nickname that implied aw-shucks simplicity and down-home charm. The charm, at least, was apparently genuine. Cousin Leslie was famous for hosting buyers (and likely prospects) at Spendthrift's sumptuous pre-auction soirees, for steering enchanted onlookers through the farm's magnificent limestone stallion barn, and for making money hand over fist. At a time when the average auction-yearling price was $4,500, his young horses brought an average of $21,000, thanks not only to his reputation as a horseman and the quality of the bloodlines he offered, but also to his shrewd salesmanship.

In 1947, Combs did something revolutionary. He put together a syndicate to buy a foreign stallion named Beau Pere. It was a simple maneuver that allowed Combs to put up more money to outbid rival buyers, and it also allowed the partners to spread the risk if anything went wrong. And Beau Pere, who cost the syndicate $100,000, went badly wrong. He died before he ever covered a mare. But Combs had hit on a good business model, and it wasn't long before his great rival in the breeding business, Claiborne Farm owner Arthur "Bull" Hancock Jr., followed suit.

Like Combs, Hancock had an illustrious family background in Thoroughbred breeding. The Hancock name ran like a gold thread through histories of some of America's greatest races, starting with Knight of Ellerslie's victory in the 1884 Preakness. The Hancocks' vast farm near the tiny hamlet of Paris, Kentucky, outside Lexington, housed the brightest stars in Thoroughbred breeding's firmament, and those assets drew top owners and their valuable broodmares. Inevitably, thanks to the bloodlines of their stallions, the Hancocks became closely entwined with the racing successes of Phippses, Guggenheims, and Woodwards, names that embodied America's financial, social, and Turf establishment.

Two years after Combs syndicated Beau Pere, Hancock did the same with a more expensive stallion, an Irish horse named Nasrullah, who cost a record $340,000. Nasrullah had an enviable race record, but he also had something else that Hancock particularly wanted: the blood of Nearco, an undefeated racehorse, a descendant of Eclipse, and a prominent European stallion regarded as one of the century's most potent sires. Best of all, Nearco appeared to be passing along that priceless ability to sire high-class racehorses, which put his sons in high demand. When Hancock and his partners made their offer, Nasrullah's first runners already had hit English racetracks with astounding early success. Clearly, Hancock thought, this was the kind of thriving genetic material that could put some additional vitality in Claiborne's venerable old bloodlines. Nasrullah was as sure a thing as you could get in the breeding game.

When Hancock and his syndicate bought Nasrullah, they divided the ownership into 32 shares. Each shareholder got one annual breeding right, or season, for every share he owned. One of the investors, banker and Jockey Club chairman William Woodward Sr., used a Nasrullah season in 1951 to breed his mare Segula and got a champion. Woodward's son, William Jr., inherited the colt, named Nashua, on his father's death in 1953.

Nashua, one of the most celebrated runners of the 1950's, gave Nasrullah immediate cachet in America. Though he failed to win the 1955 Kentucky Derby, finishing second to Swaps, he otherwise dominated his rivals, was named champion twice, and eventually earned more than $1 million from purses. But in the fall of 1955, a year before Nashua's complete race record was in the books, a shocking tragedy altered the trajectory of his racing career—and, more importantly for the breeding industry, his stud career. On October 30, 1955, Woodward was shot to death in his Long Island mansion by his wife, Ann, who later said she mistook her husband for an intruder.

The lurid story filled pages of newsprint, and to most of the public who devoured the press coverage, Nashua was a sidebar. But to a number of sharp-eyed Bluegrass horsemen, he was the main issue. When the Woodward estate's executors decided to sell the family's storied bloodstock, Kentucky stud-farm owners sharpened their pencils, called their accountants, and arranged lunch with their bankers.

A sealed-bid auction for the Woodward bloodstock dynasty was set for December 15, 1955. Nashua whiled away the days leading up to it in a paddock at Claiborne Farm, where, had events taken their natural course, he probably would have ended up as a stallion. But Woodward's death had put this potential genetic diamond mine up for grabs. The colt already was a massive success and, at only age 3, he had another racing season ahead of him before he retired to stud. The moneymaking potential was staggering.

"He was the most valuable piece of Thoroughbred property that was available for sale in the world," Thoroughbred auctioneer Humphrey Finney, who conducted the sale, later wrote. "No animal of that value had ever been offered at public auction."

When Woodward's executors announced the auction, one of the men who started raising money was Hancock's archrival, Leslie Combs II.

Finney had estimated Nashua's value at $1.2 million, and Hancock privately had arrived at about the same figure. When Finney opened the 11 bids for Nashua at 11:00 A.M. on the appointed day, he found five for more than $1 million. The highest one, for $1,251,200, belonged to Cousin Leslie's group. It was the first seven-figure syndication the Thoroughbred world had ever seen, and, with it, Combs had launched breeding's corporate age. Soon, a single unproven yearling would fetch a price far beyond Nashua's syndication value. Owners would sell stallions for amounts that previous generations would have spent buying entire companies. Horses would be not merely bred but designed and manufactured to suit the tastes and needs of these high-flying investors. And the truly special stallion prospect would become a commodity more valuable than ever before.

The Thoroughbred-industry boom that began with Nashua's million-dollar syndication traveled along the Nearco male bloodline like a flame burning through a dynamite fuse, and it threw off golden sparks for farms like Claiborne that held the bloodlines. Nasrullah begot Bold Ruler, a champion and dominant Claiborne sire for 15 years, and then Bold Ruler begot Secretariat. Another son of Nearco, a Canadian horse named Nearctic, begot Northern Dancer, who became one of the century's most influential sires. Those two Nearco-line horses, Secretariat and Northern Dancer, permanently altered the Thoroughbred-industry landscape.

In the beginning, Northern Dancer did not seem destined to become a star. He was the result of a last-minute mating between Canadian champion Nearctic and a stakes-quality filly named Natalma, both owned by Canadian industrialist E. P. Taylor. In a way, it was bad racing luck that brought Nearctic and Natalma together that year. Taylor had sent Natalma to Kentucky to run in the prestigious Kentucky Oaks in 1960, but while training for this distaff version of the Kentucky Derby she injured her knee. It was already April and late in the breeding season, but Taylor retired his filly and rushed her back to Canada, where Nearctic was standing his first season at stud.

Nearctic's first foals were eagerly anticipated, but Natalma's colt was something of a disappointment. Having been conceived late, he naturally was born late, on May 27, and that made him smaller than his peers. Unfortunately, he stayed small: Fully mature, he only stood a shade over 15 hands, about four inches shorter, on average, than other mature male Thoroughbreds. Taylor put him up for sale as a yearling, but no one met the $25,000 price, so Northern Dancer joined Taylor's racing stable. There, the small package luckily turned out to be stuffed with Nearctic's brilliant running genes. Northern Dancer went on to win 14 of his 18 races, including the 1964 Kentucky Derby in a record two minutes flat, and the Preakness. He never finished worse than third.

Northern Dancer retired to Taylor's Canadian farm, Windfields, where he stood for $10,000 and was expected to become a creditable sire. No one would have predicted what happened next. From his first crop of runners, which arrived at the racetrack in 1968, Northern Dancer got 10 stakes winners from just 21 foals. It was a shockingly good strike rate, made more impressive by the fact that one of those runners, Viceregal, was voted 1968's Canadian Horse of the Year at age 2.

This was good stuff, but even better things were in store for the chronically underestimated little stallion. At a 1968 sale in Canada, Irish horse trainer Vincent O'Brien spotted a yearling Northern Dancer colt he liked, and he bought him for $84,000. Two years later that colt, Nijinsky II, became the first horse since 1935 to win England's Triple Crown, vaulting his Canadian sire straight to the top of the English stallion rankings.

Nijinsky II started a full-blooded run on Northern Dancer yearlings that would last for two decades and bring droves of British, European, Japanese, and American buyers to the Kentucky and Saratoga auctions. And the prices soared. Taylor, for his part, struck while the iron was hot. When Nijinsky II blazed gloriously across England in 1970, Taylor quickly took advantage of the moment and syndicated Northern Dancer in 32 shares for a total of $2.4 million. Taylor undoubtedly knew that the stallion's fortunes could change at any moment, but, in retrospect, he underestimated the horse's seemingly endless capacity for siring expensive future champions. Two days after Northern Dancer's syndication deal was announced, his son Nijinsky II was syndicated for $5.4 million.

It would not take long for that figure to be surpassed. In 1970, the same year that Nijinsky II won his English Triple Crown, Secretariat was foaled in Virginia. He became the first 2-year-old to be voted Horse of the Year, and as a son of the brilliant racehorse and sire Bold Ruler, who had died the previous year, he had great appeal for American breeders.

Bull Hancock's son Seth syndicated Secretariat for more than $6 million in a daring gamble that immediately confirmed for everyone that the breeding shed, and not the racetrack, was now the seat of financial power in the Thoroughbred business. What made the deal daring was not just the syndication value, but also the fact that it took place so early, in the winter of 1973, before Secretariat had even started his 3-year-old racing season. He was already a 2-year-old champion, but many 2-year-olds fail to maintain their worth at 3. When Seth Hancock started calling prospective investors and offering them $190,000 shares in Secretariat, the colt was still a significant gamble.

What made Secretariat's syndication revolutionary was that its terms required the colt to retire at the end of his 3-year-old season, so his investors could limit the risk of depreciation through poor performance or injury (and start receiving income from breeding fees). Secretariat's total syndication value was $6,080,000, more money than he could ever recoup by winning purses. Even later, after he won the 1973 Triple Crown, the first horse to accomplish that feat in 25 years, Secretariat still was worth far more in the breeding shed than he would ever be, in strict financial terms, on the racetrack.

The Secretariat deal unabashedly identified the stallion as a financial commodity, an asset that could appreciate or depreciate, that could be speculated on, cashed out of, bought, and sold like any other product, and for more money than ever. And it was the breeding side of the Thoroughbred sport, not the racing side, that could confer the most value on a horse, because unlike racehorses, stallions could bring in profits for a decade or two.

The engine that drove the breeding business and gave it the clout to set such extravagant values was the yearling market.

The year before Secretariat's syndication, Leslie Combs's Spendthrift Farm became the first seller ever to gross more than $2 million at an auction. The year after the syndication, Spendthrift sold a yearling colt at the Keeneland July sale for a world-record $625,000, quickly shattering that mark the next year with one that brought $715,000. In 1976, a colt from Secretariat's first crop broke the $1 million barrier.

Within a decade, $1 million would become the opening bid on many Keeneland yearlings. Most of those seven-figure babies bore the genetic stamp of Northern Dancer, whose one-time breeding fees were now also selling for $1 million when shareholders offered them. In 1981, when the great horse was 20 and nearing the end of his breeding life, a new syndicate approached Northern Dancer's owners and offered to buy the stallion, who now represented unprecedented moneymaking power, for $40 million. Taylor's group said no.

The stakes at auction and in the breeding shed were higher than ever. And now the gamblers included not just the horse's owner or breeders, but also speculative investors who hoped to turn a quick profit by selling their stallion seasons to breeders who hadn't been quick enough or rich enough to buy into the syndicates in the first place.

A number of factors contributed to the blazing bloodstock market. Favorable tax laws made it a haven, for a start, and the market for yearlings was expanding. Imported stallions such as Nasrullah had made American pedigrees more familiar to European buyers; the success of Northern Dancer's runners in Europe convinced them to buy at American sales if they wanted to win; and horses they bought in Kentucky or Saratoga could now be flown back to Europe more easily than ever.

The yearling prices were otherworldly, but they made a compelling point for the business-minded investor considering a stallion share. This may, in fact, have been the whole point. Industry insiders privately questioned a number of the more outlandish yearling prices. The conditions of sale allowed anyone, including sellers, to bid on any horse, and it was widely suspected that some sellers involved in stallions would run the yearling prices up in the auction ring, either by paying an agent to push his unwitting clients' bids up or by buying the horse back themselves through a seemingly legitimate "buyer." The stallion owners could then trumpet the inflated sale price as evidence of their horse's ability to generate profits for people who bred to him.

Legit or not, the dazzling sales helped draw novice investors into the business. They piled into syndicates, and the number of shares per horse expanded, from 32 to 40 and beyond. The old Thoroughbred world—the cloistered, clannish sport familiar to Whitneys and Woodwards, where bloodlines did not get tangled up in bottom lines—was bursting along its seams like an old silk purse overstuffed with new money. The modern age belonged to speculators, businessmen, and entrepreneurs, some of whom would build their own dynasties on the simple principle that blood equals money. The Thoroughbred world was still a playground for sheikhs and queens, but now it also belonged to men like D. Wayne Lukas.

Lukas grew up in Wisconsin, where he had stamped himself as a go-getter from an early age. At 9, he leased a small plot of land from a relative, raised a crop of beans on it over the summer, and sold them at a profit. He delivered papers from the back of a white pony named Queenie, he raised rabbits to sell at Easter, he bought a goat so he could sell the milk. And he traded horses.

Like any horse-crazy boy, Lukas spent as much time as he could in the saddle. He camped out on the trail and did some rodeo-style trick riding at county fairs. He bought horses at local sales and raced them in all-breed events at the neighboring Menominee Indian reservation. As a teenager, Lukas hung out at a local slaughter auction, scouting for prospects he thought he could buy cheap, brighten up, and resell as riding horses. He bought wild mustangs for meat prices, then spent months breaking them to the saddle. They'd buck, kick, and slam him around, but Lukas kept at it, and at the end of the process he had horses he could sell to cowboys and pleasure riders for profit.

In the 10 years after his 1958 graduation from the University of Wisconsin, Lukas coached high-school basketball, got a master's degree in education, and invented a basketball shoe called the All Star Trainer, but he never quit horses. In 1968, he went to the racetrack full time, starting on the Quarter Horse circuit, where the horses run like a cavalry charge down a quarter-mile straightaway. He came to dominate that sport, training 23 champions and a two-time Horse of the Year, Dash for Cash. But in late 1977, smelling an even better business opportunity, he switched to Thoroughbreds in California.

In a decade of Quarter Horse racing, Lukas won just over $4 million. He got $4.3 million in his first three years with Thoroughbreds.

Lukas had made it to the big time, but soon he was butting his head against his owners' financial limits. What he needed was a whale, a fearless entrepreneur with a love of action, who could bankroll Lukas's vision: a national expansion of D. Wayne Lukas, Inc., that would make his barn the most profitable factory of winners and breeding prospects the Thoroughbred sport had ever seen.

Lukas found his whale when he met Eugene Klein, a self-made man who made his first fortune selling used cars and his second one owning a chain of movie theaters. Klein knew little about racing except that his wife liked it and it looked like more fun than he'd had owning the San Diego Chargers: The horses, at least, wouldn't have cocaine problems and contract negotiations.

The Lukas-Klein program was simple. They would mine the yearling auctions for genetic and physical gems, using a rating system and Lukas's experienced eye to settle on their top prospects. They were prepared to pay $1 million, without flinching, for a horse they rated highly. Their purchases would go to a Lukas-operated training center in California that could stable hundreds of horses at a time. There, Klein's yearlings would get their early training, which would help reveal what circuits they belonged on. Lukas had racing stables on every major circuit from Florida to New York to California, each under the capable eye of a hand-picked, Lukas-trained assistant. Lukas and his assistants would run the horses where they could win and earn money. The best of them, the men knew, could earn a *lot* of money, increasing their value as breeding stock. When they were at their peak value, Klein could syndicate the colts, auction the fillies as broodmare prospects, and plow the profits right back into the yearling sales.

This starkly commercial approach to the noble Thoroughbred,

even the champions, took the sporting world's old guard aback. Klein was a gambler who made much of the fact that he loved to take risks—"I am not a safe player," he once said—but the Klein-Lukas program was, in fact, designed to control as many variables as possible by dealing in large numbers of the best possible stock, all trained by one of the sport's most accomplished horsemen. It was expensive to buy so many well-bred horses, but that made it harder for pesky bad luck or human error to trip you up, at least until the starting gate opened. If the horses won, the rest of the plan was straightforward: Sell high and reinvest the profits.

"I buy so many because I believe strongly that the law of averages is going to work," Klein was once quoted as saying. "I don't know if it will be the million-dollar colt or the $150,000 colt. Some of them will make it, some will not. But if I have enough of them going, and they're all selected by Wayne, I feel we'll win our fair share."

It worked. On Lukas's advice, Klein spent an estimated $39 million on bloodstock in the six years of their partnership. He won about $27 million in purses, became the first owner ever to win $5 million in a single season, campaigned six champions, got three coveted Eclipse Awards from the Thoroughbred industry as the nation's leading owner, and took the 1988 Kentucky Derby with Winning Colors, one of only three fillies ever to win the race. When Klein dispersed his 114 horses in 1989 due to declining health, they made another $29.6 million. And those were just the figures on public sales, excluding earlier private sales or syndications whose values were never disclosed.

Lukas and Klein launched their program at the 1983 Keeneland July auction, at the hot and airy center of the bloodstock market's bubble. They competed against the most formidable buyers of the era, including oil-rich Sheikh Mohammed al-Maktoum, who had just taken up racing seriously in Europe, as well as the Irish-based partnership of Robert Sangster, John Magnier, and the famed trainer Vincent O'Brien, founders of Coolmore Stud.

Those three competing forces made up the yearling boom's prevailing weather system in the 1980's. On July 23, 1985, two of them collided over a Northern Dancer-line colt in a hurricane of bidding. The result was a world-record price so preposterous it may never be equaled. The lightning rod that afternoon was a bright bay colt, the color of rich milk chocolate, with only tiny points of white: a sliver rimming his left hind heel, a small star on his forehead, and an even tinier trace between his nostrils, as if his brown paint job needed finishing touches.

Most importantly, his sire was Northern Dancer's fabulously successful son Nijinsky II and his mother, My Charmer, was also the dam of Triple Crown winner Seattle Slew. And both Nijinsky II and Seattle Slew were highly successful studs. To buyers contemplating his glowing catalog page, the colt, later named Seattle Dancer, looked like a flawless 50-carat diamond. He reflected everything that breeders had been striving for since the time of his ancestor, the Darley Arabian.

The market had reached unprecedented heights two years before Seattle Dancer's momentous sale. Sheikh Mohammed had outbid Lukas and Sangster in 1983 for a colt later called Snaafi Dancer, paying a then world-record price of $10.2 million that one commentator called "a world record for irrationality." Snaafi Dancer never raced and then turned out to be completely sterile to boot—an extraordinary run of bad luck that obviously had not discouraged Sheikh Mohammed or his auction rivals.

But until Hip Number 215 strode into the auction ring, the boiling market actually seemed to have cooled in 1985. Earlier in the year, Sangster, O'Brien, and Magnier had flown to Dubai for a desert summit with Sheikh Mohammed, whose competition was driving up the prices for horses they wanted. The end result of the meeting was a kind of détente that understandably worried high-end sellers. When the 1985 Keeneland July auction opened, things looked ominous for those with a taste for Veuve Clicquot and caviar, especially when one of Sheikh Mohammed's agents was spotted shuttling between his seat and Sangster's preferred bidding spot behind the pavilion, apparently confirming the plan to divide up the yearlings equitably. Sure enough, none of the first 214 horses through the ring sold for more than $2.6 million, a drop from the last couple of July sales. The Sangster-Maktoum policy of "one for me, one for you" was having its intended effect.

No one had counted on D. Wayne Lukas and Eugene Klein to crash the party. The bidding on Hip 215 opened when two spotters signaled almost simultaneously to the auctioneer, Tom Caldwell, that they had bids of $1 million. Caldwell recognized the one from behind the pavilion, where Sangster was bidding through his agent, Joss Collins. In less than a minute, the price had escalated to $7 million. This was a surprise, considering that the market had seemed comparatively sleepy. What was more surprising was that the man batting Sangster's bids back at him was not Sheikh Mohammed. Lukas, wearing his trademark dark glasses and no expression, was sitting in the pavilion with Klein and L. R. French, for whom Lukas trained champion Landaluce. He was also representing a fourth partner, the absent Mel Hatley, who owned another Lukas-trained star, Life's Magic, with Klein.

Lukas bid with such unexpected aggression that Sangster, unable to see his competitor from behind the pavilion, suspected that Sheikh Mohammed must have broken their agreement. On Lukas's $10.3 million bid, Seattle Dancer had shot past the world record.

Now in uncharted territory, Sangster and Lukas made irregular raises, plumbing each other's determination. The bids bounced from $11.2 million to $11.5 million, then bumped sharply to $11.7 million. Inside the pavilion, Klein's forehead was beginning to glisten with sweat. Finally, at $12.5 million, Caldwell boldly asked for $13 million. Lukas, attempting a coup de grace, agreed. Sangster, after a brief, chagrined pause, fired back with $13.1 million. Lukas exchanged an intense look with Klein, then stiffened his spine and said, "No."

"Wayne Lukas," Sangster said later, "was a very brave bidder."

As the receipt made its way into the history books, some people debated whether Lukas's courage was based on desire to buy the colt or perhaps to run up his price. Before Seattle Dancer sold, Lukas has said to have met privately with sellers Warner Jones Jr. and William Farish III in their barn at Keeneland. There was speculation that he and Klein had bought an interest in Seattle Dancer before the sale, then ratcheted the price up as far as they could. A $13 million bid, while not beyond possibility for a man like Klein, was somewhat out of character for a client Lukas himself had described as a bottom-line fellow. The rumor, never proven, put a possible new interpretation on Klein's nervous sweating: He might also have been afraid Lukas would press too hard and crack

Sangster like an eggshell, sticking Klein with the colt.

But Lukas made it clear that he had rated Seattle Dancer "an eight-plus" on a scale where 10 was equine perfection.

"The thing I had marked against him was a thin hoof wall," he explained to the *Daily Racing Form*. "He was a threat to be shelly-footed."

His clients, Lukas said, had definitely wanted to buy the colt, at least until the bidding went past the previous world mark of $10.2 million.

"When it got above the record, Gene Klein says, 'That's it, no more for me,'" Lukas said. "But French whispers to keep going. Hatley isn't there, and I've got my whole net worth tied up in my 25 percent. I am on my own. Gene is a bit hard of hearing, but I couldn't raise my voice. It would have given away our intentions. I made my last bid at $13 million, and they came back at $13.1 million. Money was no object to them. But it had become to us."

Whichever story you believed, Lukas had played high-stakes poker very, very well, and the obvious beneficiaries were the sellers.

"Sometimes their feet go wrong, their knees go wrong, the dogs run them through a fence, they get struck by lightning," Jones told the press that surrounded him after the sale. "It always seems to be the best one that something happens to, but he got up to the sale in good shape and we were fortunate that true interest was shown by the people most able to own him and that they liked him and bid on him."

Seattle Dancer, who went on to earn just over $164,000 and sire a handful of European champions, is mainly memorable as the pinnacle of the yearling boom. Yearling prices topped out with him, and the market bubble burst in the late 1980's. There was a brief market slump, but by the mid-1990's, prices were back on the upswing. Innovations such as simulcasting made it possible for bettors to wager on races nationwide without leaving their local track, and the increased handle gave purses a healthy boost—a factor that encouraged bidders to pursue horses they felt could earn their keep at the racetrack, and, if they were good enough, make big money.

Thoroughbred breeding has grown from pastime to industry over the last two centuries, transforming the horse into a commodity along the way. But the horseman's goal—whether he is a breeder, a trainer, a seller, or an owner—has remained the same: to get the home run horse, the one that can change your life by bestowing glory or money or both. If Eclipse's owner, Dennis O'Kelly, were to haunt the plush pavilions of today's Thoroughbred auctions, he would find the blood of his great stallion still flowing through the pedigrees on offer. He probably also would recognize a bit of himself in the high-rollers who gamble on such bloodlines in hopes of finding another Eclipse. If John Madden's ghost could stroll through Keeneland's sale barns, he would find his descendants among the sellers serving free cocktails outside their consignments, tempting a buyer to stay a moment more, when the perfect yearling might happen to come out of a stall and catch his eye.

The modern racehorse market has become slick and corporate since the days of O'Kelly and Madden, but the Thoroughbred investment fundamentally remains a gamble on hope and potential. The difference now is that today's breeders and sellers can select and tailor their horses more closely to a buyer's fantasy, and they can mint more of those dreams than ever.

4 On the Production Line

HILL 'N' DALE FARM'S stallion manager, Aidan O'Meara, was born in 1977, the same year Vindication's sire became the first and, so far, only undefeated Triple Crown winner. O'Meara's life intersected with Seattle Slew's briefly 25 years later, after he left his native County Tipperary, Ireland, for better opportunities in Kentucky. O'Meara will never forget the month from April to May in 2002 when he got to know the stallion.

Then, as now, O'Meara—tall and pale with a soft, boyish face, a quiet mover who never wastes motion—handled on-the-ground management of Hill 'n' Dale's growing stallion roster. When he first came to the farm, O'Meara knew immediately he had landed at a promising springboard, a good operation with stallions that were probably going places. But it had nothing of legendary proportions until April 1, 2002. That morning, at about 6:00 A.M., Seattle Slew arrived at Hill 'n' Dale to live out the last month of his life.

It was a strange and sad procession. Seattle Slew, 28 years old and ailing after two surgeries to relieve arthritis-related pressure on his spinal cord, rolled up in a van with his longtime groom, Tom Wade, who protectively installed him in a quiet corner of the farm. Seattle Slew's owners, Karen and Mickey Taylor, had stood him for the previous 17 years at another Bluegrass farm, Three Chimneys. But they became increasingly convinced that Slew's stall there, which was within sight of the Three Chimneys breeding shed and its alluring activity, was hindering the retired stallion's recovery.

The Taylors had asked Hill 'n' Dale's owner, a former professional hockey player named John Sikura, if he would take Slew in. Sikura, honored by the request, agreed immediately. And young Aidan O'Meara got a close view of the racing and breeding hero as he helped Slew's silent, serious-minded groom care for the old horse.

Seattle Slew died at 9:00 A.M. on May 7, 2002, exactly 25 years after his Kentucky Derby victory. When they buried the massive body just outside the courtyard of Hill 'n' Dale's stud barn, it was Aidan O'Meara who cradled the stallion's head, lowering it gently into the grave.

"I'd always wondered why people got so upset when somebody like Elvis or Princess Di died," he said, "and I didn't realize why until we buried Slew that day. There's just something about a thing that great passing away that makes you emotional."

From the tall back window of his apartment atop the Hill 'n' Dale stud barn, O'Meara can look out on Slew's grave, which even in the dead of winter is piled with fresh wreaths and flowers his devotees have left. So when O'Meara was sent to the Lexington airport in a horse van a little more than a year later to pick up Slew's champion son Vindication, he understandably felt a tiny shiver of anticipation about the new arrival.

"The thought was always in the back of the mind when Vindication came here, like maybe it was the second coming," O'Meara said. "He's pretty much the heir apparent. Vindication is set up to be the flagship horse that can carry the farm into the future."

The memory of Seattle Slew was also on John Sikura's mind when he first made his bid for Satish Sanan's colt.

"He was a workmanlike horse who emerged from nowhere, like the small-town boy who becomes president," Sikura said of Seattle Slew, who was a $17,500 yearling before he won the Triple Crown and became a multimillion-dollar racehorse-production industry unto himself. "He was the equine example of the American dream.

"I would never be so arrogant to think I could have the next Seattle Slew," Sikura added. "I don't think there ever will be another Seattle Slew. But when Seattle Slew came here, I thought he came here for a reason. I just didn't know what the reason was. When we did the deal for Vindication, I really felt there was a connection between the two things. At least, that was a motivation for me when I talked to the Sanans about Vindication and Seattle Slew. I knew something about it. I saw the horse take his last breath."

Sikura, 45, is no novice in the horse world. His father, a Canadian self-made millionaire who died in a car fire in 1994, launched the original Hill 'n' Dale Thoroughbred farm in Ontario, Canada, then expanded it to Kentucky so he could have a foothold in the breeding world's most important business center. His son John took over the Kentucky operation after the elder Sikura's death and dedicated himself to raising the farm's commercial profile. John Sikura is young and highly aggressive by Bluegrass hardboot standards, and his style suits racing's entrepreneurial owners, businessmen like Satish Sanan who consider themselves forward-thinking and open to new ideas.

Sikura's first splashy deal came in 1997, when he surprised local society by purchasing part of a famous Bluegrass property called North Ridge Farm, which had a distinguished Thoroughbred-breeding history. Sikura got his 342-acre portion through a complex deal that involved, among other arrangements, trading the original Kentucky division of Hill 'n' Dale. But the new land was considered nearly priceless. It included some of Kentucky's most treasured pastureland as well as a regal brick stud barn, whose 24 stalls surrounded three sides of a courtyard with a central fountain that in the summer spilled over not with water, but with lavish cascades of flowers. If Sikura was to realize his dream of making Hill 'n' Dale an important force in Kentucky's viciously competitive Thoroughbred-breeding business, he would have to fill those 24 stalls with as many good horses as he could.

He scored his first major coup when Michael Paulson, son of the late Gulfstream Aerospace CEO and highly successful breeder Allen Paulson, decided to move the estate's bloodstock to Hill 'n' Dale. That package included a top stallion, Theatrical. But Theatrical, at 20, was nearing the end of his breeding career. Sikura needed a young horse that could vault the farm into the Thoroughbred business's highest echelon and keep it there for a while.

73

He found his potential home run horse one bright afternoon in late July while attending the races at California's surfside Del Mar racetrack. Vindication was making his first start that day, and he caught Sikura's eye instantly.

"He just impressed me, and I liked the look of him," Sikura said.

Vindication won that race by daylight, soaring out ahead of his competition by 5 ½ lengths at the wire in a performance Sikura called "awe-inspiring."

"I have a pretty good relationship with Bob Baffert, and so when I saw him I kind of ribbed him, 'How come you didn't tell me about this horse? I'd have bet a little on him!'" Sikura recalled. "I had been totally in the dark about this horse."

He never overlooked the colt again. When Vindication ran almost two months later at Kentucky's Turfway Park, Sikura was attending the fall yearling sale at Keeneland, an hour away. But he made a point to watch the race, the Kentucky Cup Juvenile, via simulcast in Keeneland's clubhouse. And he was there for the 2002 Breeders' Cup Juvenile at Arlington, arriving early enough in the week to watch some of Vindication's prerace training.

Sikura wasn't the only one. Farm owners all over Kentucky had taken notice of Vindication's progress, and by the time Satish Sanan arrived in Lexington for Keeneland's November breeding-stock sale the week after the Breeders' Cup, he was snowed under with requests for meetings. Hill 'n' Dale was one of the farms he visited.

Sikura showed Sanan Hill 'n' Dale's vast pastures, its grand brick stallion barn, the memorial for Vindication's revered sire. He made his pitch: He talked about the farm's business and breeding philosophies, proposed a range of stud fees for Sanan's stallion prospect, discussed how many mares he thought he could get to the colt.

Sikura got no commitment.

"His visit was certainly more than cursory," Sikura said, "but we were just one of a number of suitors. Things didn't go too far for a couple of weeks. It's hard to buy a horse from anyone at any level after the euphoria of a victory, especially the Breeders' Cup. I think the Sanans just kind of wanted to take a step back and just enjoy the horse for a little while before they made a decision."

In December, after several weeks of silence, Sikura took the

74

initiative and called Sanan and told him he was planning to come to Tampa, within reach of Sanan's company headquarters in Clearwater, Florida, for a hockey game.

"We've already talked about everything we would talk about as an introduction, and I don't want to waste your time," Sikura told Sanan. "But if you'd like to make a deal, I'd like to meet with you."

Sanan agreed to meet Sikura over coffee at a Tampa hotel.

"And what started as coffee turned out to be a deal," Sikura said. "At the end of a couple of hours of going back and forth, we scratched it out on a piece of paper, and it seemed easy. A couple of hours face to face made all the difference in the world. Be they romantic relationships or friendships or business deals, you never really know what makes something click. But I think Satish knew I really, really coveted the horse and wanted him. And I think he knew that I respect him and his family, that I felt they deserved the horse and deserved to have more like him."

Such personal touches may have been even more important in this particular deal, because Vindication was never for sale outright. The Sanans would only syndicate 33 percent of the colt, so, as Sikura put it, "It was never really a matter of who was going to pay the most money."

Vindication injured himself just over a month after the deal.

"It was a real disappointment," Sikura acknowledged. "But looking back on it, a lot worse things could have happened. He's remained a hugely popular horse.

"The thing is, you never know where a top sire is going to come from," he added. "There are lots of unusual circumstances that make a farm happen to be the place a particular good horse stands."

If Vindication turns out to be a good enough sire, he can etch Hill 'n' Dale's name in Bluegrass history and, by its association with him, into Thoroughbred bloodlines.

"All the famous farms of the past are associated with a particular horse, the same way you associate a particular actor with a classic movie," Sikura said. "Bold Ruler and Claiborne, Northern Dancer and Windfields, Raise a Native and Spendthrift, Roberto and Darby Dan, and on and on. All those farms had *that horse* that defined their success."

• • •

On an achingly cold morning in late January 2004, with the high temperature hanging like an icicle below 20 degrees, Aidan O'Meara rattled the latch around Vindication's paddock gate. The colt, now 4 years old, was at the far end of the paddock cropping yellowed grass, but he looked up and pricked his ears when he heard the metallic clanking of latch and chain that usually meant to him that something interesting was about to happen. Most of those interesting things began like this, with the latch snapping and O'Meara striding down the gentle, grassy slope toward him. O'Meara was Vindication's constant companion now, overseeing the horse's transition from racehorse to stallion.

That transition is more complex than it sounds. Racehorses spend most of their lives in their stalls or at carefully regimented exercise on the track, and they are actively discouraged from showing sexual interest in anything at all. They are fit, on the muscle, and unused to running free, which makes even a simple task, such as turning them out in a paddock by themselves, a potentially dangerous activity. Not surprisingly, the first thing a fit Thoroughbred racehorse generally will do when turned loose in a field is run. He will fly along his fence line, wheel and buck, run at top speed for the fence before sliding to a stop at the last second. Ironically, the horse's sheer enjoyment of his own speed is terribly worrying to a stallion manager like O'Meara, because an exuberant colt, unused to turnout time, can easily hurt himself by crashing through the paddock fence or simply taking an awkward step.

"So we have to get them to the stage where we can get them out in their paddocks safely," O'Meara said, recounting the days he spent hand-walking Vindication in an enclosed ring "to take the buzz out of him," waiting for the summer-hardened ground to soften underfoot before he dared turn the horse out in a paddock. "That's always one of the scarier aspects, especially with a horse like this, where if anything goes wrong it's a major problem."

Vindication jogged toward O'Meara in a friendly manner, then tossed his head in a playful warning as the lanky Irishman drew close enough to attach a lead shank to the halter. O'Meara threaded the brass chain at one end of the leather lead over the noseband of Vindication's halter, a maneuver that gave him a little more leverage over the colt, who danced excitedly beside him as they headed toward the barn. In the five months since Vindication had left training, he had started to put on some of the stallion's typical bulk. His neck was thickening slightly and his belly was rounder now that he was exercising himself rather than being galloped every day around the racetrack. His mane and forelock, longer and thicker than in his racing days, gave him a slightly leonine look.

"He looked like a greyhound when we got him, and he's kind of a high-energy horse who keeps himself active, bucking and doing that sort of kiddish stuff," O'Meara said, giving the shank a quick tug to keep the stallion from outpacing him. "But he's slowly putting on some weight."

Prancing along beside O'Meara with his neck arched, Vindication looked powerful and coiled to strike, still ready to break from a starting gate if called upon to do it. He wheeled his rump to one side, threatening to buck, but O'Meara calmly steered him back on his path to the barn.

"He's a young horse, so we'll let him get away with a few things early on, just like we did with the other ones when they were young," O'Meara said. "For safety, you do have to get them to do what you want them to do, but you can't force them. You kind of have to finesse them into doing things."

Vindication was having one of his more crucial lessons that day, a practice run for the real matings he would have to accomplish soon. In mid-February, some of the best mares in the world would start arriving in vans to visit the stallion for $50,000 breeding sessions. Given the values of the horses involved, and the amount of money at stake every time Vindication mounted a mare, the Hill 'n' Dale staff could not afford to leave much to chance. The first step in ensuring a safe, successful mating was to teach the colt the mechanics of his job. That, O'Meara said, takes several weeks, a willing mare of even temperament, about five men to help things along, and a great deal of patience.

"These horses that are off the track have spent all their time being chastised for showing any interest in mares, and then we bring them here and expect them to turn around and do the exact opposite of what they've always been told, and to go on and actually breed the

11

mares," O'Meara said. "Patience is critical. The first time we take them in there, they mess around a little and don't really know what's going on. But once they get their acts together and figure out what nature wants them to do, they get more enthusiastic about it and figure out the technique to it. It's crucial that we get these practice runs in and get his confidence up, because that mare is nice and quiet and just stands there, but the mares in the breeding season—and especially the maiden mares—are going to be a lot tougher on him."

The mare that served as Vindication's practice partner, the nice and quiet one O'Meara referred to, was a shaggy pony-sized animal of indeterminate breeding. She was about 10 years old, O'Meara figured, and Hill 'n' Dale leased her to be a nurse mare for one of its orphaned foals and was keeping her on a little longer for test breeding.

The nurse-mare business is one of the breeding industry's natural spin-offs, and there are farmers who specialize in providing mares of various breeds as substitute mothers for Thoroughbred foals. After a nurse mare's adopted Thoroughbred foal is weaned, it is the renting farm's obligation to get the nurse mare pregnant again before returning her so that she will be producing milk in time for the next foaling season. Because nurse mares tend to be older and tolerant, and because they are not especially valuable by Thoroughbred-industry standards, many stud farms also find them to be the ideal test mates for young stallions.

By late January, Vindication had been test-bred three times and was beginning to get the hang of things. The bay nurse mare waited patiently in Hill 'n' Dale's round breeding shed, an enclosed pavilion overlooked by a sparsely furnished office with a microscope, a coffeemaker, and a large window into the shed.

The breeding shed is designed with safety in mind: The floor is thickly covered in loose wood chips, the room is round with no sharp corners, and potentially dangerous areas such as doorways have padding attached to their edges. Even Vindication's diminutive partner wore protective clothing for their meeting. The bay mare, woolly with two-inch winter hair and a long, unkempt black mane, had leather booties strapped over her back hooves, which would help cushion any kicks she sent Vindication's way. For her own protection, she also wore a heavy canvas cape. The brown cape was draped over her neck, reaching to her shoulders, and it ran lengthwise from behind her ears to the back of her withers. The top 10 inches or so of her tail had been wrapped tightly in a bandage to prevent stray hairs from getting in the way and cutting either her or Vindication.

One of the five attendants in the breeding shed gripped a device called a twitch, a thick stick with a rope loop on one end; he fitted the loop over the mare's upper lip and gradually twisted it until it was squeezing the lip, an ancient and supposedly painless method of restraint that serves either to distract a horse or to release calm-inducing endorphins, no one seems sure which. The twitch was a precautionary measure in this case, because the mare stood stock-still, apparently unconcerned.

Next to the mare and her elaborate garb, Vindication looked peculiarly vulnerable, despite his greater size and muscle. While several other men stood at the ready on either side of the mare, O'Meara led Vindication into the breeding shed and let him take a good look at the situation.

Hill 'n' Dale's farm manager—a wry 30-year industry veteran named Joe Ramsey, or J.R., for short—pulled on a pair of white rubber gloves as Vindication sized up the mare, who gave him a hint by lifting her tail, exposing her vulva, and releasing a small, pungent stream of urine, a universal equine come-on. When the stallion's penis dropped from its sheath, Ramsey washed it with a mass of cotton soaked in warm water.

O'Meara slowly led the stallion around the shed's wall, approaching the mare from her left side in order to avoid a direct hit if she decided to fire with a hind leg. Vindication sniffed around the mare's nether regions, gingerly nibbled at the top of her left hind leg, and pawed once or twice. He sniffed again, then stretched his neck out, turning his nose up and tossing his head. When he finally stood back on his hind legs and mounted the mare, the attendants quietly sprang into action.

In a Thoroughbred breeding shed, the sexual act itself is remarkably clinical, a revelation that often surprises new owners or shareholders who occasionally arrive at the farm, slightly embarrassed, to see their investments at work. A breeding session is more like a feat of engineering than a large-scale moment of passion. It requires delicately maneuvering an aroused stallion and a sometimes angry or frightened mare, each weighing a thousand pounds or more, into position to accomplish the mating as efficiently as possible and without damaging each other or the people around them. Breeding-shed workers—and the vast majority of them are men—who might be inclined toward shyness about the job's sexual nature get over that self-consciousness quickly. The work is hard and downright dangerous. As one longtime stud manager put it, "You get a stallion in a breeding shed, let me tell you something, he's got something on his mind, and you're in the way."

Stallions can be savage. Affirmed, winner of the 1978 Triple Crown, nearly took a groom's arm off. Another horse, Kennedy Road, once grabbed his groom by the stomach, shook him like a forkful of hay, and dragged him right down onto the stall floor. A groom in that position has few options for defense and little chance of making it out alive, but that one did—barely.

Mares in the breeding shed can also be deadly. Horsemen working on the ground are most likely to be injured by flying hooves backed up by a literal half-ton of horsepower. A solid blow to the head or chest can kill instantly. If they don't kill the people around them, the horses might kill themselves. A forceful kick in the belly or head can do it. Stranger, less violent things can be fatal, too. The champion mare Laugh and Be Merry reared up during a breeding session, lost her balance, and struck her head when she crashed to the floor. She died instantly.

A farm's best protection against such catastrophic accidents is a group of employees armed only with that 10-foot leather shank and their own good sense, although there is nothing even they can do if a horse dies of a heart attack while breeding, another occasional occurrence.

Hill 'n' Dale's breeding-shed attendants took up their positions around Vindication and his test mare. One held the mare's head. Another manned her tail, holding it off to one side so it was out of the stallion's way. O'Meara, unflappable and expressionless, maintained a gentle hold on the leather lead throughout the mating.

And J.R. Ramsey, his rubber gloves white against Vindication's heaving black form, was in the key position of navigator in case the stallion needed direction. The men were largely silent and unobtrusive as the horse balanced himself atop the tiny mare, who braced herself with stubby legs splayed out, her swayback sagging lower under his weight. His forelegs hung down along her shoulders, and he gripped the cape over her withers with his teeth. He hung there for a minute, seemingly uncertain about the next step, and then he backed off the mare.

Upstairs in the office, Hill 'n' Dale's general manager and resident veterinarian, Dr. George Mundy, watched the young stallion through the long window overlooking the shed floor. Mundy's distance from the scene belied his important role in it, both as an executive and a scientist.

Mundy is a middle-aged, preternaturally tidy man who has an air of rigorous discipline about him. His handwriting looks as if it has come off a printing press. His dark, slightly wavy hair is divided by a perfectly linear part and lies neatly on his head as if he has just come from the barber's chair. In khaki trousers and a clean navy-blue sweater, Mundy is a jarring contrast to the grooms below, who are dressed to be buffeted by the weather and the horses: jeans, Carhartt overalls, thick-soled work boots, and bulky knit ski hats or grimy baseball caps—all of which bear the smears, dark stains, and abrasions a person gets from working closely with horses and their biological functions.

Mundy is a veterinarian with plenty of blood-and-guts experience, but his executive side is more obvious at Hill 'n' Dale. Mundy's highly organized mind is well suited to the intricacies of the modern breeding shed, from the science of fertility to the scheduling challenges of breeding 30 mares a day. Talking about the Hill 'n' Dale stallions, he combines the languages of a psychologist, a physician, and a risk-management consultant.

"These young colts off the racetrack are a little apprehensive about this, because they think they're going to get reprimanded," he said as the stallion dismounted and half reared again. "So we have to undo some of that training. What we're trying to get this horse to do is just to cover the mare, so we're not going to discipline him too much right now. We just want him to learn to get the job done. But the more he does, the more professional we'll require him to be. We'll let him do a little rearing right now, as long as it's not dangerous. But you have to be careful, because if you let them, a horse will come in here and take over the whole show. That can't be. Someone will get hurt."

The biggest risk, Mundy said, is that a mare will kick the stallion. At best, that could discourage a horse; at worst it could cripple him permanently.

"His first live mares, it's early in the year, and some of them aren't really right," Mundy explained. "I mean, they're in heat, but they're not dead *perfect* in heat. They might be having an irregular cycle, but people want to get them bred anyway. Some of those mares, we have to tranquilize them or restrain them to get them bred. What you hope for with a young guy like this just starting out is that his first mares are some old barren mares, or even foaling mares, that are in heat just perfect.

"Even this mare," he said, pointing to the nurse mare standing patiently below the window, "she wasn't right on, but we've given her hormones, and that makes a difference. We have mares that we lease for this purpose, and when we're done with them, they're gone again. We can't be choosy about what we get."

Led by O'Meara, Vindication repeated the gradual, oblique approach to the mare and mounted her again. This time, after a few awkward moments and a little help from Ramsey, Vindication entered the mare.

"There! That's right! See, he's doing everything right," Mundy said enthusiastically, leaning toward the window. "See how he's grabbing onto the cape? That's a smart horse. He's doing the bio-mechanical things right. There's a lot of things that have to go just right, and he's helping himself do it. Some horses don't figure out that there are things they can do to make the process better. One is, if they can grab on to the cape and anchor themselves and pull themselves, that's great. And they've got to learn to work those hind legs to get the positioning right. In some breeding sheds, you'll see the guys actually have to get behind a horse and push him. Some horses just don't figure it all out.

"J.R. is the quarterback of the whole thing. The guy guiding the horse dictates how everything's going to go. He tells Aidan when to let the horse mount, when to back him off, what to do. He's in control."

One of the handlers quickly pushed a thick cotton-covered cylinder called a breeding roll between Vindication's pelvis and the mare's rump to prevent the stallion from penetrating too far and bruising the mare.

"It all looks a little haphazard, but it's actually good," Mundy said. "J.R. is trying to let the horse figure out what he's got to do. We can't show him a video and say, 'Do this.' We just want every experience to be a good experience. We don't want to do anything to discourage him."

Vindication's tail flagged upward briefly, the classic sign of ejaculation, and he backed down again. In a flash, Ramsey pulled a paper cup from the pocket of his overalls and deftly caught a dribble of the stallion's semen in it. He handed the cup off to an assistant who bolted up a flight of stairs, ducked into the office, and handed the cup to Mundy. O'Meara, meanwhile, had his hands full trying to get Vindication out of the breeding shed again. The horse pulled back as O'Meara tried to lead him out, reared back on his haunches, and then lurched forward and bucked, lashing out with both hind legs.

"Look at that, he doesn't want to go home," Mundy said with a smile. "That is *great*, because libido is the limiting factor to a horse."

A fertile horse with a poor libido can be maddening for stallion managers, and he can be difficult to help. When 2002 Kentucky Derby winner War Emblem went to stud in Japan at the end of his racing career, he caused great consternation by showing little interest in breeding mares. Eventually, the farm that stood him resorted to showing him a parade of mares and breeding him to the ones that aroused him. It was a time-consuming process that any stallion manager would prefer to avoid. A stallion that enjoyed his job, as Vindication appeared to, kept the production line moving.

One of Hill 'n' Dale's shed attendants now stood at a safe distance behind Vindication and swung a leather lead shank at him. The stallion rolled his eye backward, lashed out resentfully with a hind leg, then hopped forward and finally followed O'Meara out of the shed again. The mare, quiet as ever, was led away through a separate door to have her various trappings removed. The entire process had taken less than 20 minutes, and, ideally, that would drop to about 10 minutes per mare as Vindication became more efficient at his new job. With books of more than 100 mares, speed is important in the modern breeding shed. One slow breeder can back up an entire day's appointments, which are timed as closely as possible to each mare's ovulation.

At Hill 'n' Dale, Mundy has fine-tuned the scheduling by refusing to make firm breeding appointments several days in advance, the traditional booking method developed years ago, when stallions were bred to fewer mares each season. Hill 'n' Dale customers are asked to keep checking each mare until it is nearly certain that she is on the point of ovulating, and then Hill 'n' Dale assigns that mare a time slot that is most likely to match egg with sperm.

But the pressure to fit so many mares into just over four months of breeding is still acute for stallions and farm staff alike. The scheduling leaves little time for stallions who are shy, slow, or highly romantic about their job.

"It takes him 10 minutes to get ready to breed, and when he's ready he wants to get up there right away," Claiborne Farm's stallion manager, Jim Zajic, once groused about the farm's expensive ($150,000), successful, and quirky stallion Seeking the Gold. "So he'll mount the mare, and he'll enter two or three times, but then he'll dismount whether or not he's bred the mare. It's what I call foreplay, and it's a pain in the neck."

To speed things along, stallion men try to determine what each stallion's preferences are. In this regard, the modern stallion manager has become as shrewd about fetishes as a Las Vegas madam. Quick arousal means quick action, and time is money.

"When they walk in here, let them tell you what they like," an old stud manager told Zajic when he first started work at Claiborne.

"He showed me tricks," Zajic said. "Little tricks."

The tricks are largely psychological. One of Claiborne's stallions, Devil's Bag, liked to watch the stallion ahead of him breed a mare before he himself came into the breeding shed. The highly successful sire Unbridled liked to nuzzle and tease mares. Several others have preferred to have the cotton-covered breeding roll between themselves and the mares before they would breed. As odd as they sound, such details help keep a stallion interested in his job, which is crucial to an efficient breeding shed. A stallion with enough libido and enough bookings might breed three times a day.

The packed schedule adds to the job's physical risk, too. Breeders eager to get to a stallion early in the season might present mares who are, as one stud manager put it, "only borderline receptive." Those mares, hastily pushed into production before they have come fully into heat, are more likely to kick.

"I understand the economics of it," said Bill Sellers, the stallion manager at Lane's End Farm, where Seattle Slew's son A.P. Indy stands for a $300,000 fee and covers about 100 mares annually. "Probably the hardest part of our job is determining whether a mare is safe to breed. But the fact of the matter is that they're going to keep coming, and we have to try to get them covered and try to get them in foal."

Mundy tipped several drops of Vindication's ejaculate from the paper cup onto one glass slide, covered it with another slide, and pushed the stack under the brackets of the microscope near the window.

"After every cover, when the horse comes off, we get a little dismount sample," Mundy said. "You don't need much. But it's the only way you know the horse ejaculated. He can go through the motions and do everything, but this is your proof that he did it or not. I'm just looking for whether they're there or not."

In this case, they were. The view through the microscope's eyepiece showed a landscape of tiny sperm that looked like shivering, fine-ground pepper. Whether or not they were actually fertile remained an open question. Neither the farm nor its equine-insurance agent ran a fertility test on Vindication once he arrived at Hill 'n' Dale.

"The insurance company requires that the horse can't be test-bred or evaluated or have covered a mare before the insurance starts," Mundy said. "They will ultrasound them and look at them physically, and they might make their rates higher if, say, the horse only has one testicle. Or they may not, depending on the consistency, whether it's a normal testicle, the orientation of the testicle. They might even do hormone testing.

"But unless there's something obviously abnormal physically, it's very, very hard to determine something like fertility, especially in these young horses coming off the track."

The difficulty of assessing fertility through a microscope was made clear when Secretariat began his stud career at age 4. Two early analyses showed his sperm cells to be immature, a bit of information that undoubtedly caused plenty of sleepless nights for those at Claiborne Farm and the stallion's syndicate members. Claiborne added a stipulation to its syndication that investors whose mares turned up empty after breeding to the Triple Crown winner could get a full refund plus interest. In exchange, shareholders agreed to drop any additional testing and let Secretariat get on with his job. In the end, he got 32 of his 36 mares in foal during the 1974 breeding season, an excellent fertility rate by any standard.

Two-time Horse of the Year and Breeders' Cup Classic winner Cigar, on the other hand, was a complete dud as a stallion. Coolmore Stud bought the horse privately and brought him to its Kentucky farm with great fanfare. Fans and media flocked while the champion runner was displayed like a jewel in the crown. The farm understandably was horrified to discover soon afterward that the stallion was completely infertile.

The insurance payment amounted to $25 million. Cigar now resides at the Kentucky Horse Park in Lexington, where he is a living legend paraded daily for his fans. For his insurers, who now own him, Cigar is like the sword in the stone. If they could solve the riddle of his problem, if they could make the sperm magically alive and potent, they could have a horse well worth what they paid in the settlement. Every fall, just in case something has changed, the company arranges to van Cigar to a local fertility specialist, who examines him to no avail and sends him back again. The horse remains the nation's pet and the insurer's direst nightmare.

Racehorses straight off the track might have any number of reasons for showing signs of subfertility, ranging from simple stress to the effects of drugs.

"But the biggest things are fitness and stress," Mundy said. "You have a horse that has no body fat and is at a top level of fitness. That's a whole different focus than on making sperm and being able to cover mares. The way we got this horse was perfect, because we had six months to let him adjust, to let him gear down from his race-track routine and put him into this routine. Time is the best thing.

"What goes against us is the shortening of the day length, because stallions a lot of times are geared to daylight, just like mares. Their natural cycle is to be as fertile as they can in April and May, which is what the mares also do. But we want to make them more fertile ahead of schedule. Some people actually extend the daylight for the stallions by putting them under lights at night.

"But there's no question that the best stimulus for a horse to produce sperm is to breed them. That's exactly what we're doing with Vindication, and we'll let some of our other horses breed a couple of times before breeding season starts, too. It gets the cycle started: The hormones surge, and things get going.

"The only definitive test is, can he get his mares pregnant?" Mundy added. "And we'll know that 15 days after he breeds his first mare. Normal stallions run at about 50 percent, so if we breed 10 mares, we'd expect five of them to be pregnant, and that would be the breed average. So you start with a hundred mares, and you'll probably get half of those. So then you have 50 you breed a second time, and you'll probably get 25 or 30 of them, and then you've got the rest you have to breed a third time. That's how it works, and you never get them all."

In Mundy's experience, the increase in stallions' book sizes has made more difference to scheduling than to fertility. But the two things are also related, as Mundy pointed out.

"If you're breeding right on top of ovulation, that's your best shot at getting the mare pregnant," he said. "It takes less sperm volume and it increases efficiency. We don't double, which is breeding a mare back again because she didn't ovulate."

Mundy's careful, on-the-egg scheduling program at Hill 'n' Dale is as much about not wasting the product—the sperm—as it is about fertility. On the industrial scale of Thoroughbred breeding, that can also help preserve a stallion's libido. And for a horse like Vindication, who was expected to breed about 130 mares in his first season, libido is an important job requirement. If they haven't got that—Mundy shrugs—there's not much a stallion manager can do.

Mundy knows Hill 'n' Dale's product well, including its sell-by date. He has to.

"The industry standard says that sperm is viable for 48 hours," he said. "We know from experience how good our horses are, how long their sperm lasts. Some horses are notorious for lasting a long time. Woodman, over at Ashford Stud, is the classic one: He's said to have had sperm last 14 days. When you have a horse like that, believe me, it makes your job easier.

"We know how long our stallions' sperm is viable because we've had cases where we bred a mare, she didn't ovulate for five days, and we didn't double her—and she still got pregnant. So then I know my guy lasts for five days. The other way we know is if a mare comes up with twins that are different ages, which you can tell by the relative sizes of the vesicles. If a mare comes up with a 21-day vesicle and a twin vesicle that's five days smaller, then, again, you know your horse lasts for five days. So if someone wants a double after two days, I know my horses well enough to tell them to wait four or five days and check again."

These complex accountings are part of a stud manager's daily life. Mundy combines a farmer's knowledge of nature and livestock, a veterinarian's scientific method, and the efficiency obsessions of a factory floor manager. He keeps a ledger for every stallion's breeding season, filling in the name of each mare, which heat cycle she was bred on, the breeding date, and various reference notes.

"I put all sorts of notes in here, like this one here had to be tranquilized," he said, pointing to a mare with "TQ" next to her entry. "Or if I don't like something I see in the dismount sample, like if there's urine in it, I note that down, too. This mare"—he ran his finger down to another entry—"we had to restrain her by an ear when we bred her on a four-day double. She wasn't happy to be here, so she'd probably ovulated by the time she got here."

An uninterested or unhappy mare can be dangerous, but there are things that worry Mundy more than that. Namely, disease. Breeding sheds take every precaution to prevent disease, and Hill 'n' Dale is no exception. Disease outbreaks such as equine viral arteritis, a highly contagious problem that can cause abortion, have on occasion shut Kentucky's entire breeding business down as veterinarians struggled to contain them. Routinely, breeders bringing their mares to stud farms present health certificates, and the mares are washed and examined before being brought to the breeding shed. Mundy also takes weekly bacterial cultures from three sites on each stallion's penis to monitor possible pathogens. The cultures are sent to a lab, which reports back any suspicious findings.

"The biggest thing we worry about is a stallion having a venereal infection, because that can compromise a mare getting pregnant," Mundy said.

But the precautions are surprisingly simple. Hill 'n' Dale's breeding shed has a cabinet filled with plastic bottles of Ivory liquid soap, which is a staple of the farm's disease-prevention campaign; they use it to wash the mares. Another weapon: vinegar.

"Most of the things we come up with on our stallion cultures, we're able to take care of just by changing the stallion's pH," Mundy said. "All it might take is a little vinegar and water. After he breeds a mare, we'll just spray him with that. If the pH is out of balance, then it allows the bad stuff to take over. We used to treat them with antibiotics systemically and topically, the whole bit, but we've found that actually less is better. But if it's something really detrimental, then we'll take a stallion out of the line to deal with it."

With that, Mundy removed the slides that trapped a fraction of Vindication's $50,000 ejaculate and dropped them unceremoniously into a plastic trash jug labeled "Sharps," for discarding used hypodermic needles and similar veterinary detritus from the breeding shed's routine operations.

"We're enthusiastic about what we see with this horse," he concluded. "He's just got it, you know? Some horses just don't put it all together. I remember I had one horse that we actually had to take the mare to his stall and had him follow her out of his stall. He bred her right outside of the stall. Until then, he had had no interest and just didn't get it. We worked with him for weeks and tried everything, and finally when we did that, boom! The light came on.

"That's why you get a little anxious with a first-year horse. Boy, you hope he's a fast breeder, because if they're slow, the process takes a half-hour and it's a pain. We've got 10 horses. We can breed all 10 of them in an hour and a half, about 10 minutes a horse. You have one guy washing, one guy bringing in the next horse—it's a production line. If a slow breeder comes in, it backs the whole thing up. A fast horse, he comes in, drops down, is ready to go, and, if the mare's right, it's bing, bing, bing, as fast as they can breed."

Back in the stallion barn, young Aidan O'Meara was in his own "office," next to one of the stud barn's tack rooms, where the stallions' thick leather-and-brass halters hung on hooks and extra feed bags were stored in stacks. O'Meara's office had a refrigerator humming on one side and a window looking out across the stallion paddocks on the other. It also had a leather chair pulled up to an inexpensive metal desk of the kind you would find in a strip-mall H & R Block office, but O'Meara wasn't off his feet long enough to use the furniture for much except hanging a jacket on. The desk had a well-thumbed Larousse Spanish pocket dictionary on it—a necessary tool in an industry where the workers increasingly are Hispanic—and a few computer-printed pedigrees detailing the produce records of some mares.

O'Meara's real office was outside the door and down the walkways of the stud barn. His job there was to learn the personal habits of Hill 'n' Dale's 10 stallions and to keep the horses healthy, happy, and efficient. That had less to do with science than art. It started with careful observation and good horsemanship, and it would develop into a mutual understanding and a sort of constant negotiation, once Vindication became a full-fledged stallion. The horse's first breeding season would turn him into that. The strapping colt would put on 300 or 400 pounds, his neck would thicken further, and he would grow more possessive about his paddock and his stall. He would command a certain respect, and part of O'Meara's job would be finding ways to cater to the horse's natural and instinctive requirements, without letting the stallion take over. It would be a delicate task, day in and day out.

"Stallions are very territorial creatures, and you can see it if you look out at one of their paddocks, you'll see four or five big poop piles on the corners in front of the fence," O'Meara said. "They're still herd animals, and they do a lot of things they'd do out in the wild. To keep the stallions happy, we encourage some of that and try to keep the environment as close as we can to what they'd do in the wild. But, obviously, we can't do it exactly like the wild, but we do let them have their little idiosyncrasies every day."

O'Meara already liked what he saw of Vindication, and it pleased him that the horse was drawing crowds of interested breeders as well as fans. In November 2003, a year after John Sikura had first taken Satish Sanan on a tour around the farm in hopes they could strike a deal for the Breeders' Cup Juvenile winner, O'Meara had shown Vindication to 35 visitors in a single day.

"So far, they've been blown off their feet by him," O'Meara said. "They're so impressed by him, physically, and his whole attitude."

The attitude, O'Meara noted with some amusement, is familiar.

"He's a lot like his daddy," he said. "He has his dad's personality and some of the same quirks, like he doesn't like you rubbing on his belly. Seattle Slew wasn't a big fan of that, either. He's a pretty smart horse who picks things up right away, but he does like to do things his own way. So we have to find a balance and get along with each other."

If Vindication proved as successful as his sire, he and O'Meara might have to get along with each other for a long time.

"He's got the best group of mares he possibly could get, lots of Grade 1 winners and producers," O'Meara said, ticking off the list of outstanding mates that were signed up to visit Vindication. The list included at least one who was a two-time champion, a mare named Silverbulletday who won titles as top 2-year-old and 3-year-old filly as well as the Breeders' Cup Juvenile Fillies in the 1990's.

"With the likes of that, he's going to get every shot he can to make it as a sire," O'Meara said. "He's one that could be in the same league as his daddy down the road. But, obviously, it's a tough business, and there are many horses who had the same credentials as his and didn't make it.

"Vindication has to have a serious shot. There's been a changing of the guard lately. A lot of good, older stallions are coming to the end of their terms, and a number of good stallions have died recently, so there's a real opportunity there for a young horse to rise and fill that void. But it's a fickle business."

Nature is also fickle, as Hill 'n' Dale owner Sikura and general manager Mundy well knew. But they all believed that Vindication was as good a gamble as there was, for reasons ranging from the genetic to the spiritual.

"To have the champion son, from his last crop, standing where he could see Seattle Slew's grave," Sikura mused. "I don't mean to sound New Age or anything like that, but there's something there about the spirit of Seattle Slew in that."

91

But Hill 'n' Dale also has nine other stallions, including another promising son of Seattle Slew named Doneraile Court. And there were an additional 302 advertised stallions in Kentucky alone who were also heading to the breeding shed that year.

"You never know where the good horse comes from," Sikura said. "It may not be Vindication. Maybe it's another horse, maybe it's at another farm. But if you can get that one special horse, and if he stays healthy, and if he does as well as he should and isn't beset by any weird circumstances, you can build your success around that special horse.

"If you have one of those, opportunities abound. You have favor with established breeders and new people alike. More people call you, and there are fewer calls you have to make. But the great thing about it is, you just never know."

5 The Fragile Factory

IT IS HARD to imagine, as one takes in the panorama of central Kentucky's rolling pastureland and palatial barns, that fortunes can be made by selling such airy stuff as equine pedigrees and human hope.

But they can, and one need only visit 1,600-acre Taylor Made Farm near Lexington to see how well racehorse owners' dreams fuel the industrial manufacture of Thoroughbreds. Taylor Made is aptly named, not just because the four brothers who own it are named Taylor, but also because, as a modern commercial breeding operation, the farm is engaged primarily in providing horses that are tailor-made for the demanding Thoroughbred marketplace. In that regard, Taylor Made Farm is similar to many other nurseries, large and small, in central Kentucky. But it is far bigger and reaps a vastly larger income than the average breeding farm.

At the end of foaling season, when the farm's population is at its peak, Taylor Made holds about 650 horses for some 100 clients. Almost all of those are mares, their foals, and yearlings. Six are stallions. Taylor Made's equine demographics indicate the extent of the farm's involvement in Thoroughbred breeding. From conception to weaning to the auction ring, Taylor Made handles it all, and it does so on an industrial scale.

By dealing in high volume as well as attracting clients with superior bloodstock, Taylor Made has hit on the golden exacta that improves a farm's chances of success: quality *and* quantity. The farm's list of distinguished "graduates"—a handy catch-all term farms often use to refer to runners that were bred, raised, or sold by them—is studded with champions: Unbridled's Song, Anees, Farda Amiga, and on and on. For Taylor Made and the commercial breeders who make up the majority of the farm's clients, the definition of a big horse is not limited to champions or Grade 1 winners. It also means a home run moneymaker in the auction ring. By this standard, Taylor Made also has done well: Its operators estimate that, in the 25 years since it opened, Taylor Made has sold more than $830 million worth of horseflesh, most of it at public auction. In light of this success, the farm's motto is particularly apt: "May prosperity lie in this transaction."

The Taylor brothers—and their two sisters, one of whom also works full-time at the farm—are the children of a legendary Kentucky horseman, Joe Taylor, who made his mark as manager of a prestigious Lexington farm, Gainesway. Taylor's boys grew up working with horses for their dad, and his influence, in terms of both knowledge and business connections, was thorough.

In 1976, the oldest son, 19-year-old Duncan, spotted an opportunity. The Thoroughbred market was growing, new investors were buying mares to support the stallions they held shares in, and the mare population was starting to outnumber the stalls and acreage available at some established farms, including Gainesway. Young Duncan Taylor, equipped with stalls on a small farm his father owned, started a modest business boarding overflow mares that were booked to Gainesway's stallions. His contact with Gainesway's high-class clientele and their horses gave him an enviable platform to build on, and he did, gradually expanding from keeping mares to prepping their foals for auction.

Duncan's younger brothers later joined him, and within five years of opening its barn doors, Taylor Made had sold three horses for $1 million or more at auction. After another five years, Taylor Made was a major consignor, selling as many as a hundred horses at larger sales such as Keeneland's September yearling auction. In 1997, Taylor Made opened a stallion barn, too, and made juvenile champion Unbridled's Song its first resident—finally extending the farm's reach into the last corner of the commercial Thoroughbred market.

The farm now stands six stallions at its Nicholasville, Kentucky, facility. Their fees range from $10,000 for champions Artax and Real Quiet to $125,000 for Breeders' Cup Juvenile winner Unbridled's Song. Together, the Taylor Made stallions sired 409 foals in 2003 for North American breeders. If they sired the same number again in 2004, and if all of those breeders were to pay the full stud fees, Taylor Made's stallion barn alone would generate $18,575,000.

Taylor Made is renowned for a mixture of slick marketing and down-home customer service. Every Taylor Made client with a mare at the farm gets a monthly statement that includes a photo of her foal; the Taylor Made team's detailed assessment of the foal's progress, including both its attributes and areas where it could stand a little improvement; and the monthly bill, including any special shoeing, feed supplements, or corrective and cosmetic surgeries the foal might have needed as part of that improvement.

"The people who own these horses might not know anything about horses or how to handle them," one of their yearling managers said. "But they are proud of their horses, and they like to see how they're progressing, maybe put each month's photo up on their wall, sit back, light up a cigar, look at them, and say, 'That's my horse.' It's important to us and to them to let them know how their horse is doing."

The office's computers hum with programs that track mares' runners and their close relatives, its phones are lively with staff updating clients on their horses. The barns are swept bare of dirt and stray straws; their white cinder-block walls gleam with disinfectant after a foaling; every barn has a blackboard with detailed descriptions of each mare, her foaling date, the covering stallion, and any special medicine she might need; and at every hour, day and night, there are numerous eyes and hands checking and rechecking the mares, foals, yearlings, and stallions that are Taylor Made's profitable but perishable product.

Every participant in the high-stakes Thoroughbred industry is gambling, but breeders arguably take more risk and have a longer wait for their payoff than anyone else in the game. The reason is purely biological: It takes 11 months for a mare to carry a foal to term. Most commercial breeders sell their young stock as yearlings, meaning they have at least a two-year wait from conception to pay-day. The period between mating and the auction ring is a yawning stretch of financial wasteland in which mare and foal—assuming the mare actually conceives and produces a healthy one—rack up about $11,000 in routine health care, feed, board, and, in many cases, some form of surgery or other veterinary care for the foal. The hope is that the foal's eventual auction price will cover those expenses and the stud fee, but the sale is a long way off, and there are myriad risks in the meantime.

Catastrophic foaling injuries are just one of the unforeseeable problems that can strike a breeder's equine investment, even in such scrupulously managed surroundings as Taylor Made's. A $1 million mare with a $500,000 stud fee in her is still a horse that has to be turned out to graze and exercise, even though she might be struck by lightning or fatally kicked by another mare while she is in the pasture. Mares abort foals or deliver deformed ones, regardless of how much you have invested in them. And even seemingly ideal foals can grow up to be afflicted with unpredictable, and sometimes fatal, problems.

One worker at Taylor Made recalled a yearling so physically perfect that the Taylor brothers proudly gathered the farm's yearling managers around just to look at him. He later came down with wobbler syndrome, a developmental disease in which the vertebral column pinches the growing spinal cord, causing the horse to lose his coordination. Needless to say, the colt never made it to the races.

Not surprisingly, the breeding industry has spawned a thriving equine-insurance business that can help offset some of the crushing losses that can afflict breeders. About 90 percent of the mares, foals, and yearlings at Taylor Made are insured, though sometimes the cost of coverage can be expensive. One common form of insurance, for example, covers a foal from 42 days after conception until 30 days after birth, at a rate of about 16 percent of its insured value.

Some mares simply do not conceive at all, an especially frustrating problem that can have multiple causes or no readily identifiable explanation. Barrenness, which might occur only once in a mare's lifetime or become a perennial problem, has plagued breeders for centuries. In a business where the uterus is the factory and the foal is the sellable product, a habitually empty mare spells doom for a breeder, and sometimes for herself.

97

Gervase Markham, an Englishman who published a book on horsemanship in 1683, offered a range of "cures" for barrenness that included such ingredients as sparrows' dung and turpentine. In one recipe, he suggests mashing "a good handful of Leeks" into five spoonfuls of wine, "then put thereunto twelve flies, called Cantharides, then strain them all together with a sufficient quantity of water to serve the Mare therewith two days together, by pouring the same into her nature with a Clyster-pipe made for the purpose."

Thankfully, treatments for many equine reproductive problems like barrenness and spontaneous abortion have advanced significantly since the 1600's, but the causes can still be as mysterious as they were in Markham's time. And the costs can be huge, both for breeders left without a product to sell and for stallion owners, who generally collect their fee only when a mare produces a live foal.

"If the factory is closed down, you've got no product to sell," as one breeder put it.

In the spring of 2001, a disease of unknown origin caused thousands of mares in central Kentucky to abort their fetuses, wiping out approximately a third of the state's entire foal crop that year, or about 2,700 fetuses. Hundreds of other mares produced sickly foals that later died. Most of the mares never showed any sign of illness, except perhaps for a slight fever. The abortions occurred primarily between April and June, and by the time the mares lost their fetuses, it was too late in the season to wait for them to come into heat and breed them again. For many commercial Thoroughbred breeders, the mysterious wave of fetal and foal deaths—known as mare reproductive loss syndrome—was the equivalent of the 1929 stock market crash, especially for those who had borrowed heavily against returns they had expected those foals to make at future auctions. The Kentucky Department of Agriculture estimated the disease's total economic impact— including stud-fee losses, future auction losses, and the value of the dead foals, among other things—at more than $300 million.

Farms tried to explain to clients why their fat, dappled, and apparently healthy mares had, without warning, expelled their fetuses, but there was little to go on. Some scientists thought it might have been a weather-related bloom of mycotoxins in the pastures, and so breeders brought their mares in from pastures and fed them hay instead. Other researchers suspected the culprit was a massive springtime infestation of Eastern tent caterpillars, a compelling theory that sent farm workers out with insecticides and blowtorches to rid their trees of the silky, baglike nests. When someone pointed out that the caterpillars ate cherry leaves, which were known to produce cyanide, breeders hacked down the pink-flowered trees.

In fact, no one really knew why the abortions had occurred, and as they scrambled to eliminate every possible culprit, the professional breeders were left reminding their clients of a truism that often got overlooked in the golden dream of million-dollar sale prices: Thoroughbred breeding is an *agri*business, and like every other kind of farming, it is subject to the whims of nature. Mares, it turns out, are more like farm fields than factories.

The vast majority of hands-on breeders (as opposed to those who simply own mares as an investment) know as well as any whale at the mutuel window that there is no such thing as a sure bet with horses. Like their high-rolling counterparts who study race replays and the *Daily Racing Form*'s information-laden past-performance lines, breeders too are obsessed with risk-reduction. Their eyes naturally spot danger in mundane objects that other people would never notice at all, and, what's more, breeders will work out ways to eliminate that risk or at least buffer their mares from it.

The Taylors are particularly zealous in this. One of the first things a Taylor brother is likely to do with a visitor to the farm is hand him a copy of the family's own risk-reduction textbook, *Joe Taylor's Complete Guide to Breeding and Raising Racehorses*, written by their father. Published in 1993, the book is exhaustive, covering everything from buying property and building barns to managing stallions and training yearlings. The topics in between reveal a staggering array of potential disasters and mishaps that might be prevented by proper attention to detail. Joe Taylor's thoughts on gate latches and hinges alone cover three pages. "Hinges for horse gates have always interested me," he explained, adding, "I have examined hinges all across the United States and in my travels to Europe." (His recommendation, incidentally, is a pipe-sleeve design, mainly because it has no protruding edges that might injure a horse and is still strong enough to hold the gate up properly.)

The catalog of risks makes for intimidating reading. Asphalt floors in a wash stall, Taylor warns, are risky because they don't drain well and can allow bacteria to accumulate. Stall doorways should have rounded edges to prevent a mare from injuring herself as she enters and exits. Proper ventilation is crucial, because "horses are sensitive to the ammonia, dust, and molds that accumulate in a barn. The result may manifest itself as pneumonia in a foal. Older horses may develop more deceptive problems: allergies, emphysema, and various maladies labeled as chronic obstructive pulmonary disease."

Horses apparently are ingenious at finding ways to maim, sicken, or kill themselves indoors, but even outdoors in their natural setting there is a multitude of dangers. Trees are a particular hazard, and breeders should try to build their pastures to exclude them wherever possible, Taylor writes. If trees can't be fenced out, they should at least be surrounded by protective fencing, because horses will otherwise run into them, chew on them, or stand under them and get struck by lightning. Beware groundhog holes that can snap a leg. In winter, muddy ground that is heavily pocked with hoofprints can freeze over and cause a mare or yearling to injure an ankle—and in horses, of course, a fractured ankle can be fatal. If you build your pasture fences with the posts facing the inside, it's almost guaranteed your mare will knock her knee on one and cripple herself.

If they are unable to kill themselves on fences, trees, frozen mud, or groundhog holes, horses can simply kill each other. In early 2004, two Kentucky broodmares—one of them the dam of a champion—accidentally collided in a field, injuring each other so badly they both had to be euthanized. Clearly, investing in mares is more dangerous than it looks to the tourists who stop by pasture fences to photograph mares and foals capering in the grass. "The horse business," as a participant once observed, "is not for boys in short pants."

The longest chapters in *Joe Taylor's Complete Guide to Breeding and Raising Racehorses* have to do with broodmare management and foaling, and they, too, reveal an alarming number of ways that everything can go tragically awry: uterine infection, retained afterbirth, foal deformity, fatal incompatibility between the mare's colostrum and the foal's red blood cells, a too-big foal in a too-narrow birth canal.

"The actual mechanics of reproduction are quite complex," Joe Taylor advised novice breeders in his book. "You need to understand only two important points: (1) Mares are delicate and highly unpredictable . . . and (2) you must employ qualified veterinarians and other personnel who understand the systems and individualistic nature of mares."

No one knows the intricacies of equine birth better than Charlie Barron, Taylor Made's broodmare manager. In his 18 years at the farm, he has helped with more than 7,000 births. The vast majority have gone well, but, inevitably, some have not.

"We've seen a little bit of everything," Barron said as he piloted his enormous, growling pickup truck from foaling barn to foaling barn one moonless February night. The pastures he drove by were like a black rolling ocean, and the distant foaling barns, their square stall windows yellow with light, looked like lonely ships. "We've had babies upside down that we've had to turn. We've had red bag, which is a thick, leatherlike bag over the placenta, and we've got to bust it and get the baby out pretty quick to get it some oxygen. We've had them with their feet folded back. We've had them with their head folded back. Just different ways they're laying, and there are some you've got to correct even before the mare can lay down and have her baby."

Barron learned long ago that some things, like a foal's position in the womb, cannot be controlled or predicted; they can only be dealt with. He always leaves his pickup truck running while he's foaling one mare, because another mare is likely to "go" minutes later in another barn, and a foaling always has the potential to become an emergency in no time flat. Charlie Barron is matter-of-fact, tranquil, experienced, and good-humored, but there are some things that send a chill even through his stout heart.

"The worst thing, and I don't even like to talk about it, is what you call the dog-sit position," he said. "The back feet are actually hooked over the mare's pelvis. You don't really detect it until you get the baby half out. You'll get its nose and front feet out to the shoulders, and then you're stuck. You can't push the baby back in, and you can't get it out. Usually, in that scenario, you lose the baby and you're just working to save the mare. The only way to do it is the mare's either got to go to the clinic or you've got to get her flipped onto her back. But usually they're gonna fight you, because they don't want to lay there with all four feet in the air like that. But if you can do it, you might be able to push the baby back and the feet will drop down from the pelvis enough to release. It's a mess. You seldom ever save a baby like that, and if you do, you got real lucky."

The previous season, two mares at Taylor Made ended up in this situation.

"And I got lucky with one of them," he said. "I knew what was wrong as soon as the baby got halfway out and came to a dead stop, with no give, I knew what was going on. The mare evidently knew something was wrong, because she laid there and started wallowing, and she rolled up against the wall and got cast there. That gave me an opportunity, so I laid down, pushed that thing back in, got my arm up in there, and dropped those feet below the pelvis.

"I was able to get the baby out with just a torn ligament. The mare just laid there till we got the baby out, and then we just turned her over again. We did pretty good on that one. We got real, real lucky.

"But the other one, we lost the baby and the mom, because she got down and couldn't get up, and we couldn't get her on the van to go to the clinic. She was paralyzed. So."

Modern life has given breeders many lifesavers: antibiotics, veterinary surgical techniques such as equine caesareans, and even the homely telephone have all made a crucial difference to horsemen in their constant battle for a safe, successful harvest of their annual equine crop. Major farms often have resident veterinarians dedicated to their mares, and Lexington also has two world-renowned equine clinics with surgical facilities to rival many human hospitals. Joe Taylor himself noted that sometimes a breeder's best tool is a horse van parked right outside the foaling barn, ready to speed a troubled mare or foal to the veterinary hospital.

Lexington's two equine clinics, Rood and Riddle Equine Hospital and Hagyard Davidson McGee, get plenty of customers during the peak foaling season between March and May. Dr. Bill Bernard, who oversees Rood and Riddle's neonatal intensive-care unit, estimated the hospital treats between 100 and 200 foals a year. Some are premature, others suffer from ailments such as colitis or enteritis.

The fact that such a neonatal intensive-care unit exists at all suggests how much value breeders place on their commercially bred Thoroughbred foals. As bloodstock values have climbed in the last decade, breeders have had more incentive to rehabilitate or save a well-bred foal, especially if the foal is a filly who might make a promising broodmare prospect even if she never races. Neonatal care can run from $200 to $500 a day, and, for potential sale-ring or racetrack prodigies, it can be worth the gamble. But cheaply bred stock is much less likely to make it to a clinic, because the economic equation, the guiding factor for most commercial breeders in the modern Thoroughbred industry, simply doesn't add up.

"The level of intensive care can get pretty high," Bernard acknowledged. "But if, for example, you have a foal that has a $100,000 stud fee in it, those owners can be willing to spend $5,000 to $10,000 to attempt to save it. We can tell someone that, if the foal is valuable enough to spend that $5,000 to $10,000 on, we're not wasting their money. We're not always successful, but often we are. Many of these foals can surprise people and be athletes. They can turn from scrawny individuals to strong adults."

Bernard spoke outside a roomy stall holding a dark bay filly delivered three weeks early by caesarean section after veterinarians discovered her dam was dying of an irreparable small colon rupture. The filly, who could not stand yet, was barely visible among a pile of blue blankets, diaper pads, and pillows that cushioned her head and hooves. She was festooned with lengths of tubes connected to intravenous drips and an intranasal oxygen supply, and a heating lamp hung over her.

Most of the hospital expenses for foals like this one go for nursing care at a cost of around $8 an hour. A neonatal staff of about 10 works in three shifts of eight hours each, weighing and cleaning the foals, monitoring their vital signs, conducting blood tests, and turning the foals over every two hours to prevent bedsores. It's labor-intensive work that requires great attention and gentleness.

"The nursing care is very important," Bernard said. "Without that, all the medication I can give them won't be successful."

Most of the breeders who send foals to Rood and Riddle or Hagyard Davidson McGee are gambling that the foal will turn out to be worth saving, in cold financial terms. A good number have been, and some have even turned out to be home run horses. The clinics are chary of revealing their patients' identities; the Lexington farm that sent the premature filly's dam to Rood and Riddle for the caesarean, for example, threatened a lawsuit if the dead mare's name was published. Other farms—revealing a widespread culture of paranoia about any information that might damage a horse's future value—had been known to request that the identification cards on their horses' hospital stalls be labeled falsely, to prevent word of the illness or injury from getting out. But Bernard acknowledged that former Rood and Riddle neonatal patients have included $1 million sale yearlings and Breeders' Cup winners, though not a Kentucky Derby winner yet.

His own goals, and that of the nursing staff, are more modest. "My wish," he said, "is that every foal we get in here gets to go home again."

During the traditional foaling season from January to June, Charlie Barron and his Taylor Made staff of seven—one person watching in each foaling barn and three men like Barron driving around the farm—oversee the births of about 250 foals.

No matter when they are actually born, all of those foals share the same official birthday: January 1. The Thoroughbred registry at The Jockey Club established the January 1 birthday for orderly record-keeping. All of the foals born at Taylor Made in 2004, for example, would become yearlings on January 1, 2005, and they would all be eligible to run in their first races after they officially turned 2 on January 1, 2006. By neatly placing foals in "crops" by year, the single-birthday system eliminates the headache of having to determine, for example, which horses are *actually* 3 years old at the Kentucky Derby, which is open only to 3-year-olds.

The system is orderly, but it requires a certain manipulation of nature. The breeding season runs from roughly February 10 until early July, so that mares will begin foaling on schedule the following January. Much of the breeding season takes place in winter or early spring, a time when mares are not naturally at peak fertility.

"To breed horses that will satisfy the rules of racing means we must first frustrate the rules of nature," as Joe Taylor put it in his book. "In February, we must 'trick' the systems of the mare into believing it is late May or June. . . . As you might guess, fooling nature can be a touchy business." Breeders accomplish this trick partly by putting their mares under artificial light for part of each day from December until May. The idea is to expose them to at least 16 hours of light a day in the hopes that their bodies will maintain peak-season fertility.

Understandably, the January 1 requirement puts a premium on foals born as close as possible to that date each year, because those foals really will be yearlings when the official birthday rolls around the following season. Their pasture-mates born in May will also be yearlings officially, but physically they will be smaller and less mature—in other words, less attractive than their peers at a yearling auction. To ensure an early foal, commercial breeders strive to get their mares mated to a stallion as soon as the breeding shed opens in February. After 11 months, the ideal result is a strapping foal that would at least avoid one of the common strikes against sale yearlings.

The practical effect of all this, from broodmare manager Charlie Barron's point of view, is that most of Taylor Made's 250 foals are due to arrive in February, March, and early April. Barron doesn't sleep much during foaling season. Six nights a week, he spends his 7:00 P.M. to 7:00 A.M. shift driving from barn to barn, crouching in the deep golden straw that beds each mare's stall, peeking underneath the horses' huge bellies to see whether their udders are dripping with milk, and pulling on foals' forelimbs to help them come into the wintry world. Every Saturday, he takes the night off to sleep, leaving his second-in-command, a taciturn, gray-bearded man named Jackie Davis, to oversee the broodmares.

A day or two after a healthy foal is born, Barron's team rotates the mare and her baby out of the foaling barn and brings another pregnant mare in. There is always a crowd of mares ready for a stall

in the foaling barns, and sometimes they can't wait. This is one reason that Barron's three other drive-around men carry spotlights
with them as they make their nightly rounds, so they can sweep the
beam over the mares still out at pasture full time, just in case one
has started to foal outside. This is also why Taylor Made's grooms
braid the tails of mares within a couple of weeks of foaling, so that
anyone walking or driving near a field during the day, when the
"imminent" mares are turned out, can immediately see which ones
are closest to their due dates.

At night, the heavily pregnant mares return to their stalls, where
they are under constant surveillance by a night-watcher, who
spends much of the time picking manure out of each mare's stall
and simply walking up and down, waiting for someone to show any
signs of impending labor. The job's duller hours are offset considerably by the hustle when a mare has a foal or the outright terror
when something goes wrong during a birth. But by far the biggest
part of the night-watcher's job is close, detailed observation.

At Taylor Made's Whitehouse division, where two 20-stall foaling barns sit next to each other, the responsibility falls on 20-year-
old Stephanie Robb's shoulders. In her capacity as night-watcher
for the Whitehouse mares, Robb is a critical cog in Taylor Made's
giant machinery. Her best assets are a sharp eye for equine behav-
ior, an ability to stay calm in a crisis, and a willingness to stay up all
night—preparing the mares' 3:00 A.M. feed, vigorously grooming
the ones that return mud-caked from their afternoon at pasture,
and always, always noticing.

On this particular mid-February night, with a stiff breeze blowing
and temperatures in the teens, Robb wore black canvas overalls that,
by her own description, have been "covered in blood, pee, and placenta"; an oversized jacket in Taylor Made maroon; and several layers
of shirts, the outermost a black turtleneck. A thin silver cross on a delicate chain hung over the top of the turtleneck. Her brown hair was
pulled back in a ponytail, revealing a face that looked too chipper for
all the wearying hours spent examining mares' udders, looking for the
waxy buildup of milk on the teats that suggests foaling is at hand.

"They are *so* unpredictable," Robb said of the 40 mares she
oversees from 7:00 P.M. to 7:00 A.M. six nights a week. "In
December, before foaling season started, the Taylor Made guys

met with us and told us, 'Here's what will happen: They'll wax up, they'll drip milk, and then they'll go.'" she said. "Well, so far, none of my mares have gone according to the plan. I've had mares wax up and drip milk for two weeks before they foaled. And I had one maiden mare that didn't do anything at all. One minute she was just standing there in her stall, and the next minute I saw two front feet sticking out of her."

Robb, who grew up barrel-racing Quarter Horses and lambing ewes in Moses Lake, Washington, had never seen a foal born before she landed her Taylor Made internship five months earlier. She arrived in Kentucky knowing nothing about racing or the commercial Thoroughbred world, entirely unaware of the huge sums of money that changed hands over the horses. Central Kentucky's shrewd, unsentimental focus on the bottom line had taken her aback. Riding in the back of horse vans with Taylor Made mares on the way to breeding appointments, Robb was stunned by the rolling view of lavish wealth she sometimes got at the bigger farms: grand stone pillars at the entrances, stallion barns with mahogany doors and brass fittings, the graceful Georgian- or plantation- or Tudor-style mansions from which fabulously rich horsemen could overlook their green acreage dotted with horses. She was equally astonished when someone casually mentioned one morning that the plain bay mare she was holding had been insured for $8 million.

"I was like, 'Whoa, take this lead shank back!'" she said, her eyes widening, her arm extended in a mock attempt to hand off the responsibility. "Eight *million* dollars."

Then she shrugged. "But you get over that pretty fast. It's a horse, and you have to treat it like a horse."

By February, Robb had foaled about 25 mares, and she'd been surprised at the variety of behaviors they had exhibited beforehand. Several had weaved back and forth or circled repeatedly in their stalls. One, disturbingly, had stood in her stall and knocked her forehead against the wall.

Robb's most immediate fear was that she might miss a mare foaling, something that was surprisingly easy to do. Most mares, heeding some primeval instinct, have their foals at night (which is why night-watchers are so necessary), and they can take as little as 15 minutes to deliver a 100-pound foal. When a mare's water would break, Robb's job was to immediately radio Charlie Barron or another driver, who would come oversee the birth. On occasion, when three or four mares foaled at once or when there was an especially difficult case that required men and time, the crew wouldn't get to the Whitehouse barns fast enough, and Robb would have to help the mare as well as she could, gently pulling on the foal's forelegs as the mare heaved, removing the placenta, clearing mucus out of the foal's nose, and praying that there was no serious hitch in the natural process.

In recent years, many night-watchers have gotten electronic help thanks to automatic mare-monitoring devices such as Foalert, a system that involves stitching a transmitter onto the mare's vulva a week or two before she is due to foal. When the vulva opens immediately before the birth, it automatically activates the transmitter, which sends a signal to a receiver wherever the night-watcher is. With a little extra equipment, it can even be made to page several beepers. The obvious appeal of devices like these is that they allow the breeder to regain something the old night-watching tradition steals in great quantities: sleep.

But at Taylor Made, in this regard at least, things are still done the old-fashioned way: a wakeful night-watcher, a barn full of mares, and a lot of coffee. And so, from January until the last foal is born in late May or June, Stephanie Robb and her counterparts in the other foaling stables make their rounds up and down the barn aisles every 10 or 15 minutes, looking for the same signs that horsemen have always waited for. Each barn has a room at one end where the night-watcher can duck in and get warmed up on winter nights, but the accommodations are deliberately spartan: a closet-sized bathroom, a telephone, a battered desk with a pile of tiny leather foal halters on it, a metal filing cabinet holding information about the mares, a microwave oven, a stainless-steel sink, and a small refrigerator used mainly for storing equine medicines.

In Stephanie Robb's barn, the room's most attractive feature was probably the coffeemaker and the red 2 ½-pound can of McDaniel's Old World Classic ground coffee on a shelf above it. Robb could take breaks in here to recharge the caffeine need, sipping a mug among the triple row of wooden shelves that displayed bottles and jars of a veterinary nature: gooey yellow Corona ointment for cuts and scrapes, rubber-stoppered glass tubes for collecting blood samples, jugs of Clorox bleach, white bottles of sulfamethoxazole pills, plastic bottles of neon-blue Nolvasan antiseptic or molasses-brown Prodine solution.

A black plastic toolbox, about a foot wide and two feet long and with a removable shelf, held Robb's work kit. There was a pair of royal-blue nylon straps with detachable metal handles, used when a foal needed strong pulling during a difficult birth. A plastic bottle of Nolvasan and a stainless-steel cup, used for disinfecting the foal's umbilical stump. A thermometer. An Ace bandage for wrapping the mare's tail. Clear, arm-length plastic sleeves for vaginal examinations. Enemas, which are given to every foal. And a green glass bottle that used to hold the locally produced Ale 8 One soda—the empties, fitted with a rubber nipple, make great nursing bottles.

A small package of items pertained solely to the placenta, which had to be spread out and examined closely once the mare expelled it. If a piece was missing, however small, it had to be retrieved from the mare so it would not cause infection. If it was odd in any way, it had to be sent to the University of Kentucky's Livestock Disease Diagnostic Laboratory. And so the foaling kit included a small scale for weighing each placenta (12 to 16 pounds is normal for a 100-pound foal, and a placenta weighing substantially more than that might indicate disease); twine for binding the afterbirth up into a neat package; and black trash bags for disposing of it or sending it to the lab.

But all of this equipment sat idle for now. A plastic clock hanging over the bathroom door ticked loudly.

"You get lonely, you get tired, you never see the daylight, and if you're not moving you *will* fall asleep," Robb said.

But the job had its rewards, she added. Tearing open the placenta and getting the first view of a foal—Is it a colt or a filly? Does it have white markings?—was like opening a present on Christmas Day, every time.

"I never get tired of it," she said. "No matter how cold it is, as soon as you see that baby coming, you don't even feel the cold. You're working, you're pulling on it, and then you open the placenta and see the baby come out. When it takes its first breath, when it latches on to its mother's teat for the first time and its little tail wiggles, well, it's just the sweetest thing. I don't think I could ever get tired of it."

Robb was keeping a special eye on Pinetop, a chestnut mare who had started dripping milk around 8:30 and had been circling and pawing in her stall, occasionally buckling her legs slightly as if considering where to lie down. She was six days overdue. When Robb stopped by Pinetop's stall again at 9:20, the mare still had small milk drops falling at regular intervals from each of her two teats, but she had stopped circling and was now calmly eating her hay.

Robb rolled open the mare's front door and looked in at her. "It's hard to say," she said. "She could pop any second or she could go for two more weeks. You really just never know."

At about 9:30 P.M., Adriel Mathews, the night-watcher nearby in Taylor Made's Springhouse division, sent a crackling message over the radio: foal on the way. The transmission brought Jackie Davis and another driving watchman, Woody Clem, identically dressed in Taylor Made jackets and caps. It also brought Charl Koekemoer, a South African intern who had recently been promoted to a yearling-manager's position for some of Taylor Made's less expensive young stock.

By the time they all got there, the mare—a deep bay named Charlie My Girl, in foal to the young stallion Stormy Atlantic—was still on her feet, but a single white hoof, slightly larger around than a silver dollar, was protruding from her vulva. Mathews stood in the stall's open doorway, hands thrust into the edges of her overalls, and watched as the mare circled around the stall, looking for a place to lie down. When Charlie My Girl swung her rump perilously close to the cinder-block walls or to the grille of her front and back doors, nearly scraping the tiny leg, Mathews stepped in and smacked her rump lightly to make her move on. This was necessary, but the disadvantage was that it might give Charlie My Girl the idea that she was not allowed to lie down at all. Most mares would know better, but Charlie My Girl was a maiden mare, a first-time mother. Mares had been known to develop the unfortunate habit of foaling while standing up, which required the staff to catch the foal as it came out.

109

There are other reasons for caution with a maiden mare. Mathews, an intensely serious 23-year-old who was studying to be a vet, had a terse assessment of them as a class: "It means a lot of hard work, and it's usually going to be frustrating."

Maidens had narrower pelvises and were more likely to have trouble foaling, she explained.

"Sometimes they tend to have smaller foals, which is good for the mare because she's not very big, but then the foals tend to have weaker legs and find it harder to stand up at first, so you have to hold them up. Then the mare doesn't want to stand still. And because they've never had a foal before, you don't know what they're going to do when they foal."

Mathews had extra reason to be wary of maidens. In her first season at Taylor Made, the previous year, she had had a traumatic experience with one.

"The foal was upside down, and it was a maiden mare, so she was very, *very* tight," she recalled. "My hand barely fit in there. I was terrified."

Things quickly got worse. The mare's straining pushed the foal's hoof, and then its nose, through her rectum. Mathews and Barron tried to correct the situation, but they couldn't. The foal died.

Mathews now regarded the maiden Charlie My Girl with narrowed eyes. So far everything looked all right, but it was early yet.

Jackie Davis pulled an arm-length plastic glove on, stepped into the stall, and tried to work his left hand into the mare.

"In tight, huh?" Mathews asked him.

"Yeah, it is." Davis felt around until he found the foal's second forefoot, which he gently pulled out. It was white, too. A gush of pale amniotic fluid spilled out of the mare as Davis withdrew his hand again. He was out of breath just from the effort of working his arm around in the narrow mare. "It's going to be pretty good-sized," he said quietly.

Charlie My Girl finally toppled onto her right side in the middle of the stall, her rump pointing toward the open stall door. This was the call to action for Mathews and Davis, who knelt down behind her. The mare started to push, and the two quickly wrapped the bright blue foaling straps around the foal's slowly emerging legs. They pulled when the mare pushed. A nose emerged, followed by a damp head with blinking eyes. But the mare was struggling, and progress was slow. Clem and Koekemoer joined the effort, but even with four people pulling, the foal was not moving. Its shoulders seemed stuck in the birth canal.

"Push, mare, push!" shouted Mathews. The hapless mare, wet with sweat and groaning loudly, was not making much headway.

The four humans hauled on the foal: two on one leg, one on the other leg, and one tugging a slippery ear. Their progress was painfully slow, but the foal was emerging by half-inches. As the team pulled, they backed up, gradually dragging the prone mare around to one side of the stall as they went.

"Where are we? The hips?" panted Davis, who couldn't see the foal from his position as anchor, his back nearly against the wall.

"Not yet," said Koekemoer, who cradled the foal's head so it wouldn't scrape along the floor of the stall. The foal's shoulders, a dull chestnut color, came free, and then, with a sudden gush of blood, the foal slid out of the mare, its hindquarters still wrapped in the white placenta. Mathews rushed to pull the bag off the foal, which, though tired and wet, appeared healthy. It was a colt.

It all looked much cleaner on John Prather's laptop screen. To Prather, a highly respected bloodstock adviser, Charlie My Girl would have appeared as a pedigree, a screenful of names, some highlighted by colored bars if they occurred more than once in the first six generations, revealing a rainbow of inbreeding patterns.

Grand themes emerge when Prather scrolls through 10 or 12 generations of a horse's pedigree, and those themes are what he uses to create a mating. The sweaty, bloody upheaval that took place in Charlie My Girl's stall almost certainly had similarly ethereal beginnings on a computer very like Prather's, with someone doing just what he was doing now, splicing pedigrees together in hypothetical matings to see what patterns emerged from two mingled bloodlines. Finding "the power of the pattern" is what Prather, 57, calls it.

Conversing about pedigrees, female families, inbreeding, and great American speed sires, Prather, a large man with white hair and a white mustache-goatee combination, becomes animated. His hands gesticulate rapidly and return frequently to his keyboard to call up the color-coded strains in certain pedigrees he likes for their symmetry, class, or balance of speed and stamina.

Prather is not a scientist and has no training in genetics. He is more of a historian, which probably would have been his profession after college if he had not gotten sidetracked by a passion for horses, a tendency to skip class in favor of card games, and a tour in Vietnam with the Ninth Infantry Division, in roughly that order. Instead, he ended up as a sought-after pedigree analyst, a Merlin in the cult of breeding theory who helps farms conjure winners out of ancient family clusters that have produced successful racehorses in the past. Prather hunts out "nicks," or bloodline crosses that work well together, and tries to combine them to improve the resulting foal's chance of becoming a champion.

Prather has had enough success to be considered one of the best pedigree advisers around. He views his ultimate job in simple terms that belie its difficulty: "To breed a stallion factory." In other words, to put together a mating that, when it yields a filly, results in a mare that consistently can produce high-caliber stallions—essentially, creating the Golden Goose.

One of Prather's most successful hits came in the late 1990's when he advised the breeder Harold Harrison to mate his $240,000 mare, an unraced daughter of Mr. Prospector named Mr. P's Princess, to the stallion Nureyev, who was a son of Northern Dancer. That mating employed one of the most favorable modern nicks, crossing the bloodlines of Mr. Prospector with those of Northern Dancer. But the specific cross of Nureyev with Mr. Prospector mares had not produced much at the time from seven or eight attempts, Prather said. Nonetheless, he recommended it for Mr. P's Princess, and the mare's first foal by Nureyev turned out to be a proper home run horse. Coolmore Stud bought him as a yearling for $450,000 and named him Fasliyev. He became an undefeated champion 2-year-old in England, France, and Ireland, then the runaway leading first-crop sire of 2003 in Europe, and now he commands a stud fee of 75,000 euros, or about $87,000. The next foal out of Mr. P's Princess sold for $3.9 million, and Harrison later sold the mare privately to Coolmore for what Prather demurely described as "quite a bit of money."

"It's all about trying to pick good bloodstock, mate it properly, and create stallions," Prather said. "After the mare's first foal was so good, everything that came after it was just considered golden.

"We strongly believe that each mare is an individual, and this mare was very different to me from the seven or eight other Mr. Prospector mares who had gone to Nureyev and had no stakes winners," Prather explained. The key to successful breeding, he said, was to locate such crucial differences, however tiny, and exploit them.

Prather's search routinely takes him along the oldest branches of the Thoroughbred tree, back into the thickets where horses' birth years are recorded as "16??" or "about 1701." Other pedigree advisers discount the effects of patterns that old, but Prather feels strongly that bloodlines are valuable regardless of age. One knot of bloodlines that has produced winners in the past, or that has worked well with another knot of bloodlines to get those winners, is a building block. By doubling or tripling up on those old bloodlines, Prather argues, a breeder can enhance even an ancient influence.

"We're intensifying the genes by having duplications, and we like those duplications to come forward through different sources," he said, explaining that while he would not want to see the same stallion's name showing up repeatedly in a horse's pedigree, he likes to see a prominent stallion's or mare's close genetic relatives—their "equivalents," as he put it—repeat. "We love to stack things in the tenth generation that will give us variations of different horses in the sixth generation, to reinforce things."

He refers to this as "packing and stacking," as if he were a sort of genetic stevedore. But his occupation is more ephemeral, artistic, and complex than that.

Prather, one of a generally collegial group of a few dozen elite pedigree advisers worldwide, usually labors in the background, providing research that breeders might or might not use. Bloodstock advisers who unearth creative or previously unnoticed patterns that appear to be keys to success can be protective of that knowledge, like an archaeologist who has discovered a rare shard of pottery from a little-known civilization. The satisfactions are often more intellectual than financial.

"There's a lot more money in brokering horses," he said, a slightly mournful note creeping into his exuberant disquisition on the influential virtues of Myrtlewood, a champion mare from the 1930's. "But research is what I love to do, even though I'm probably nuts to do it."

Pedigree advisers' reputations get a lift when a mating they recommended produces a Fasliyev, and they take pride in their contributions to a champion. But they get little in terms of financial bonuses when that horse turns out to be a diamond.

Prather, an informal man who favors khakis, sweatshirts, and comfortable shoes, generally works out of his home, in a room off the kitchen. But sometimes, as on this day, he heads to the library at the Keeneland Race Course and auction company, which houses copious tomes of pedigree and race records dating back to the 1600's. One of Prather's most important tools is a software program called TesioPower 5.0—named after Nearco's legendary breeder, Federico Tesio—which allows him instant access to tens of thousands of six-generation pedigrees. It also gives him the ability to slice and dice those pedigrees according to certain characteristics he is interested in, such as particular names or families that repeat in six generations or horses in the tree that are half-siblings to each other.

Mares' names are listed with a number beside them that represents the female family the mare comes from, a quick-reference guide to a female group and its dominant attributes.

"In the late 1800's, an Australian by the name of Bruce Lowe tracked the major classic winners in England through their tail-female line back to the first mares registered in the English Stud Book, and he assigned family numbers to them," Prather explained. "It helps us know what the female lines of these horses are."

Each time Prather clicks on a name in any pedigree, the software pulls up a six-generation chart for that horse, too, revealing new names. Groups of horses inevitably recur throughout 10 or 12 generations of Thoroughbreds, and these repetitions are what attract Prather's attention. Concentrations of profitable blood, or recurring bloodline patterns that have been successful in the past, can increase your chances of striking gold again, Prather believes. In effect, Prather uses long pedigree trees the way handicappers use the *Daily Racing Form*'s past-performance lines: to look for patterns in a horse's career that suggest what conditions he needs in order to win—a muddy track, a distance under a mile, three weeks between races, or whatever other factors have combined previously for a victory.

Some bloodline patterns are well known, such as pairing Mr. Prospector blood with that of Northern Dancer. Others are obscure and highly complex, and there are theoretical variations on how they should be used. In "sex-balanced" breeding, Prather explained, a breeder might mate a stallion by a son of Mr. Prospector to a mare who carries Mr. Prospector blood only through a female line, not a male line, creating a kind of symmetry that pleases many artistic-minded pedigree theoreticians.

"We like to bring together horses that have two common ancestors within three generations, the equivalents," Prather said. "You know, sometimes I'll be mating a mare, and all of a sudden way back in the pedigree I see something interesting, and I'm off and running. I say, 'Wow, this fourteen tribe seems to be working with the eight family.' For example, a key to Storm Cat, a great way to reinforce him and he just *loves* it, is a mare called Honeysuckle, from the eight family, but, see, I'm digressing."

One of Prather's favorite pedigree building blocks is the famed American speedster and successful sire Domino, who was foaled in 1891. Another pedigree researcher had recently published a work showing that Domino's family had produced the most classic winners—winners of races such as the Kentucky Derby and the Epsom Derby—from 1914 to 2001, Prather said.

"Matter of fact, our last Triple Crown winner, Affirmed, his eighth dam is champion 2-year-old Correction, a full sister to Domino. He's loaded with Domino. He had at least 15 shots of Domino in his pedigree."

But does such elaborate embroidery really improve a mating's chances of producing the Kentucky Derby winner? It's hard to tell, but Prather and his clients believe that breeding sensibly—i.e., intensifying good influences along established patterns that have succeeded in the past—is bound to be more productive than breeding at random, or because a certain sire, who might not suit your mare at all genetically, has come into fashion.

A breeder who is a slave to market fashion, some advisers say, is relying too heavily on chance. Oddly, market buyers often seem to favor unproven new stallions over older, less-hyped horses whose progeny have built up a track record. This market demand, Prather says, encourages many breeders to breed to stallions they gamble will be fashionable, not ones whose records suggest that, mated with a particular mare, they will produce winners.

"Most yearlings at sales have eclectic pedigrees that don't go together," he said. "Mares bred like that are hard to work with, because the different aspects of their pedigree don't particularly go together like they would if there was a grand, unifying pedigree pattern. You can see the ones right away that the guy either knows something or he's had a professional do it. Those just jump out.

"It's harder mating for the market, because you're trying to breed pretty," he added. "The sales ring is a beauty contest. A lot of the buyers aren't that concerned with what's six or seven generations back, if the foal looks like a model. If you have a mare that throws pretty, you could almost breed her to the teaser and get a good price. But what is it Forrest Gump said? Pretty is as pretty does."

Whether a client is breeding to sell or to race, mating Thoroughbreds in hopes of a big winner is a "low-percentage game," as Prather put it, so his job is to find the highest-percentage patterns for a breeder to try.

"When we looked at sending Mr. P's Princess to Nureyev, that mating looked like it should work," he said. "But maybe we were just as lucky as all get-out. We can get the pattern right and still come up with a maiden claimer. There's a fine line between winning the Derby and being a maiden claimer. It's a genetic roll of the dice: Is the horse going to get the good things from the pattern or not? Full brothers can have very different abilities, but if a mare has produced a Derby winner, I'll buy that full brother. Odds are, she won't produce two Derby winners, but we know the pattern's good."

Pedigree advisers have countless theories they use to sway the genetic odds in their favor, and although they range from breathtakingly simple to mind-bogglingly complex to downright eccentric, they all share the view that, while the mysteries of pedigree cannot be entirely controlled, they can be influenced profitably.

Federico Tesio, the famed Italian breeder who died in 1954 with 20 Italian Derby wins to his credit, did some "stacking and packing" of his own. He preferred to concentrate the blood of a great 19th-century sire, St. Simon, as often as possible in his pedigrees, though he was generally opposed to very close inbreeding, believing that it could cause sterility. He also was a believer in nicks, comparing them in his book *Breeding the Racehorse* to harmonious strains of music or color.

Tesio was an amateur student of Mendelian genetic theory, but as the Italian Turf correspondent Franco Varola, writing in the sporting magazine *Horse and Hound*, noted, "He admits that in breeding his mares to almost every top sire in France and England for about 50 years he has never had in mind theories and principles, but he believes in choosing the right sire for the right mare by practically applying his own impressions regarding the size, conformation, the temperament and the individuality, as a whole, of each animal." However it came about, Tesio's breeding program is responsible for some of the most vibrant bloodlines in modern sporting history.

Among the eccentrics was Colonel William Hall Walker, later Lord Wavertree, who was famous for consulting astrological charts as guidance for his horses' matings in the early 1900's. A prim-looking English gentleman with a wide, carefully trimmed white mustache and a flawlessly formal mode of dress, Lord Wavertree appeared unlikely to go off on such a mystical tangent. But so strong was his fervor that he built his stud barn with skylights, purportedly to expose his horses to beneficial starlight. Unbelievably, he was immensely successful. He bred the 1909 Epsom Derby winner, Minoru, among other notables, and his program yielded some of the era's best stallions, but no one seems to know exactly why.

This sort of randomness offends the sensibilities of many pedigree theorists, who will sometimes go to great lengths in search of a pattern that might not exist. Breeding historian Abram Hewitt attempted a strained analysis of Wavertree's methods: "This suggests that inbreeding to the best strains can be successfully exploited, though the direct results of such inbreeding, that is, the inbred animals themselves, may not be very successful on the track. It is when the closeup descendants of these inbred animals are mated to sires of classic stature . . . that great successes on the track, and even more so at stud, are realized.

"Perhaps," Hewitt concluded hopefully, "this pattern could even be regarded as a kind of 'wave motion,' starting with the best classic animals at the crest, declining through the trough of their inbred descendants, and rising to the crest of the wave again, first through mares with a closely inbred ancestry showing racing ability above expectations, then mated to first-class classic stallions."

Perhaps. A hypothetical pedigree seems orderly and compelling on paper, but its practical application, starting with a foal's birth, is considerably messier. The genetic combinations pedigree advisers balance so carefully are buffeted, and sometimes swamped, by things that happen in the harsh world beyond the brilliant names in their family trees. Horses get lung infections or throw their shoes during a race. Sometimes they are not born at all, thanks to diseases like mare reproductive loss syndrome. Nonetheless, three centuries of pedigree students, since the breed began, have insisted—and not without evidence—that a thoughtful mating can help swing the odds at least a little in the breeder's favor.

"When you get the pattern right, just repeat it!" Prather exclaimed. "I like to breed on a good pattern three or four times. If it's a good pattern, you might not know it will work, but you can *expect* that it might.

"Pedigree is a tool," Prather added. "It's an inexact science. Has the best pedigree mating ever been done? I don't think so, not by a long shot. But we're getting better. A friend of mine once said his knowledge was like a pea rolling around in a boxcar, and when he dies, it'll be like a marble rolling around in a boxcar. There's so much to learn. Someday, maybe genetics will break the code, and then it'll just come down to who's got the most money, and they'll get the best horses."

His thoughts echoed those of analysts before him, who, like all other Thoroughbred gamblers, sense instinctively there is a grand but often obscure plan.

"That there is much uncertainty, and ever will be, attending the best mode of breeding, there can be no doubt; and this remark cannot be more strongly or more shortly exemplified than by the frequent occurrence of one horse being in high form and his own brother good for nothing," pedigree theorist Nicholas Hanckey Smith wrote in 1825 in *Observations on*

Breeding for the Turf. "Yet [the author] must beg leave to differ from the opinion of many, that all depends on chance."

At the modern Thoroughbred breeding farm, as little as possible is left to chance. Pedigree advisers help supply the blueprint for the breeder's product. Working together, advisers and breeders plan a mating that will minimize the risk of failure and maximize successful patterns. But the resulting physical animal may need some tweaking, especially if the foal is destined for the highly selective auction ring, where even a minor flaw can make the difference between a profitable sale and no sale at all.

At Taylor Made, where most of the annual foal crop is bred for auction, perfecting the results of nature's whimsy begins early.

"Pretty much as soon as they hit the ground, we start evaluating them," Charl Koekemoer said. "If a foal is born tonight, a manager will evaluate him in the morning. But it's hard to do foals, because as soon as they hit the sunshine, they start changing. Sometimes they're more correct after a few days out of the womb."

About 10 days after birth, the foals get their first visit from the farrier, who trims their hooves. Hooves are more malleable than they seem, and a skilled farrier can use his rasp much the way podiatrists use corrective baby shoes.

"It prevents some angular deformities if you start corrective shoeing early enough, while the growth plates are still soft," Koekemoer said. "You can correct a lot of problems early like that and get a horse that's less likely to break down later at the races, just by fiddling with the feet, maybe by rasping a millimeter more off of one side of the hoof than off the other."

Taylor Made's managers evaluate the foals about twice a month, monitoring changes in conformation and intervening when they think it is necessary. Those interventions can include cosmetic surgery to straighten a foal's legs. The jury is out on how helpful such surgeries are. Some vets claim that a conformationally correct leg, whether created by nature or surgically altered, promotes soundness, while some buyers believe cosmetic surgeries simply mask problems. But they are enormously popular among commercial breeders, whose horses are intensely scrutinized and frequently rejected for conformational flaws at auction. Equine surgeon Dr. Michael Spirito of Hagyard Davidson McGee was not certain how many cosmetic surgeries the firm performs each year to correct flaws in young Thoroughbreds. But he acknowledged that it runs to "hundreds and hundreds" annually.

The two most common cosmetic surgeries are transphyseal bridging, commonly called screw-and-wire, and periosteal elevation, known as stripping. Both require general anesthesia and careful postsurgical care and are done anywhere from 90 days to 14 months after the foal's birth.

In transphyseal bridging, a staple or a figure-eight formation of screws and wires is implanted on the knee to restrict growth on one side of the joint, allowing the other side to grow freely and "catch up," straightening the knee in the process. The staple or screw-and-wire device is later removed in a second surgery, and the procedure costs about $2,000 for both knees. Periosteal elevation, which is less invasive and generally more common than transphyseal bridging, involves making a pair of incisions in the periosteum, the elastic tissue that covers bone, and peeling the tissue back from the bone. The idea is to allow for freer bone growth that can speed conformational correction of the joints. Stripping, which can be done in ankles and knees, costs about $450 per joint pair.

"With awareness that these procedures are reasonably safe and effective, there's been a large demand for their use," Spirito said. "If the horse has a crooked leg, you can straighten it. That's a good thing."

Certainly, many top runners have had one or the other surgery, including 1998 Kentucky Derby winner Real Quiet, who had transphyseal bridging. Horses that are bred to race for their breeders, rather than to sell, are far less likely to go under the knife for cosmetic reasons, because only their racing performances—and not their looks—matter.

Mark Taylor, one of the brothers that own Taylor Made Farm, estimated that about 20 percent of the farm's yearlings would undergo stripping, and about 10 percent would have the screw-and-wire surgery. But surgery is not always necessary, he said.

"A lot of preventative stuff can eliminate having to do a screw-and-wire or a strip later on: having your nutrition right, leaving the horse outside as much as possible so they're not 'hot-housed' up in a stall, and really looking at those feet every two weeks during those critical stages," he said, noting that, during the hot summer months, Taylor Made will even daub mud on the foals' and yearlings' joints to cool them. The mud also shields the legs from fly bites, which in turn stops the horses from stomping—a potentially injurious activity.

"From the moment the horse walks into the yearling division at about nine months old, we start evaluating them," Koekemoer said. "We pull the yearling out of the stall once a week and do a sight analysis. We might start at the neck, and we look at them according to what we'd like to see at the sales: a long thin neck, a nice low head, an aggressive walk. We want the horse to jump out at you when you see it. We want to give the owner an idea of what he might expect to make for it.

"We grade the horses on their body and we grade them on their legs. So a horse might have a good body, maybe a B+ body, but if he's really crooked he can still have C legs. When we look at the legs, we might decide that he needs screws and wires or he might need to be stripped. Or maybe he toes in a little on the left or the right leg, and we might decide not to worry about that if he has a narrow chest—as he grows his chest will widen and that will naturally straighten his legs.

"Short cannon bones are a very good thing, because when they extend them, if they have a long forearm and a short cannon bone, they get more reach. We like a nice short pastern because it protects the sesamoids and it means the deep digital flexor tendon doesn't extend too much.

"We'll note the tail set," he continued. "It might be a little too low or a little too high. If we have a horse that's a little bit hunch-backed, we'll organize a chiropractor to come out and work on its back. We set up a game plan for what we're going to do from the time we first look at the yearling until he sells, so that we can minimize the amount of work we have to push into those two sale-prepping months. Thinking ahead helps things to go more smoothly."

It all starts with a grand plan. An adviser somewhere conjures a foal out of the smoke of two historic pedigrees. In theory, the paired bloodlines combine to bring out the strongest strands of genetic material from stallion and mare, double- or triple-dosing strengths while weaknesses fade, one hopes, into insignificance. It all looks orderly and compelling on paper. But even if it shows such thrilling names as Eclipse, Nashua, Northern Dancer, and Seattle Slew in its thickest, oldest branches, the paper tree does not account for foals like the one Stephanie Robb found one day in a large, manicured, safe, and mineral-balanced pasture at one of the world's most successful and prosperous Thoroughbred nurseries.

A mare came into Robb's barn that morning with discharge under her tail. The discovery sent a jolt of anguish through the Taylor Made staff. The mare must have aborted during the night. Stephanie headed out into the pasture, where the trees were fenced off for the mares' safety, the water supply was clear, the gates had latches with no protruding edges, and the grass was naturally infused with the bone-strengthening minerals of Kentucky limestone. But there it was, in the safest environment in the world: a dead fetus, about two feet long, with legs and the nubs of hooves. That was the dreadful end of a breeder's carefully planned mating and thoughtful investment, supported by hours of Taylor Made's attentive care. It was not immediately clear why the mare had aborted. That might never be known. Robb did the only thing that could be done with the dead foal at that point. She buried it.

6 The Good Eye

MORE THAN 2,000 years ago, an Athenian cavalry officer named Xenophon who was eager to protect his readers from being cheated by horse dealers set down criteria for judging unbroken young stock. His treatise, called "On the Art of Horsemanship," urged horsemen to carefully observe the various bones and joints of the horses they were considering, because that observation could, he strongly believed, tell them a lot about how the horses would perform.

"The bones [of the pastern] above the hooves and below the fetlocks should not be too upright, like a goat's: such legs give too hard a tread, jar the rider, and are more liable to inflammation," Xenophon advised. "Nor yet should the bones be too low, else the fetlocks are likely to become bare and sore when the horse is ridden over clods or stones.

"If the colt's knees are supple when bending as he walks, you may guess that his legs will be supple when he is ridden, too," Xenophon continued, "for all horses acquire greater suppleness at the knee as time goes on. Supple knees are rightly approved, since they render the horse less likely to stumble and tire than stiff legs."

The hindquarters "must be broad and fleshy, that they may be in right proportion to the flanks and chest, and if they are firm all over, they will be lighter for running and will make the horse speedier."

Xenophon's advice, it turns out, is not very different from the bloodstock agent's today. Neither is the quandary that has faced horse judges and gamblers before Xenophon and since: That horse looks all right, but can he run?

Good conformation does not necessarily translate into good action. As the 19th-century English sporting editor J. H. Walsh wrote ruefully in *The Horse in the Stable and the Field*, "It will sometimes be found that the frame which looks nearly perfectly symmetrical while at rest becomes awkward and comparatively unsightly while in motion, and the horse which is expected to move well will often be sent back to his stall with, 'That will do, thank you,' after a single run." Even good conformation and action together have never been certain proof of racing talent.

Horses have been running counter to their looks for time immemorial, as Walsh pointed out. "The winner of the 1860 Derby went a-begging, and was at last bought for a very moderate price," he wrote. "So also with Butterfly, the winner of the Oaks; no store was set upon her until she came to be tried; and even on the morning of the race she was not thought good enough to win. The celebrated Blink Bonny was a mean-looking mare, and would not have fetched fifty pounds at Tattersalls, from her appearance alone."

Appearance definitely counts at a horse auction, particularly at yearling sales, where there is little way to analyze a horse's running ability. Historically, horsemen have judged certain appearances to be actual physical flaws, as in the long-standing prejudice against horses with white feet. For centuries, they considered white feet to be softer and therefore less hardy than dark ones. That impression was so entrenched that a proverb about it was already timeworn in 1659, when a printer published it in a book of beloved maxims:

A four white-foot horse is a horse for a fool
A three white-foot horse is a horse for a king
And if he hath but one, I'll give him to none.

Today's buyers are less apt to dismiss a horse with four white feet, but there are new bugaboos such as entrapped epiglottises and OCD lesions (a problem caused by improper cartilage development) that make them reluctant to bid.

Horse shopping is no longer a life-and-death issue, as it undoubtedly was for Xenophon's cavalrymen, who essentially were selecting weaponry when they bought a horse. But, financially speaking, the stakes for today's buyers are higher than ever, especially if they are seriously seeking a horse capable of making the seamless transition from million-dollar yearling to champion to profitable stallion.

To have a shot at championship status, a horse must win Grade 1 races, the sport's highest level of competition, which includes (but is not limited to) the Triple Crown and Breeders' Cup events. And those starting gates can have a pretty steep admission price. Between 1987 and 2002, the average cost of publicly sold Derby winners was $472,636, ranging from 1998 winner Real Quiet, sold for about the price of a Toyota Corolla at $17,000, to the 2000 winner, Fusaichi Pegasus, who cost more than a garageful of Bentleys at $4 million.

The point, as bloodstock agents and trainers repeatedly tell their clients, is this: In general, your best chance to succeed in racing is to buy the most proven bloodlines in the most athletic body. And that combination costs money. Satish Sanan's splurge on Vindication, who then went on to be a champion and the early favorite for the Derby, was just the most recent example to shore up that point.

Even though he did not make it to Churchill Downs, Vindication's success in the Breeders' Cup helped guarantee him an enthusiastic reception in his first year at stud. A passionate buyer such as Fusao Sekiguchi or Satish Sanan may feel his heart flutter over a horse he has decided to bid millions for. But like a bridegroom with a prenuptial agreement for his intended, he also is coolly calculating more practical issues. In the case of a Thoroughbred, those issues include residual value.

A well-bred yearling who never gets near the Derby starting gate can still become a moneymaking stallion if he can string together a few impressive wins. In fact, the market for stallions now is so vast that even a well-bred horse with a limited race record can sometimes find a home as a stud in a smaller market such as, say, New Mexico, or overseas. A spectacularly bred colt who has a race record to match, well, that's the ultimate home run horse, a runner that can turn his race record and genetic material into a profit-making business for as long as he lives and is fertile.

The same is true for fillies who become great broodmares, but their prices and moneymaking value are necessarily less than a stallion's, because a stud can produce millions annually in breeding fees while a mare can have only one (potentially imperfect and unfit for market) foal each year.

At least since the commercial Thoroughbred market shifted into high gear in the mid-1980's, a horse's residual value has been a key consideration for almost every major auction buyer who is serious about both winning and turning a profit in the game. Prices have skyrocketed for those gifted horses with promising pedigrees and athletic bodies combined, and business-minded buyers such as Satish Sanan have entered the game with an eye toward making those horses not just winners, but also profitable winners. Consequently, the competition has intensified to correctly identify which yearlings eventually will be great and which ones merely mediocre, or outright duds.

But looking for a Derby horse at the yearling sales, as one regular buyer put it, is like recruiting a professional football team out of a class of third-graders. It is a highly speculative and subjective process. With so much money on the line, and with so much room for error, it is hardly surprising that an entire industry has grown up to help owners separate the equine wheat from the chaff.

Like bettors looking for a "perfect system," buyers flock to new technology and theories they think might improve their chances of picking a winner. There are biomechanics specialists who measure key aspects of the horse in search of ideal proportional relationships that suggest balance and efficiency of motion. There are researchers who study the relationship of heart size and breathing capacity to racing performance. There are X-rays, endoscopic exams, and heart monitors. All the theories and machines, and all the experts behind them, are geared toward helping the buyer minimize his chance of picking a loser.

The desire to reduce that risk keeps veterinarians such as Dr. Craig Van Balen busy and well paid. Van Balen, who is based in

Lexington, Kentucky, frequently travels the circuit of major year-ling auctions. He and his colleagues can be seen at every big horse sale, moving rapidly from barn to barn, towing luggage dollies with complicated-looking devices stacked on board, electrical cords and flexible endoscope tubing looped over their shoulders.

The stronger the market for yearlings, the more grueling Van Balen's schedule is. His three-member vet team examined about 100 horses, or nearly half the catalog, at Saratoga's 2003 auction, and that, Van Balen said, was a slow sale for him. The vets' job description often covers both sides of the auction transaction. They do pre- and post-sale exams for bidders, but they also help con-signors with sale horses that develop fevers or colic.

Consignors often complain that buyers can be too selective. But Van Balen pointed out that a bidder's decision to pass or fail a year-ling for what he called a "bloodstock portfolio" comes down to much the same issue an investor faces with a stock portfolio: his attitude toward risk.

"A little radiographic lesion doesn't scare some clients, but oth-ers aren't risk-takers and want a horse to be absolutely radiograph-ically clean," Van Balen said.

For much of the last decade, auction companies like Fasig-Tipton have offered repositories for consignor-provided X-rays (also called radiographs) and endoscopic videos on the sale year-lings. That has not prevented bidders from wanting their own vets to examine the horses. But Van Balen said the repository system has speeded up vets' and buyers' understanding of what flaws are likely to compromise a horse's eventual racing career.

"We've learned a lot, and our level of comfort with certain radiographic lesions has gone up considerably," he said. "We realize now that particular kinds of lesions have a great prognosis and have no detriment to a horse's racing career.

"Clients come off horses for a number of different reasons: con-formation, the horse looks tired and is dragging his feet, the client didn't like the way the horse handled the challenge of being at the sale ground," he added. "The idiosyncrasies of buyers are very wide. But I think buyers as a whole at yearling sales are much more educated and have a better understanding now of what the results of these examinations mean. If anything, I think they're better informed and more tolerant of things not being exactly textbook perfect. They want things to be within a range of normal, but that range has expanded for them."

Today's Thoroughbred buyer, armed as he is with veterinarians, trainers, and pedigree analysts, has an unprecedented amount of data and technology to help him pick a winner out of the yearling sales. But his primary tool, the one he will use first, is the same one that countless generations of horsemen from Xenophon to Sheikh Mohammed al-Maktoum have used: the "eye for a horse."

Even J. H. Walsh, having provided the bruising list of rejects who went on to English sporting glory, returns nonetheless to the "good eye," saying, "Still, it cannot be denied that a good judge will select the ten best horses out of twenty, or perhaps out of a hundred; but he will possibly leave the very best out of his list. The theoretical rule is simple enough, but it requires great experience and a good eye to carry it out in practice. It is simply this . . . the horse which is formed in the mold most like that of the greatest number of good racehorses, will run the best."

In the Thoroughbred auction world, the person with an eye for a horse is king. He is almost always for hire. And, no matter how lofty his reputation, he will begin the same way Xenophon did: by pulling a horse out of the stall and watching him walk.

Buzz Chace consulted the catalog page, then considered the yearling before him. It was a warm, cloudless September morning in Lexington, and the Keeneland Association's stable area was a hive of activity in preparation for its two-week September sale, the largest Thoroughbred yearling auction in the world. The colt Chace pondered was one of nearly 1,800 currently on the grounds, and one of almost 4,300 that ultimately would go through the ring. In the course of the auction, the rest of the cataloged yearlings would rotate through Keeneland's green-trimmed cinder-block barns, and Chace would look at roughly a quarter of them in hopes of finding some good horses—and, if possible, some bargains—for his clients.

Chace, one of the Thoroughbred business's most successful bloodstock agents, is a 30-year auction veteran. During his long career, he has selected horses for some of the world's most daring spenders, including game-show mogul Roger King, Oregon timber executive Aaron Jones and his wife, Marie, and real estate investment trust owner B. Wayne Hughes.

Chace has half a dozen regular clients who buy horses at prices from $25,000 to $2.5 million, and he often picks up additional work from several other buyers and agents who recruit him while he is at a sale to look at or bid on horses. The wide economic spread of his clients, and the fact that he is an inveterate bargain hunter, make the Keeneland September sale a perfect market for Chace. The two-week auction offers yearlings of every kind: cheap and expensive, horses bred to sprint and to run long, on turf and on dirt. There will be something for almost everyone on Chace's shopping list. He will sift through the sale's first two days—the so-called select days, where the stock has met stricter pedigree and conformation criteria—for clients like Aaron and Marie Jones. The Joneses, like many players at the highest level of the market today, are primarily interested in blue-blooded racing prospects that can be parlayed into high-class, moneymaking stallions, a program that demands good, though expensive, pedigrees.

But Chace will also buy on behalf of clients like West Point Thoroughbreds, a public stable that targets horses in the $50,000 to $200,000 range, syndicates them, and races them for the ownership groups. West Point's primary emphasis is on the thrill of racing, rather than on long-term breeding potential, and that means they will compromise on pedigree more than on athleticism. For them, Chace will leaf through the sale's later catalogs, looking at literally hundreds of yearlings in search of a promising horse that has slipped through the cracks, maybe because of a slightly obscure pedigree or a cosmetic flaw that Chace feels the horse can overcome on the racetrack.

Chace's strengths, his clients agree, are an exceptionally sharp eye for a horse and a tireless work ethic, a pair of essential requirements for bargain hunting. Those two assets have helped him become unusually adept at turning profits for his clients, and that keeps him on the road. Chace has houses in New Jersey and Florida, but he rarely gets to enjoy time off at the beach. The mailbox is constantly full of new sale catalogs, and Chace's clients are hungry for horses. Walk into a Thoroughbred yearling or 2-year-old auction in Maryland, Florida, New York, Kentucky, or California, and chances are you'll find Buzz Chace, catalog in hand, looking at horses. Before flying to the 2003 Keeneland September auction, Chace bought six horses at Saratoga for $1,755,000. Earlier in the year, at a Miami 2-year-old sale, he signed for three that cost a total of $1,250,000. That spending ability makes Chace a commanding presence in a seller's barn.

This particular Keeneland yearling—a tall, rangy chestnut colt— looked pretty good to Chace when he first came out of the stall. But he began slipping out of favor the longer Chace looked at him.

"He's a nice, big horse, but then you start pulling him apart," Chace explained, gesturing with the ballpoint pen he carries to make conformation notes on catalog pages. "He's got one heel lower than the other. Looks like he's got a clubby foot there. But all in all, he's not a bad horse."

Chace turned to the handler, a blond woman dressed like all the other handlers in this consignment, in khaki pants and a button-down oxford shirt.

"Can you go down there with him, please?" Chace asked.

The handler turned the colt and walked him away from Chace, down one side of a dirt walking ring in front of the barn. Silently, Chace watched the yearling's back end, his hocks, where and how his back hooves fell in relation to his front hooves and in relation to each other. The handler turned the colt again at the end of the straightaway and strode back toward Chace, who now had a head-on view and was scrutinizing the colt's knees.

So was the seller, who stood at a discreet distance behind Chace. He was holding a black three-ring binder that bristled with color-coded tabs, one for each horse in the consignment. The binder contained notes that were not included in the catalog pages, either because they had happened too late to be printed or because they were not part of the catalog's standard information: fast workouts, promising race results, and good sale prices that this yearling's relatives had achieved, anything that added luster to the horse on offer. The seller was overseeing five or six yearlings that were being shown simultaneously to various buyers and agents, but he was keeping an especially close eye on Chace, whose approval of a horse could make a significant difference to the consignment's profit margin.

"I'm taking too much time with him, really," Chace said in a low voice as the colt walked toward him. "He's got bad knees, he's too narrow up front in his chest. But sometimes you have to be diplomatic. The seller's right there looking at them, too."

Before the handler could stop the horse in front of him again, Chace nodded at her and said, "That's fine, thanks," the universal words of dismissal at a horse sale. The handler kept walking and took the colt straight back to his stall. The consignor, who also held the list of horses Chace had requested to see, silently beckoned toward the barn and another handler immediately brought out another colt.

Chace had been making his way from consignment to consignment since 6:30 A.M., and he would keep going until the barns closed down to feed the horses around 4:30 P.M. He would look at every horse selling in the first four days, a total of about 1,300 yearlings, plus a handful selling later, in the auction's less fashionable second week.

"You have to look at that many," Chace said. "You don't want to miss the individual."

By the end of the sale, Chace would buy just 16 of those "individuals" for prices ranging from $25,000 to $300,000.

Sifting through so many horses is tedious, tiring business. At big auctions like Keeneland's, Chace is on his feet almost constantly for 10 hours or more, turning catalog pages, scribbling hieroglyphic conformation notes in the white spaces, watching—and usually rejecting—yearlings as they stride up and down the walking ring.

The reasons Chace rejects a horse are highly variable.

"See that pig eye?" he said of one nearly black colt, a grandson of the redoubtable and much sought after stallion Storm Cat. "He's no 'count."

Chace warmed to a handsome colt by former 2-year-old champion and new sire Anees, whose first yearlings were on offer, until he saw the colt move. "How 'bout that walk?" he said to no one in particular, shaking his head. "He throws that hind leg out pretty good."

He made a note in the catalog. "Too bad, because he's a nice horse."

Chace's criteria for a good horse are hard to describe, but, like every agent, he knows one when he sees him. "I like for all the parts to fit together," he said. He likes a refined head; a body that looks as if it will improve with time and growth; a large, bright eye; a powerful rump; and a back that isn't too long.

"A neck like Cher, and a butt like Charles Barkley," a nearby consignor offered helpfully.

"Yeah, that's it," Chace said, smiling.

Chace prefers good, straight legs, because crooked legs and offset joints can add stress during training and racing. But most horses are not flawless, and Chace can forgive some faults.

"Horses run through most everything," he said. "I can live with an awful lot of stuff."

It is Chace's job to weigh the various aspects of each horse's pedigree and build, then to come up with an overall rating and estimated price range, and advise his clients on whether or not to bid. He will also arrange veterinary inspections for short-listed horses, bid for his clients, and arrange to ship the horse from the sale grounds to its next destination, usually a farm or training center. Understandably, Chace's time is valuable, and he is quick to dismiss a horse that doesn't catch his experienced eye.

"I like to be nice about it, but as soon as a horse comes out of its stall, I either like it or I don't," he said.

That's not to say he's not flexible. Looking at one gray colt who stood with his front feet turned slightly out, Chace told the consignor, "He toes out, but that doesn't bother me much. Last horse I faulted for toeing out is racing now in Maryland, and every time I look up, he's beating me."

A filly by Irish-bred grass-racing champion Theatrical gets rejected on her pedigree, even though it's a good one. Her dam is by Kingmambo, an expensive stallion who is himself the son of the legendary female grass champion Miesque. It's a high-class family that would appeal to the British and European racing scene, where grass racing dominates. But Chace's clients all race in America, where there are fewer races for turf runners, and therefore less opportunity for their owners to make purse money. In America, many horses are pointed to turf racing only if they are unsuccessful on the more common dirt surface.

"This horse is grass only," he said, pointing at the pedigree. "I can't use her."

What Chace can and can't use is largely dictated by how his clients define a home run horse.

"I'm looking mostly for colts that will make a stallion or horses that look like they'll really run," Chace said. "That's what everybody's looking for. Most of the people I'm looking for would love to have a stallion. People like the Joneses go into a yearling sale thinking way long term. A lot of my other owners are mainly looking for runners, and it would be a big dream for them to have a horse that could also go on and stand at stud."

Chace lived that dream himself, starting in 1994 when he bought the gray yearling that is largely responsible for his clout as a buying agent today.

Buzz Chace's eye for a horse is not just a mystical gift from the heavens. It is the product of a lifetime with horses. Chace grew up in southeastern Massachusetts, where he got his start riding high-stepping three- and five-gaited Saddlebreds at a show barn. At 16, he dropped out of high school to make his living full-time with horses. He found work at a Rhode Island Thoroughbred farm, learned how to gallop racehorses, and eventually ended up at the track, which offered a faster pace, unlimited opportunities to learn about horses, and niche jobs with which a racetracker could string a living together. Chace exercised racehorses and groomed them, and then he took a job that accelerated his understanding of the consequences of poor equine conformation: assistant to a racetrack veterinarian. Chace saw more than 100 horses a day, an exposure rate that inevitably revealed patterns any horseman would learn from: which conformational flaws contribute to which injuries, what physical traits horses can and can't overcome, and what faults are purely cosmetic.

Working for the veterinarian, he did X-rays and learned equine dentistry, a job that involves fitting the horse's mouth with a brace that keeps it open while the practitioner reaches in with a six-inch rasp, then files down rough-edged teeth that can actually cut a horse's mouth. It was hard work, but Chace learned about horses from the inside out, and he began to form opinions about what flaws really matter to performance and what faults can be fixed or even ignored. In his years on the racetrack, he also shod horses, a job that gave him a close-up perspective on the all-important equine hoof. He trained a few runners, bought and sold some for a handful of clients, and lived off his betting a time or two.

By the time he was 50, Chace had put together a solid career as a bloodstock agent and was making a good enough living to raise two children. And then, suddenly, he got the big buyer and found the big horse.

The big buyer was Ernie Paragallo, a 36-year-old Long Islander. Like Chace, Paragallo was a high-school dropout, but he waited to get into the horse business until after he had made his millions in investment banking and computer-software development.

Paragallo, an intense man with glowering eyebrows, wavy black hair, and a fondness for wearing black ensembles with black cowboy boots, had never bought a horse at auction before. He had gotten Chace's name from a New Jersey horse trainer and gave him a try partly because he knew Chace had identified and bought a nice stakes winner named Meadow Flight for another client.

Paragallo may not have had experience, but he was game and ready to take risks. He loved the action enough to try "pinhooking," the high-wire art of buying yearlings, breaking them and giving them their early training, then reselling them at a profit the following season as ready-to-race juveniles. Yearling-to-juvenile pinhooking is one of the riskiest avenues a horseman can take. When he buys his inventory, he has to scratch up bargain horses that others have rejected or overlooked but that have the potential to mature quickly and turn a big profit six or eight months later. Even when a pinhooker buys exactly the right yearling for the task, he runs a greater risk that the horse will injure itself in the process of breaking and training; he also runs the risk that once the horse is ready to be clocked over short workouts it will simply be slow. But Paragallo was fearless. He also had enough money to secure the better resale prospects, which made Chace's job somewhat easier, and he trusted Chace's judgment absolutely.

Chace found Paragallo's star, Unbridled's Song, at Saratoga's 1994 yearling sale. The colt was one of the first foals of 1990

Kentucky Derby winner Unbridled, who was himself well bred and clearly accomplished, but as yet unproven as a stallion. Chace liked two things about Unbridled as a sire.

First, he came from a long male line that was legendary for its quality. His father was Fappiano, a blazing speedster who set a record for six furlongs but also won classy races going beyond a mile, and his grandsire was the great Mr. Prospector, another speedball. That brilliance had been harnessed and stretched out effectively through the influence of Unbridled's dam, Gana Facil, so that Unbridled had received the golden genetic combination of speed and stamina. Given the sire records of Unbridled's father and grandfather, Chace thought it was a good bet that Unbridled would also pass along his talent.

135

Second, Unbridled had won first time out at age 2 in dramatic style, leaving his rivals behind by 10 ½ lengths. That told Chace the colt he was considering could mature quickly enough to become a precocious young racehorse or a showpiece at a 2-year-old sale.

All that potential was offset somewhat by the yearling's dam, a nondescript runner named Trolley Song who won just once, going a distance on the grass. She had been offered at auction while carrying the Unbridled colt, but her seller had bought her back when bidding stopped at $90,000.

But the sire line had potential, and, most of all, Chace just loved the way this yearling looked. There were no real faults, and the horse had an impressive, confident bearing that Chace found irresistible.

Paragallo bought the Unbridled colt for $200,000 and added him to a draft of horses destined for the following spring's 2-year-old sales in California.

Chace was right about Unbridled's Song. Once the colt got a saddle on his back and started working, it quickly became obvious that he had million-dollar talent. By the time he reached the Barretts auction facility in Pomona, California, Unbridled's Song was blitzing through his eighth-mile workouts in times so fast his owner began making wild predictions.

"He's going to sell for more money than any 2-year-old ever has," Paragallo told reporters. "I'll be disappointed if he doesn't make a million dollars."

Turf and auction-ring regulars snickered. But when selling started at Barretts in March 1995, it turned out that Paragallo's flamboyant prediction had been too conservative. The hammer fell at
$1.4 million, a world-record sale price for a 2-year-old.

The sales world was stunned, but the story wasn't over. The
buyer, Japanese racehorse owner Hiroshi Fujita, had ordered post-
sale X-rays of the colt's legs. An X-ray of the right front ankle came
back with a shadow that Fujita said was a bone chip. Fujita wanted
to return the colt. Such a difference of opinion usually leads to
arbitration, but Paragallo, again to the astonishment of his peers,
immediately took back his world-record colt.

"They've just made the biggest mistake of their lives," he said
afterward. "They'll never find another horse as good as this one. I
didn't want to sell him anyway. We're going to win the Breeders'
Cup with this colt, and they're going to wish they never brought the
matter up."

"But I was devastated," Chace recalled. "I knew there was nothing there in the X-ray. Maybe they just wanted to offer us less
money for the horse. So now I'm feeling bad, because in the beginning Ernie said, 'I'm going to give you 5 percent for buying him
and 10 percent for everything we sell.' I was going to get $140,000
for my 10 percent—so I also felt bad about *that*."

Even without Unbridled's Song, Paragallo and Chace had an
enormously profitable year. In their first season of pinhooking, the
team made $4 million by selling 2-year-olds they had bought for
$1.7 million just eight months earlier. Their success was unprece-
dented. Paragallo was brash, but he had turned out to be right
when it counted, thanks in large part to Chace's eye for a horse.

It turned out Paragallo was right about the Breeders' Cup,
too. Eight months after his failed sale, Unbridled's Song won the
$1 million Breeders' Cup Juvenile by a neck and immediately
became the hot favorite for the 1996 Kentucky Derby.

Unbridled's Song had become a star with seemingly unlimited
potential. Paradoxically, Ernie Paragallo had been lucky to have a
bad X-ray at the auction. The hapless Hiroshi Fujita, meanwhile,
had been tripped up by the precision technology intended to help
him. He unwittingly had tossed away a winning lottery ticket whose
stud value was now worth between $10 million and $20 million.

Even veterinary X-rays, after all, were subject to the eye's interpretation.

In the Breeders' Cup win picture, the smiling man holding the trophy was Buzz Chace. He had good reason to smile because now he also owned 10 percent of Unbridled's Song.

"A week after the Barretts sale, Ernie said to me, 'About Unbridled's Song. You own 10 percent of him right now, for whatever he does: stallion, racing, whatever,'" Chace said. "So that $140,000 I would have gotten from the Barretts sale, forget it. I owned 10 percent, and that equals four shares in him as a stallion, too."

Those shares, which include one breeding right apiece for each year Unbridled's Song stands at stud, have appreciated considerably. In 2004, the stallion carried a $125,000 stud fee.

"I think Buzz Chace has the best eye for a horse of anybody in the country," Paragallo said after the Breeders' Cup trophy ceremony. "With the results we've gotten in racing and pinhooking, I don't think too many people should argue with that."

Chace had found Unbridled's Song, but he couldn't hold off the stresses of training and bad racing luck. Paragallo's amazing run petered out eventually, and at the worst possible time: Derby Week. The problem started as a small crack that trainer Jim Ryerson discovered in Unbridled's Song's left front hoof after the colt handily won his last Derby prep race. Such cracks are fairly common and easily fixed. Ryerson had it patched with acrylic, the standard treatment, and the colt was sent to Churchill Downs as the Derby's heavy favorite.

Things promptly got worse. Six days before the race, Unbridled's Song came in lame from a routine gallop; the acrylic patch had caused a bruise and a small infection where it folded under the hoof. Ryerson hastily arranged to put different shoes on the colt to relieve pressure on the area. Chace pitched in to help, soaking the colt's sore foot in a tub.

Two days later, at the traditional draw for Derby post positions, Unbridled's Song was unlucky again: he got post 20, on the far outside of the track. When another horse scratched, Unbridled's Song got to move in one path to post 19, but no horse had ever won the Derby roses from there, either.

It all added up to defeat. Unbridled's Song, considered even by rival trainers to be the best horse in the race, finished fifth.

"It was a shame," Chace said. "It was bad timing, and timing's everything."

Even so, Unbridled's Song was exactly the sort of life-changing horse everyone wants. Bob Baffert—whose first Derby starter, the gelding Cavonnier, was stabled in the same barn at Churchill with Unbridled's Song—got a tantalizingly close view of the strapping gray every morning during Derby Week as the horses went to and from their morning workouts.

Cavonnier was a big runner for Baffert, but he literally lacked the cojones to complete the magic circle from racing hero to profit-making stud. It was a critical difference that made Unbridled's Song the bigger horse, and Baffert knew it.

The day before the Derby, Baffert made a confession that wasn't very elegant but probably spoke for most of the owners and trainers at racetracks across the nation.

"Unbridled's Song," he said reverently. "I'd swim in a river of gasoline with a torch up my ass to get that horse."

The Unbridled's Song story is about the triumph of the good eye, and about the limits of technology. But where does the good eye come from and how does it work? Many people—veterinarians, breeders, and even engineers—have tried to explain it, duplicate it, and, where possible, bottle and sell it.

In 1998, a research team at Colorado State University began a study that is attempting to analyze equine conformation objectively, with the help of computer software. The goal, according to research chief and veterinary orthopedic surgeon Dr. D. Wayne McIlwraith, is to develop a more standard and objective approach to conformation analysis for the average horseman.

The study analyzed five crops of foals born in the late 1990's, from the successful breeding program of Daniel Wildenstein. The team measures 39 lengths or angles on each horse annually—including withers height, foreleg length, and shoulder, fetlock, and pastern angles. They also attach markers to a specific set of "anatomical landmarks" that served as reference points, and they photograph the horses with the markers in place each year. Analyzed by computer, the photographs and measurements have revealed how a horse's conformation changes with age.

The findings so far have been interesting but not revelatory for horsemen like Chace: Angles tend to straighten as a horse grows, and many of the horse's bones work together in motion, so proportionality is important.

But the researchers, like Chace and every other person who has tried to find a good racehorse, have been unable so far to find the foolproof system.

"We do find exceptions to everything," McIlwraith said. "You can't be dogmatic about it. We've seen some horses with bad conformation go on and do quite well. We'll end up with percentages, predictabilities. What we're doing is validating what some of the experienced horse people know themselves and putting numbers on what has always been a subjective feeling."

If he were dropped onto a modern sale ground, the ancient horseman Xenophon would spot a sympathetic soul in Buzz Chace. But he probably wouldn't know what to make of Cecil Seaman. Neither did many sellers in the 1970's, when Seaman first started asking to go in their yearlings' stalls with a tailor's measuring tape. The idea of a "subjective feeling" about a horse's conformation is anathema to Seaman, who has labored for more than 30 years to compile a firmer standard for predicting performance.

People have been measuring horses for more than two centuries, trying to find correlations between bone length and performance. But only a few have been able to make an entire profession out of it. Seaman has, mainly because of two things: the computer and the buyer's eternal desire to find an edge.

Since about 1972, Seaman has been taking horses' measurements, plugging them into a computerized database, and running them through formulas he has devised. The result is a system Seaman believes can predict racing success more accurately than the subjective human eye.

"There are a lot of old wives' tales and traditions that don't really amount to much in the Thoroughbred racehorse," Seaman said. "Every horse person you talk to has a different opinion about how a horse should be made. It's deceiving, because you can take the

139

same horse and show it to eight or ten different people, and you'll get eight or ten different opinions."

What Seaman's formulas give him are scores for three factors he believes are critical in racing performance: point of gravity, efficiency, and leverage. At its most basic, Seaman's work attempts to determine which horses are the most balanced and efficient movers—exactly the same thing the good eyes are looking for. But Seaman is convinced such things can be determined objectively, and that objective measurements and comparisons, unlike the biased eye, make far more accurate judgments.

Seaman won't divulge the details of his formulas. But he describes his database as a file that started with the measurements of a core group of champion racehorses and has expanded to include more than 60,000 horses. Seaman's program essentially stacks a horse up against the known measurements of the sport's great runners. Horses that are built like champions should, in theory, run better than those who are vastly different from them; horses that are like their relatives should run something like those family members, and ones that are out of kilter with their families will probably perform differently, too. It sounds like common sense, but Seaman believes his measuring tape and computer database can turn up surprising information that the eye won't find on its own—in other words, that the database creates an edge.

The son of a photoengraver in Springfield, Ohio, Seaman grew up among the slide rules, proportion scales, and complex cameras his father worked with, an experience he called "pretty good training about the importance of proportionality."

Like his father, Seaman also had a mechanical bent. He designed part of a rotary engine when he was still in high school.

"That was before the Henkel engine even came on the market," he said. "I was going to try to get patents on part of my design, but it was going to cost something like $60,000 to build the prototype, so I didn't."

Seaman also liked horses, and he eventually bought a Quarter Horse foal for himself in the 1960's. It wasn't long before he was training a few at Ohio's Quarter Horse tracks.

"But there wasn't any money in Quarter Horses, not in Ohio," he said. "So then I got some cheap Thoroughbreds, and I started wondering why some cheap Thoroughbreds would get outdistanced by 20 or 30 lengths by the competition. I started asking these questions. I already had the exposure to proportions and mechanics from working on that rotary engine, and then I got into biomechanics. There's gotta be a reason everything works."

The reason some horses work better than others, Seaman figured, has to be related to the way their various parts operate together. The more he thought about the engine analogy, the clearer it seemed to him.

"I forget how many moving parts there were in a regular V-8 engine, but I tried to make a rotary engine with less moving parts, less friction, so it would be more efficient," he said. "It's the same way with horses. When one horse has 20 percent more leverage in some bones than other horses, and there's less mass, they're just a lot more efficient."

Seaman started reading anything he could find on racehorse biomechanics, starting with historical measurements from some of the great racehorses. The practice of taking superior runners' lengths and angles was not a new idea. A prominent veterinarian named St. Bel took extensive measurements of Eclipse twice, once when the horse was 24 and again for confirmation after the horse's death in 1789. Seaman also found references in texts from the 1890's, including one that compared the skeletal structure of the cheetah with that of the racehorse. Federico Tesio, generally regarded as one of the greatest breeders of all time and the man responsible for breeding the great sire Nearco, took meticulous records of his foals' measurements. And another veterinarian, Dr. Manuel Gilman, had recorded champions' basic measurements in a reference book called *The American Racing Manual* for several decades.

"But all that was before they really had computers, so no one was really doing much with the measurements, and everybody measured things differently," Seaman said. "They were just measuring different things they thought were important at the time. They would measure the angle of the shoulder compared to the ground, the angle of the pastern compared to the ground, and the length of the pastern. I did that for a while, too, but I didn't find any correlation with the measurements and performance.

"When I worked on engines, I knew that everything was about relationships, how the parts were proportioned and how they worked together. The angles of bones to the ground isn't as significant as everybody thinks they are. That kind of describes the horse, but they were really just measuring different parts of the horse that they liked, not the relation of parts that function together. We're measuring proportions."

St. Bel's analysis of Eclipse revealed the great racehorse and sire to be oddly configured: long and set on a slight downward slant, with hips higher than his withers, and an unusually long neck. Even today, there are buyers who wouldn't like the looks of such a horse, particularly that downhill build. But Seaman points out that looks can be deceiving, as they might well have been with Eclipse.

"There's no way you can just *look* at a horse," Seaman insisted. "You have to measure them. When you look at them, there's an optical illusion. There's an optical illusion when you look at just about everything. A horse that is fit will look taller and longer than one that is let down and has a little belly on him. Nobody can tell just by looking at a horse exactly how tall it is or how much leverage they have. You have to actually physically measure a horse to determine those things."

Having decided back in the early 1970's that proportion was the issue, Seaman began taking his measuring tape to every possible Thoroughbred. On a visit to Newmarket, England, he even got special permission to measure a life-sized bronze of the famous English champion sire Hyperion.

"It was very funny," Seaman recalled. It certainly must have been funny, the intense, wiry, middle-aged American clambering around the statue with a tape, as if trying to fit it for a suit. But that wasn't what Seaman meant. "It was funny because that bronze measured almost identical to Northern Dancer. Northern Dancer has Hyperion in him. He had Native Dancer in him, too, but he took after Hyperion."

Cecil Seaman measures about 2,800 yearlings annually, looking for horses that his formulas tell him fall within the top 12 percent of the equine population—in other words, those that are closest to champion proportionality. He begins his year at Keeneland's January sale, a week-long auction populated mainly by heavily pregnant mares and young horses that were weaned in the fall and officially became yearlings on the universal Thoroughbred birthday, January 1. The temperature on this particular day was in the 20's, and recent snow had been plowed into foot-high mounds along the edges of the walking rings between the barns.

Seaman and his assistant, a tall young woman named Martha Hamner, whose face was barely visible between her wool hat and a scarf wrapped thick and high around her neck, had been at Keeneland since about 8:00 A.M., getting the first view of the season's new yearlings. Seaman's hands were bare. "Can't measure with gloves on," he explained.

Hamner carried a clipboard of papers, including a list of barns and hip numbers the pair would visit, but Seaman carried only a handful of metal-cased tape measures, which he kept in the pockets of his green canvas coat.

"I've got two or three of them in here," he explained, patting one of the pockets, "in case we have a mechanical breakdown. We buy them by the gross from Stanley. Some last longer than others. Some, the spring will break in two or three weeks, and others will last three or four weeks."

In his khaki baseball cap and Gore-Tex hiking shoes, Seaman looked more like a racing fan than The Thoroughbred Analyst, the descriptive subtitle he uses on the business cards for his Cecil Seaman & Co. Partly this was because he carried none of the accessories that subtly distinguish the tire-kickers from the serious buyers—most notably, the traditional dog-eared sale catalog, a small stack of coil-bound supplements that provide extra information on the catalog's pedigrees, and an ink pen on a cord around the neck.

"I don't carry a catalog," Seaman said. "I just have a list of barn numbers and hip numbers. I don't want to be influenced by pedigree or anything when I look at a horse."

Seaman walked through barn after barn, deftly wending his way around the groups of muffled bloodstock agents, breeders, and farm managers who were looking at horses. The in-foal mares, slow and stately, cruised around the walking rings or stood nobly for examination, their bellies hanging almost to a point underneath them. Yearlings, electrified by the hubbub and the frigid breeze, leaped this way and that on the ends of their lead shanks, and everywhere horsemen were patting horses' necks, running their hands down legs, consulting catalog pages.

Seaman arrived at the Eaton Sales consignment, one of the largest agencies on the grounds. At Hamner's request, the barn foreman directed Seaman to a particular stall, where a groom was snapping a bit onto a yearling's halter, preparing to take the woolly chestnut colt out in the yard.

"No, that's all right," Seaman said. He always measures horses in the quiet of their stalls, a peculiarity that confuses grooms, who are used to standing their wares up in the walking ring for scrutinizing bidders. At Seaman's direction, the young woman stood the colt against the wall, so Seaman could measure along his left side.

"Pull the head over this way, please, so the head, neck, and back are in a straight line," he said to the groom.

He rubbed the colt's nose. "I like to let them smell my hand, so they know I'm not a veterinarian," he explained. "After I do that, they relax."

Seaman then pulled out one of his tapes and quickly angled its yellow line around the horse's left side, working from shoulder to rump, then along the back, calling out the number of inches as he went. Hamner dutifully wrote the numbers down on her clipboard.

To measure the legs, Seaman gently pushed bedding straw away from the colt's hooves with his foot, stepped on the end of the tape, and reeled it upward to the top of the leg. "Twenty-four and one-half, hock. Thirty-two and one-half, front legs. Fifty-nine, height."

The yearling looked startled and rolled his eye back toward Seaman as the tape wound and unwound with a faint rustle. Seaman had the groom press one end of the tape against the point of the colt's shoulder while he reeled it out to the farthest point of the rump.

"Seventy-six and one-half, length," Seaman said.

He dropped the tape over the colt's withers, caught it under the belly, and read out the distance around the colt's barrel: "Sixty and one-half, heart-girth." That measurement, combined with the one for the length of the colt's barrel, would determine his mass, Seaman explained. The length of the colt's femur and tibia would help deter-mine his leverage. The comparison between mass and leverage would be crucial to show how efficiently he would move.

The groom, watching all this, asked shyly, "What is this for?"

"This? Oh, it's biomechanics, just to see what they're going to do," Seaman said absently. He pushed his fist up under the colt's throat, measuring the space between the two sides of the jaw. "Four, jaw," he told Hamner.

"Some work was done a few years ago that claimed that if a horse is too narrow in the throat it puts too much pressure on the nerves in the windpipe area, and sometimes that nerve can become paralyzed and they'll have wind problems," he explained. "I believe there's probably some truth to that. We haven't checked the bearing that has, and we're getting ready to look at 15,000 horses in our database to see if it does have bearing. We revise our stuff many times. We're always looking."

Seaman does like to see horses walk, but unlike his colleagues who silently write notes to themselves on their catalog pages, Seaman calls out his thoughts in coded language to Hamner. He directed the groom to walk Hip 439 straight down the shedrow, not in the more usual walking ring. When the colt came back, Seaman walked around him, hands in pockets, firing out obscure comments.

"KK one-half, KO one-half," he said. "Check, check on feet. A on bone."

Then, to the groom, "That's fine, thank you."

The whole examination took less than five minutes. At the end of it, Hamner had a sheet with numbers and letters filled in for 15 measurement categories, including lengths of scapula, humerus, femur, and tibia; the length from shoulder to ischium, the point of the hip; and the distance from hock to ground, stifle to ground, and flank to ground.

"KK," Seaman explained as he left the barn, means that the colt was knock-kneed. "KO" refers to an offset knee. Bone is classified as light, average, or heavy. There is a ream of other designations, all of which are basically familiar to all horsemen who judge conformation. Seaman considers conformation, but he believes it is only helpful when considered in relation to biomechanics.

"Conformation and biomechanics aren't related at all," he said. "That's why you can have some horses with terrible conformation that still run. But what helps a horse with bad conformation that has some faults—the kind of horse a lot of people will turn down—is if he has a good point of gravity. If their point of gravity doesn't accent their conformation faults, then they can go on and stay sound and make a lot of starts. If they have a bad point of gravity, even if they're correct, they'll make less starts because the weight is too far on the front end."

For Seaman, pedigree is icing on the biomechanics cake. A good pedigree might add talent to a horse, but he will still have to be built properly in order to win. Once he does win, a good pedigree will increase his value.

"We don't take pedigree into account for what they'll do physically," Seaman said. "A lot of horses are trained wrong, because they've got a pedigree that says 'grass' or 'long,' and so they get trained that way when, in fact, they're made to do something else.

"We look at horses completely differently from most people," he acknowledged. "Most people are looking for a reason to turn the horse down. We're trying to find reasons to buy the horse. We want to buy a horse that has good biomechanics, a good point of gravity, correct enough that we think it will make it to the races, and as much pedigree as we can afford, because pedigree is your residual value. If you have a horse with a great pedigree that wins graded stakes, it's worth more than one without a great pedigree that wins graded stakes."

Seaman said that his program, feeding off the measurements of more than 60,000 horses and that raft of champions, can even tell him specifics: what distance a horse is biomechanically suited for, how competitive that horse's body proportions will allow him to be in graded-stakes company, even whether the horse would do better running marathons on turf or sprints on dirt.

"The computer generates all of this information, based on the raw measurements we put in," he said. "And we can buy horses right off of the information on these sheets. They tell you where it falls in the population conformationally, their soundness rating, what level of racing the horse can run to, how much the horse is overweight or underweight, what distance and surface the horse will do best on."

His rival bloodstock agents scoff at such assertions and accuse Seaman of being too dogmatic in a business they believe requires a certain subtlety of mind and eye, a notion that plainly grates on Seaman's orderly, statistically inclined mind.

"What people don't understand, they don't believe," he said, shrugging. "That's just human nature. I just tell people, 'Just look at our stats.' There are a lot of successful people from other businesses who come into the horse business and don't use the tools they could use to make them more successful here. But I'm just one consulting firm, and we're in competition with all these other agents, advisers, and farm managers. Most people have never even seen our stats. I don't know that we're demystifying horses, but we can identify the biomechanics, and we get good results.

"We've got it down to a science now," he added. "Everybody likes something that's appealing, but everybody has a bias. They like things they've been successful with. But those aren't the only things that are successful. There are lots of things that are successful. If we can buy horses that have faults, and buy them for the price of a ham sandwich, and go out there and win a lot of races with them, that makes the business work. And you have to do something that will make the business work, financially."

Seaman's average yearling-purchase price, over the last decade, was about $41,000, and most of his clients won't bid much beyond $150,000 to get a horse. They can't afford to buy a colt by Storm Cat, because no one who has paid Storm Cat's $500,000 stud fee is going to sell the colt that cheaply. So Seaman takes his slide rule to lesser pedigrees, hunting out biomechanical stars by overlooked, unproven, or unlikely sires.

Seaman's clients believe biomechanics will help them get their money's worth, and at least one statistical chart Seaman uses in his advertising suggests it might. The trade publication *Thoroughbred Times* produced the chart, which showed the return-on-investment percentages for 25 major Thoroughbred yearling buyers with 100 or more total purchases since 1990. Only six showed positive ROI's when the *Times* compared total purchase prices to total purse earnings, and Seaman's was the highest at 69 percent. Seaman spent $8,837,000 for 215 yearlings who went on to win $14,954,959.

But the chart factored in only race earnings, and not the fantastic sums that some horses can go on and generate as stallions. The clear winner in that race was Coolmore Stud's agent Demi O'Byrne. O'Byrne spent $86,475,000 to buy 106 yearlings that would earn only $12,287,485, resulting in a terrifyingly bad ROI of -86 percent. But a staggering 24.5 percent of those runners turned out to be stakes winners; most were colts; and many are now individually generating millions of dollars every breeding season for Coolmore—an immense profit not recorded on the *Times* chart. Even those stakes winners who were not good enough to make Coolmore's stallion roster could be sold privately for millions to other stud farms.

O'Byrne clearly had a talent for finding horses whose names eventually would be written in bold-face print, or "black type," The Jockey Club's coveted designation for a successful stakes performer. But he paid heavily for it. His next-nearest competitor, Canadian-based entrepreneur Frank Stronach, got 18.6 percent stakes winners from $24.4 million in yearling purchases. Sheikh Mohammed al-Maktoum got 15.1 percent stakes winners after spending $65.8 million. Black type on the racetrack equals black ink on a farm's bank statement, and the earning potential in the breeding shed far outstrips what runners can earn by racing. Coolmore obviously knew this, which was why Demi O'Byrne's -86 percent ROI had not cost the Irishman his job.

Even Seaman, who prides himself on finding biomechanically superior bargains for his clients, dreams of getting a whale like Coolmore. A buyer with that kind of financial backing could tap into rich pedigrees swollen with blank ink and end up with a flood of gold.

"I'd like to find some of those big clients, too, because our stats probably would be even better if we could buy into that next level, buy horses by stallions that are producing nine or ten percent stakes winners," Seaman said. "If we could do that, our average stakes winners would probably go up by ten or fifteen percent. Pedigree is an indication of successful horses in a horse's family. And the more successful horses there are, the more you'll have to pay for them. But it doesn't mean they're going to run, because even the top sires only get about ten percent really successful runners."

Seaman paused. "That's funny, isn't it? In what other business would ten percent be considered success?"

It was not a cheering statistic. The other 90 percent could fall victim to any number of problems, from poor proportionality, as determined by Seaman's measuring tape, to deadly illness. One of them might even be biomechanically perfect, and you would buy him, and then he could be startled during a thunderstorm and run through his paddock fence.

149

"That's true." Seaman nodded. "You can't control everything. There are so many different environmental factors: different trainers, different riders, different environments since the horses were born. There are just too many different variables, and nobody can control them all. But looking at the biomechanics, we are able to pick the right kind of horses to at least load our dice.

"We're looking at so many different factors," he concluded. "This is the combination of a lot of different parts that make up a whole. And the whole is stronger than anybody's eyeball. It's facts, it's figures, it's percentages, it's statistics."

But so far, despite the best systems of breeders, scientists, and buyers, there is still no single, objective, and fail-safe standard for creating or identifying a champion. After centuries of technological innovation and improved analysis, judging a horse is both easier and more complicated than it used to be. But the pressure remains largely where it has always been: on the person who puts up the money and on his hired eye.

Even John Ferguson, whose bids are backed by Sheikh Mohammed's seemingly bottomless account, is not immune to that pressure. His employer is an enthusiastic buyer who can spend millions on a single horse with obvious ease. That significantly increases the likelihood that Ferguson will get whatever horse he bids on, but it does not guarantee that the horse he gets will run.

In the 23 years since their arrival at American sales in 1980, Sheikh Mohammed and his brothers had spent more than $671 million on yearlings alone, but they had yet to win the Kentucky Derby, a prize Sheikh Mohammed in particular famously desires. He had bought legions of runners, most notably the champion and ill-fated stallion Dubai Millennium, who looked set for reproductive stardom but then died of a rare disease during his first year at stud in England.

Sheikh Mohammed and Ferguson both have been around horses long enough to know that such turns of luck, while sometimes devastating, are par for the course, and that no animal—not even the best-bred, best-conformed colt—is ever a sure thing. Ferguson, for one, never feels entirely comfortable, a common state of mind among people who spend their lives in close proximity to racehorses.

"Whenever you're bidding on a horse, you're constantly thinking, 'Am I making a mistake? Am I doing the right thing?'" said Ferguson, an earnest, auburn-haired Englishman with a pleasant but slightly harried manner. "You have to remember, yes, sure, I've been very lucky and we've bought a lot of nice horses over the years, but we've bought a lot of slow ones as well. I always feel, particularly when you're buying horses to race, you should have that concern, that slight fear factor. It keeps you on your toes. If you go in there totally blasé and totally believing, you'll end up having a smash, because it doesn't work like that. You have to be aware of the risks.

"Whether you're bidding for Sheikh Mohammed or Joe down the road, a horse has a value. You know going in what your last bid is. You've got to, because nothing in this world, with the exception of life, is priceless. Horses certainly are never priceless; they have a value of some kind that you have to work out sensibly, and doubly sensibly if it's not your money.

"You learn to value the entire package: pedigree, athleticism, conformation," Ferguson concluded. "And once you value that package, you walk in there thinking, 'Am I right? Am I right? Am I right?'"

There is only one objective answer to that question, and that is the finish line.

1 A Dollar and a Dream

JUST BEFORE THE sun rose over Churchill Downs on May 3, 2003, the cupolas underneath the twin spires, lit from within, seemed to hang in the sky by themselves in the final gray minutes of twilight. Below them, on the racetrack, dozens of dark, anonymous shapes, barely more than deeper shadows in the early gloom, were beginning their morning workout routine. For several hundred claimers, old sprinters, turf runners, and other everyday horses, this was just another workday. Those horses' owners had long ago lowered their sights from the famous first Saturday in May to the lesser-known contests that form the backbone of the American racing industry day in and day out.

For 16 horses on the Churchill grounds, however, this was Derby Day. Their stories were varied. The owners ranged from a Saudi prince who bred his own horses to a partnership of former high school pals who pooled their money to buy a horse. One of the runners, a short-priced contender with the unwieldy name Atswhatimtalknbout, had cost $900,000 at a 2-year-old auction and was owned by a group that included film director Steven Spielberg. At the opposite end of the money scale stood Indian Express, one of just 106 registered Thoroughbreds born in Utah in 2000. He had gone for $4,500 at a yearling auction, but after he won his first two races in Iowa by more than 10 lengths, his current owners bought him privately with an eye toward the Derby.

Whatever they were before and whatever they became afterward, those 16 horses already had done what 37,671 other North American Thoroughbred foals of 2000 had failed to do: They had gotten to the Derby. The previous year's most promising, undefeated 2-year-olds, Vindication and Sky Mesa, had not managed it. Vindication was on the sidelines with the injured ligament that would end his career. Sky Mesa had come back from the leg problem that had emerged the day before the Breeders' Cup Juvenile, only to develop a bruised hoof that took him off the Derby trail.

Only a few of the 2003 runners seemed like logical Derby candidates, the kind of well-bred, top-of-the-class horses that would have been voted most likely to succeed by anyone who saw them as youngsters. Trainer Bobby Frankel had Empire Maker, a colt by 1990 Derby winner Unbridled that had been talked up since his yearling season. D. Wayne Lukas had Scrimshaw, who had sold for $550,000 as a 2-year-old and was owned by 1997 and 1999 Derby-winning owners Bob and Beverly Lewis. And behind his unsightly name Atswhatimtalknbout boasted a classy pedigree starting with his sire, A.P. Indy, a onetime Horse of the Year.

Despite their bruising auction duels two years earlier, none of Saratoga's leading buyers had a million-dollar Derby horse to show for it. Roger King had come close. The $1.85 million Unbridled's Song colt he had exultantly outbid Satish Sanan for at Saratoga had finally made it to the racetrack at age 3, and won his first race at Churchill the day before the Derby. The horse that would have been Roger King's best shot in the Derby, ironically, was Atswhatimtalknbout. King had bred the colt and then sold him to another billionaire, B. Wayne Hughes, who was having his picture taken with Spielberg outside Churchill's Barn 41 on Derby morning.

The only other Saratoga behemoth to make it to the Derby was owner and Coolmore associate Michael Tabor, whose buying agent, Demi O'Byrne, was at Churchill Downs for the race. None of O'Byrne's seven-figure purchases for Tabor was running, but one he had bought for $375,000 was. That colt, named Brancusi, was almost 30-to-1.

It was easy to spot a barn with a Derby contender by the long saw-horses blocking off its entrances and the part-time security guard banning entry to everyone but the horse's closest connections. You could deduce the Derby contender's morning-line odds by the size of the press corps gathered outside and by whether the security guard was standing vigilantly in the barn doorway (favorite) or sitting in a metal folding chair with a cup of coffee (longshot).

Atswhatimtalknbout, a well-fancied runner in any case, also drew the press because of Spielberg's involvement. But there was an even larger group of reporters in Barn 43 next door, where the race's heavy favorite was stabled. The shedrow itself was off limits, but a quiet, watchful group of reporters had been camped outside it every morning, keeping an eye out for the Derby's acknowledged marquee horse and his trainer.

Their quarry was Empire Maker, an elegant, leggy bay with an elongated white splash on his face, as if he had been hit on the forehead with a paintball that was now running down toward his nose. Empire Maker was coming into the Derby off wins in two major prep races, and on past performances and pedigree, he looked much the best in the big race. His talent had not surprised Frankel, who had loved this horse since he was a foal at his owner's farm. Frankel and the farm employees had been high enough on the colt that they put a $2,000 Kentucky Derby win bet on him through an English bookmaker before he even ran.

Empire Maker was possibly the best-bred horse in the world, the product of bloodlines so regal that bloodstock agents generally estimated his value at $60 million, if he won the Derby as expected. He was by Unbridled, the 1990 Derby winner and successful sire who had, unfortunately, died of colic at the height of his breeding powers, aged 14. And he was out of one of history's most famous broodmares, Toussaud. Toussaud was one of just three mares ever to foal four Grade 1 winners. The other two, Dahlia and Fall Aspen, had died of old age by the time Empire Maker arrived at Churchill. But at age 14, Toussaud was still productive. Her value alone was estimated at between $8 million and $10 million, good for a world-record mare price if she came up for auction.

But Toussaud had never come up for auction, and neither had her illustrious son Empire Maker. They were the products of a powerful private breeding program, essentially self-sufficient, that minted its own golden horses under the Juddmonte Farms banner. The Juddmonte empire had begun as a Saudi prince's whim 30 years earlier, when Khalid Abdullah, a first cousin of Saudi Arabia's King Fahd, was idly sipping coffee in a French café and happened to catch a couple of trotting races on television.

"One day," he thought, "I'd like to own a horse."

By 2003, he owned more than 600 of them, as well as farms in Kentucky, England, and Ireland that covered about 7,000 total acres. His broodmare band represented some of the sport's most coveted bloodlines, the dams of numerous international champions. And Abdullah's trophy rooms were studded with silver, gold, and crystal collected from the world's most prestigious winner's circles: England's Epsom Derby, France's Prix de l'Arc de Triomphe, and the Irish Derby, all run on grass.

But, as yet, there was no Kentucky Derby trophy in Abdullah's collection. Partly, this was due to Juddmonte's propensity for breeding late-maturing horses and turf runners; the Derby, run on dirt in early May, rewarded a certain amount of precocity that Juddmonte horses often were not bred to have. Partly it was due to Juddmonte's American trainer, 61-year-old Bobby Frankel, who was famously patient with horses and refused to give in to Derby fever by rushing a promising colt too soon.

The Arab prince and the Jewish horse trainer made a paradoxical pair. Abdullah was soft-spoken and self-effacing; he preferred to be known as a "businessman" and was usually seen, if at all, in a subtly pin-striped suit and eyeglasses with thick black frames that made him look like a 1950's accountant. Frankel was outspoken and given to swearing in casual conversation. The two men had only met a few times in the 13 years that Frankel had trained for Juddmonte, but they had brought each other great success.

Frankel first arrived at the racetrack as a teenage gambler in New York. He was good at it. He once walked into a grandstand with $40, hit the daily double, and kept playing; at the end of the day he went home with $20,000.

"I put the money on my mother's bed," he told *Daily Racing Form*. "She thought I had robbed a bank."

Frankel brought the same kind of handicapping savvy to his training career, and it paid off there, too. He would claim a horse, figure out its mental and physical problems and how to fix them, and then he would run the horse back in a race it could win. He was patient, methodical, and astute about horses, and they ran for him. He turned seemingly average runners into stakes horses, and he started catching the attention of people who could give him some real stock to work with.

In 1972, Frankel moved to the West Coast. Training for prominent owners such as Bert Firestone, Edmund Gann, Jerome Moss, and Stavros Niarchos, he repeatedly won titles at Del Mar, Hollywood Park, and Santa Anita.

Juddmonte's general manager, a South African veterinarian named John Chandler, offered Frankel the training job in 1990. He selected Frankel after a computer analysis showed Frankel had a good record with turf horses and older runners—Juddmonte's specialties.

Frankel recalls his response to Juddmonte's offer with some embarrassment. "I told them I'd think about it. Can you believe it?"

After a fellow trainer who knew Juddmonte told Frankel it was the best job in racing, he accepted.

"The thing I like about him is that the horses come first," Frankel said of Abdullah. "I remember when I first started working for him, I had a filly in a $500,000 stakes that I had to scratch. I just wasn't comfortable running her. And it was no big deal to them to scratch her."

The job has also given Frankel a new respect for the power of pedigree.

"At one time, I wouldn't have believed it," he said. "But having a filly like Toussaud and then her foals, it's a little edge knowing them and training her and all her foals. I never believed in breeding as much as I have in the last few years, getting the foals out of the mares I've trained."

Frankel and Juddmonte had the perfect symbiotic relationship: He was renowned for his ability to bring out the best in horses and keep them sound, and Juddmonte's runners had the kind of talent that put the brilliant, temperamental Frankel in racing's Hall of Fame. But he hadn't won the Derby yet.

155

That appeared about to change on May 3, 2003. Empire Maker—winner of two important Derby preps, the Florida Derby and Wood Memorial—was one of the shortest-priced favorites in recent Derby history. The only hitch in Empire Maker's campaign had come, as these things often seem to, during Derby Week, when a bruised right front foot flared up and cost him a training day.

Frankel, who speculated that the injury might originally have occurred in the Wood, did not seem unduly worried.

"We're not panicking," he said. "Things like this happen every day. It just gets more attention because it's the Derby. Tomorrow, he'll be perfect. Put it this way—if he's not right, he's not going to run."

Even Khalid Abdullah, rarely seen in America, had been persuaded to come to Churchill Downs.

"I told him, 'You will never in your entire breeding life have a better shot before the race of winning the Kentucky Derby than you do right now,'" Chandler said. "'This is the best horse you've had racing in this country, and you will never have a better shot.'"

For Jackson Knowlton, it wasn't about never having a better shot. It was about having a shot at all. Knowlton, a 55-year-old health-care consultant, was the managing partner of Sackatoga Stable, which had more owners than horses. None of his nine other partners had ever owned a horse before. Now, together, they owned three. And one of them, a chestnut gelding named Funny Cide, was running in the Kentucky Derby.

It had been a magical trip for Sackatoga, which got its name by splicing the group's upstate New York hometown, Sackets Harbor (population 1,358), with Knowlton's new residence in nearby Saratoga. The syndicate got started when Knowlton convinced five friends from his high-school days to put up $5,000 each to buy a horse. They designed their silks with a diamond pattern in their high-school colors of maroon and gray. They had a little success and a lot of fun. Two of the partners split their shares to let a couple more friends in, and by the time the boisterous group arrived at Churchill Downs in a yellow school bus, the ownership group included a retired contractor, a retired schoolteacher, a caterer, an optician, a couple of health-care executives, two guys in construction, a retired mechanical engineer, and a former utility-company worker.

Their trainer was Barclay Tagg, a 65-year-old former steeplechase rider whose cunning horsemanship had earned him a name among the betting cognoscenti at Saratoga as a man with a small stable of horses that would win at big prices. Unpretentious, with a scathing tongue, he did not suffer fools or big egos gladly and had been known to "fire" owners who tried to get him to do things he thought were bad for their horses. He had made a decent living and trained some nice runners, but Tagg wasn't someone you expected to find at the Kentucky Derby—if you had heard of him at all.

The Derby wasn't really in his usual program. He didn't have clients that would spend $1 million for a yearling, so he specialized in finding horses he could buy fairly inexpensively and then improve. Like Frankel, Tagg was also known for his patience with a horse. He was much more likely to have a solid 4-year-old campaigner than a precocious 2-year-old, and he probably would never win a Breeders' Cup Juvenile. Commercial-minded owners or those who wanted mollycoddling, Tagg's history seemed to say, need not apply. But if you loved the game, loved horses, and wanted to have some fun without breaking the bank, he was your man.

Tagg was a perfect match for Sackatoga's "investors." They had no interest in making racing their business. To them, it was all for fun, and recently it had gotten fun beyond all logical probability.

Early on, Funny Cide didn't look like a home run horse. He had cost only $22,000 when he came up for sale as a yearling in 2001. He was from the first crop of foals by Distorted Humor, whose own race record suggested he would sire sprinters unlikely to run well at the Derby's 1 ¼-mile distance. Funny Cide's dam, Belle's Good Cide, was an undistinguished racehorse who didn't have any stakes-winning foals to her credit. So his pedigree was strike one for prospective buyers.

The yearling Funny Cide also was a ridgling, a colt with one undescended testicle. Some ridglings have gone on to great glory as racehorses and sires, most notably A.P. Indy. But an undescended testicle can be uncomfortable for a horse once he starts training,

and it is generally thought better to geld him before then, something a buyer would have to arrange and pay for: strike two. And
Funny Cide was born late in the foaling season, on April 20, making him less mature than the other auction yearlings. That meant
he would need time, and time, after all, is money.

Surrounded as they were by a couple hundred other sale
prospects, a lot of buyers understandably walked right past Funny
Cide, and the bidding was only moderate. Funny Cide went to a
reseller named Tony Everard who was used to taking risks. His
whole career was built on picking up horses he thought other people had underestimated, putting some training in them, and selling
them at a profit.

Tagg and his assistant trainer, Robin Smullen, were regular visitors to Everard's farm in Ocala, Florida, where they combed
through the young horses on offer. They saw Funny Cide three
times in the early spring of 2002, and they liked him better each
time. So did Everard, who had gelded the horse and now saw a lot
of promise in Funny Cide's workout times. As Funny Cide developed, his price tag jumped from $40,000 in February to $75,000 in
March.

Tagg mentioned Funny Cide to Knowlton, who thought $75,000
was too steep for Sackatoga. Then something lucky happened. One
of Sackatoga's other runners, Bail Money, was claimed for $62,500
on March 6. Sackatoga parlayed that income and some of Bail
Money's earnings into buying Funny Cide.

"He wasn't cheap, but at that point we were playing with the
house's money," Knowlton said.

Funny Cide had improved, but was still far from perfect. He had
a broken tooth that cut his mouth. And he was tough to handle on
the track, pulling so hard that Tagg's exercise riders found they
could only control him by cranking his head around hard to the left
while he galloped. One day at Saratoga, Funny Cide ran away with
one of the freelance riders Tagg had hired. By the time he came
back to the barn, the exertion had damaged the gelding's shins.
Smullen became Funny Cide's only rider after that, but, as she put
it, "You can't win an outright fight with him. You have to convince
him into doing things. The whole ride is a negotiation."

But Funny Cide had talent. Carefully brought along by Tagg and

Smullen, he was becoming a bona fide racehorse. Because he was born in New York, he was registered as a New York-bred, a designation that made him eligible for races restricted to horses foaled in the state. He won those with ease, taking his first three starts by a combined 24 lengths. He was already one of the most talked-about 2-year-olds on the New York circuit, and Tagg, a well-known pessimist, quietly began to do something optimistic: He plotted a course to the Derby.

"I wanted to give him a freshening and put him on the Derby trail and see if it would work," he said. "You don't get many opportunities, and you don't get many horses that are of this caliber. I've been around a lot of horses, but every now and then one will really, really stand out. I was pretty sure about him. We just had to give him a chance."

It wasn't a smooth trip. In his first start of the 2003 Derby campaign, Funny Cide banged into the starting gate on his way out of it and finished fifth. Then he got a lung infection and lost training time. When he came back, he ran in the Louisiana Derby, where he finished third behind a Bobby Frankel horse, Peace Rules.

They were good performances under the circumstances. But Empire Maker, in the meantime, had won a more prestigious race, the Florida Derby, coasting home by almost 10 lengths. On April 12, Funny Cide and Empire Maker met at Aqueduct racetrack in New York for the Wood Memorial, their last race before the Kentucky Derby. Empire Maker, ridden by Jerry Bailey, was favored in the betting and won as expected, beating Funny Cide and jockey Jose Santos by half a length. He made it look easy. The Wood Memorial had been simulcast to racetracks around the nation, where people turned away from the TV's, cashed their tickets on Empire Maker, and agreed that he was much the best of the horses pointing for the Derby.

But Funny Cide's camp saw something else. They saw their horse digging in, challenging the best horse of his generation, and hanging tough.

"If you looked at it very objectively, my horse was getting the hell beat out of him, and the other horse, Jerry was trying to steer Empire Maker, who was trying to lug in," Tagg recalled. "I talked myself into the fact that they were both riding as hard as they could under the circumstances, but it made it look like Jerry wasn't riding that hard because he was actually trying to steer. I clung to that faithfully so I could keep on the trail."

Whether their assessment was astute or delusional, after the Wood the Sackatogians believed their horse was worth taking to the Kentucky Derby. They knew their scrappy gelding would be a longshot against Empire Maker and the other stellar rivals flying in from California. No New York-bred had ever won the Derby. No gelding had done it since Clyde Van Dusen back in 1929. But it was still the trip of a lifetime: Churchill Downs on the first Saturday in May.

"Since the Wood," Knowlton said, "I've been counting the days and hoping beyond hope that something wasn't going to happen. I've seen so many horses get so close, and then something happens along the way."

Early in the afternoon of May 3, Churchill Downs was sunning itself in bright spring weather, and the stable area was in the thrall of Derby Day festivities. At many barns, trainers and their employees had dragged out lawn chairs and barbecues, and radios and miniature televisions were broadcasting race coverage over the pops and sizzles of chicken and pork.

Most reporters had repaired to the press box for the races, overlooking a raucous crowd of 148,530 in the clubhouse, grandstand, and infield. But a few tenacious photographers still clung to one end of Bobby Frankel's barn, and they were rewarded occasionally when he came out to take runners over to the paddock for races leading up to the Derby. By four o'clock, things were looking good for Frankel. With two hours left until Derby post time, he already had won three big races, two of them with homebred Juddmonte fillies. The photographers perched along the curb outside Frankel's barn could hear cheering from the infield, and then, a few minutes later, a smattering of applause from the backstretch crowd as Frankel and his horses, victorious again, walked back around the racetrack toward their stable.

In Barn 48, Barclay Tagg had taken his gray suit jacket off and rolled his shirtsleeves up. Behind him, in Stall Number 6, Funny

Cide stood in the doorway with his front legs in a tub of ice water—a standard prerace practice. Churchill Downs had provided each Derby trainer with a white Lincoln for the week, and Tagg was using its trunk to haul ice from the track kitchen to his barn. He poured fresh ice into the tub around Funny Cide's legs. A groom named Zacarias Quintana and a hotwalker named Raunie Hart, both already wearing the required royal-blue shirts with Triple Crown sponsor Visa's logo, knelt around Funny Cide's forelegs, adjusting stretchy black bandages that soaked the ice water all the way up around the gelding's knees. Occasionally, Hart scooped some of the frigid water into a yellow Wendy's Biggie-sized cup and poured it on Funny Cide's legs, letting it run down the bandages.

Funny Cide, a 12-1 shot, was stabled off to one side of the backstretch, and there were no photographers flocking outside his barn. Tagg was glad, because it kept things quiet and didn't distract him or the horse from the task at hand. Tagg had even told the exuberant Sackatoga clan not to hang around the barn on Derby Day.

Tagg hoped to slip in and out of his first Derby with as little change in routine as possible. He had avoided much of the circus by sending his gelding to Churchill Downs from their home base at Belmont Park just three days before the race. Once there, he had Smullen jog Funny Cide placidly around the track—no galloping, no fast breezes. All of the critical speed work had been done at Belmont.

Every morning, Tagg, slouched on his own horse and wearing a tweedy flat cap pulled low on his forehead, had led Funny Cide and Smullen around all the whirring cameras and nattering morning-show hosts and out to Churchill's track, watching for something to go wrong. Nothing did, so he kept taking his horse out to exercise in the mornings, and they were still in the race.

A group of single-engine planes growled in circles over Churchill Downs, towing banners for Green Bull ladders, Kroger supermarkets, and a local strip club called Racers. Occasionally, muffled cheers from the infield crowd wafted toward Barn 48. But, for the most part, it was peaceful at Tagg's barn. Birds chirped as they picked oats out of a nearby muck pit, and a washing machine stuffed with leg wraps and saddlecloths chugged quietly away outside a barn farther down the path. Funny Cide had actually taken a nap that afternoon, Smullen said.

Oddly, none of the Derby first-timers in Barn 48 seemed nervous. "This horse has already done so much for all of us," Smullen explained. "No matter how he runs today, he got these people to the Kentucky Derby."

It took just 2:01.19 to run the 2003 Kentucky Derby, and that slim wedge of time would be life-changing for the people who owned and trained the winner. When the starting gate opened at 6:08 P.M., Jackson Knowlton and his partners were packed into box seats next to Empire Maker's owner, Prince Khalid Abdullah, and racing manager Chandler. Abdullah's group was sober in black and gray suits, and the prince sat quietly with his binoculars focused on the starting gate. The Sackatoga box, by contrast, was a pandemonium of maroon-and-gray Funny Cide lapel buttons, pink shawls, and flowered hats. The yellow-and-blue plaid sports jacket worn by Sackatoga partner Gus Williams—"It's my lucky one," he explained—made a lot of noise by itself.

The field broke on the grandstand side of the racetrack and was carried past the stands for the first time on a thunderous roar from the crowd. As the horses and riders leaned into the first turn and headed toward the backstretch, Empire Maker was floating like a cork just outside the main flow of runners, comfortably bobbing along out of the traffic and awaiting Jerry Bailey's cue to run. Brancusi, O'Byrne's $375,000 buy for Michael Tabor, was leading the field at a quick clip; he ran the first quarter-mile in 22.78 seconds. Funny Cide, who had bumped Offlee Wild leaving the starting gate, was no worse for that and coasted along in Brancusi's wake, running fourth. Celebrity-owned Atswhatimtalknbout had dropped back almost to the end of the line, where, his fans knew, he would lurk until launching his usual late strike.

The horses ran down the backstretch, past the stable employees and their families, who had pressed up against a chain-link fence to watch. The field going by them was like a tumbling flood, and some horses already appeared to be falling back in it. As the field rolled past them, the backstretch workers dashed back to their TV's to see what would happen on the run for home.

The field whipped into the final turn. This was where things got serious, where pretenders were revealed as they faltered, tired, and fell away, and where true contenders who had been biding their time now emerged to gun for the finish line.

Brancusi was a pretender. His lead collapsed like cheap plywood when the real runners pressured him, and as the field rumbled into the final turn, Brancusi was swallowed up in the tide of also-rans. Those, according to the fine print at the bottom of the race's official chart in the *Daily Racing Form*, variously "flattened out," were "unable to seriously menace," "failed to offer a closing response," "couldn't sustain the needed momentum," and were "empty when the test came." Their Derby dream was over, but Empire Maker, in eighth position, had just gotten his signal from Bailey. Safely clear of the traffic jams created by spent and slowing horses, Empire Maker skimmed along the outside of the field and took aim on Peace Rules, his stablemate from Bobby Frankel's barn and the horse that had grabbed the lead when Brancusi shriveled.

By the time the field wheeled into the homestretch, Empire Maker had flown from eighth to third. All that stood between him and Peace Rules was Funny Cide, whom Empire Maker had recently beaten. Bailey lifted his whip in his right hand and asked for more speed from Empire Maker, but he got no acceleration. He hit Empire Maker again, but their position was not improving. The colt was at his limit.

The Sackatoga box erupted in screams, cheers, and encouraging bellows as Funny Cide, now running second only an eighth of a mile from the finish line in the Kentucky Derby, held off Empire Maker. But Peace Rules, just ahead of him, was proving tough to dislodge from the lead. With the wire rapidly approaching, the race looked like a two-on-one bar brawl with Funny Cide in the middle, holding off Empire Maker with one hand and swinging frantically at Peace Rules with the other. Peace Rules finally crumbled, and Funny Cide surged past him, with Empire Maker still doggedly in pursuit. They flashed under the wire with Funny Cide in front of Empire Maker by 1 ¾ lengths and the fading Peace Rules in third. Atswhatimtalknbout, who had indeed made his expected long rally, crossed the wire in fourth.

The Sackatoga bunch let out wild cries and raised their fists to the sky. Knowlton accidentally knocked his wife's hat askew in the riotous moment. The partners, still yelling, leaped up and down in jubilation, then collapsed against each other in a group hug that looked more like a rugby scrum. The exuberant Sackatogians formed a pocket of ecstatic joy amidst their dejected and largely silent rival owners, whose horses were now straggling in behind Funny Cide.

Bobby Frankel shrugged off the loss as well as he could. His immediate thought was that Empire Maker's foot bruise had made the 1 ¾-length difference.

"It might be that a little missed training might have cost him the race," he said.

But he pointed out that Empire Maker was young yet and had plenty of time to return to stardom. The next opportunity, he thought, would come in five weeks at the Belmont Stakes.

In their last starts before tackling the Kentucky Derby, Empire Maker and Funny Cide both raced in the Wood Memorial. One of them came out with a bruised foot and the other one didn't. It probably could have gone either way. The fact that it went the way it did may have given a $75,000 gelding and his small-time owners an edge over a priceless colt and his royal breeder, exactly when they needed it.

Barclay Tagg was a sophisticated, experienced horseman who knew what he was doing when he picked up that gelding, channeled his talent, and started planning his Derby campaign. It was not a random collision of stars that took Funny Cide from promising 2-year-old to Kentucky Derby winner. Tagg was not a superstitious man in general, and he knew better than anyone how much work had gone into those two Derby minutes, but he also knew that having Lady Luck blow on your dice never hurts, either. At the postrace press conference, suddenly caught in the camera lights, the weathered Tagg looked more relieved than ecstatic.

"Everybody thinks about winning the Derby," he said. "A lot of people who are very, very successful never have. You need a lot of luck for something like this. It was lucky that we stumbled on the horse. It was lucky that the people wanted to buy a horse at that time. It was lucky that he turned out so good. It was lucky that he never got hurt badly or anything like that. The pitfalls from the day he's born to the day he gets to the Kentucky Derby are just monumental. You can hope all you want, but things like that don't happen too easily."

But once a year it happens to someone, and in 2003 it happened to Jack Knowlton and his pals. They picked up their $800,200 share of the race's $1.1 million purse, the governor of Kentucky raised a toast to them, and Barclay Tagg, improbably, was there in the winner's circle holding the fabled trophy aloft with a satisfied smile. Funny Cide had broken the Derby's 74-year gelding drought, become the first New York-bred ever to win the race, and beaten odds that had been incalculably high when buyer after buyer passed him by at that 2001 yearling sale in New York.

"It's like the lottery," said Knowlton, his face aglow with a beatific smile. "A dollar and a dream."

Funny Cide may have been a gelding, but he was a home run horse now. More specifically, he was the one to beat in the Preakness Stakes. But even before Funny Cide rolled into Baltimore on a horse van the day before the May 17 race, his connections already had had a wild trip. The week after the Derby, while Sackets Harbor was throwing parties for its most famous alumni, a bizarre story appeared in the *Miami Herald*, insinuating that Funny Cide's jockey, Jose Santos, had carried an illegal electrical device during the Derby, a battery with which he could shock his horse into running faster. The newspaper published a photo taken soon after Funny Cide had crossed the wire that, when magnified, appeared to show a dark object between the spread fingers of the jockey's right hand.

The writer of the story contacted the stewards at Churchill Downs, one of whom called the photo "very suspicious" and promptly launched an investigation. Examining some of the hundreds of photos taken of the Derby finish from multiple angles, however, the stewards soon determined—as several other news services and publications already had done—that the "battery" was actually background color seen through the gap between Santos's fingers. Santos was cleared.

But the story had generated a tidal wave of attention. People were scandalized at first, and then, when the story was revealed as bogus, full of sympathetic outrage over the notion that the media was picking on the average Joes that had won the Derby. By the time the horses were loaded into the gate for the Preakness, it had become politically incorrect, even inflammatory, to root against "the people's horse." Even Jay Leno and David Letterman had thrown their support toward Santos and Sackatoga. Bobby Frankel earned public wrath by hastily reversing his plan to skip the Preakness with Empire Maker when it looked as if Funny Cide might be disqualified from the Derby—in which case Empire Maker would stand a chance at the Triple Crown. When the *Miami Herald* story fell apart, Frankel decided not to run Empire Maker in the Preakness, though he kept Peace Rules in.

So when Funny Cide cruised home by an emphatic 9 ¾ lengths in the Preakness, it was without his main rival, whose reputation now was on the line for the Belmont Stakes.

Peace Rules, who led for much of the Preakness, only managed to finish fourth. Frankel, now considered the deserving loser by many, was understandably irritated.

"I have nothing to say," he said with a shrug when a reporter for ESPN.com approached him after the race. "What can I say? He just got beat. He outbroke the field and he got beat. What else can I say?"

The Funny Cide road show had become a kind of national morality play. The horse, his regular-guy owners and falsely accused jockey, even the stony-faced Tagg, were suddenly cult figures in an all-American story about beating the odds, socking it to the big boys, and gaining redemption. And nowhere was Funny Cide fever higher than in New York, where the hometown horse would be trying to become the first Triple Crown winner in 25 years, and only the 12th Triple Crown winner since the series got that name in the 1930's. If Funny Cide could pull it off, Sackatoga would get one of sport's rarest honors: a not very pretty but highly desirable silver Triple Crown trophy shaped like a triangular bowl and a

$5 million bonus check from series sponsor Visa. As they approached their historic moment, the Funny Cide team was in great demand.

Santos threw out the first pitch at a Yankees game. Tagg got fan mail, including a letter from Joe Paterno, the legendary football coach at his alma mater, Penn State. Popular artist LeRoy Neiman brought his brushes and palette to Belmont and sought an audience with the potential Triple Crown winner.

The Sackatoga partners were mobbed with interview requests. They starred in an "I Love New York" television commercial and fielded merchandising proposals. Knowlton quickly moved to capitalize on the mania by signing a couple of deals and setting up a website where fans could follow the gelding's races, get inspiration from his story, and buy Funny Cide-related memorabilia.

"I got a call from a shop the other day, and this guy was telling me, 'Look, I don't care if you produce the product, I don't care if I produce it, whatever. Just get me the Funny Cide hats, because I've got hundreds of E-mails here asking me where they are,'" Knowlton told *Daily Racing Form*. "And this was a guy in Kentucky.'"

New York racing officials and Thoroughbred-industry executives everywhere in America also did what they could to cash in on the Funny Cide frenzy. Racing syndicates bought ads in general-interest magazines and newspapers encouraging readers to get in on their own racehorse. The New York Thoroughbred Breeders Association in Saratoga reminded people that New York-breds such as Funny Cide not only could win the Derby and Preakness, but they also ran for a lot of money every day in the Empire State, in races restricted to New York-breds. Joe and Anne McMahon, the breeders near Saratoga who owned the farm where Funny Cide was born, hung a sign honoring him on the side of their foaling barn. In Sackets Harbor, a sign on the road into town said, "Historic Sackets Harbor. Funny Cide Rules. On to Belmont."

The Sackatoga entourage had grown, too. This time, they were bringing four school buses and about 200 people with them to the track. In the three weeks between the Preakness and the Belmont Stakes, Belmont Park's operators had issued more than 1,000 media credentials and were expecting more than 100,000 fans to show up for the Belmont Stakes on June 7.

Amidst the tumult, Tagg was trying to train his horse to win the elusive Triple Crown. But Tagg no longer had the luxury of quiet anonymity that he had enjoyed at the Derby, and it was getting harder for him to maintain the fragile bubble of calm he needed around his temperamental charge. Just getting to the track every morning for workouts was like pushing through chest-high mud. Several dozen reporters and cameramen packed around Tagg and Funny Cide as they tried to make their way along the leafy and normally peaceful Belmont horse paths. Tagg resorted to outright trickery, telling the media he would work the horse at 8:30 in the morning and then sneaking him out of the barn for a predawn workout instead. Tagg and Smullen knew things had gotten really ridiculous when a self-proclaimed horse psychic named Maxine called the barn to set up an appointment for Funny Cide.

The horse himself was doing well. The tough Triple Crown series had put him on the road from New York to Kentucky, back to New York, on to Baltimore, and back again in just five weeks. In that time, he had won a 1 ¼-mile race, then dialed back the distance and won at 1 ³⁄16 miles. It was a grinding schedule that often wore horses down, but Funny Cide seemed even more robust during Belmont Week than he had before the Derby.

Just how fit Funny Cide was became startlingly obvious on June 3, when the gelding put in his final five-furlong speed work for the Belmont. Funny Cide was so sharp Smullen had to stand up in her irons and pull against him to keep him under control as he approached his workout's starting point. When she finally sent him forward, he soared through the first furlong in 11.18 seconds. He was pulling hard on Smullen, who gave him a little rein and let him settle into his long, flying stride. They rocketed through the opening quarter-mile in an eye-popping 21.90 and a half-mile in 45.03. The clockers had him at 57.82 a furlong later when he began pulling up, and that was the day's fastest work at the distance.

"It was a little faster than I wanted," Tagg admitted when the media horde inevitably showed up outside his barn. "But he cooled out fast. I feel a little squeamish going a mile and a half off that work. . . . He'll have to handle it."

Funny Cide's workout created a sonic boom around the stable area. Rival trainers were aghast. It sounded too fast, especially for an aggressive horse who would likely find it hard to ration his speed over the Belmont's 1 ½ miles. Frankel, talking to the *Daily Racing Form*, put it succinctly.

"Unless he's a super, super horse, he's fucked," he said.

Belmont Stakes Week was a stormy one, with hard rains that turned Belmont's dirt track into mud and then into soup. It started raining again on Saturday, June 7, the day of the race. By late morning, slicker-clad fans were already starting to fill Belmont Park's cavernous facility. There was a handicapping seminar underway in a tent near the paddock, where various experts were debating whether the hard numerical facts from the Kentucky Derby and the Preakness supported the accomplished Funny Cide or the fresh Empire Maker in the Belmont. The panel hashed out Beyer Speed Figures, fractional race times, workout performance during Belmont Week, and the influence pedigree might have on the horses' abilities to "get the distance" in the unusually long Belmont.

People crowded under the tent to listen, pulling out copies of the *Daily Racing Form* they had kept protected under their rain gear. They listened intently and wrote cryptic reference marks on the past performances. The smart money, as represented by the professional handicappers, seemed to favor Empire Maker as the most likely winner. He was well rested and over the bruised foot, he had beaten Funny Cide fairly convincingly in the Wood, he had been reasonably close behind him in the Derby when he might not have been quite fit enough, and, really, Funny Cide had not appeared to beat all that much in the Preakness.

Then again, Funny Cide had beaten Empire Maker in the Kentucky Derby and won the Preakness by an insultingly large margin. Funny Cide's supporters also cited a few more mystical handicapping factors that you wouldn't find in any objective statistics.

"Isn't he magnificent?" gushed one older lady, swaddled in waterproof material and carrying an umbrella but still bravely sporting a straw hat festooned with Funny Cide buttons. "Wasn't his Preakness magnificent? It has to be his day today. It's the 25th anniversary since Affirmed, it's a New York horse in New York. I came all the way from New Orleans to see it!"

Upstairs in the clubhouse, at 11:00 A.M., a few swells were

already filling the box seats overlooking the sodden racetrack. Nearby, the New York Racing Association was selling champagne at $10 a glass. A uniformed employee stuck strawberries on the rim of each plastic flute, and behind her, bottles of Chevalier bubbly stood row on row in green plastic tubs full of ice. Whoever won the race, NYRA would have plenty to celebrate. Even with the appalling weather, the Belmont Stakes had drawn more than 101,000 people through the gates, and they all seemed willing to take a gamble on the race's outcome. Along with simulcast viewers around the country, they would bet a near-record $48,081,346 on the Belmont Stakes alone. Some of that money came from people who bet Funny Cide with no intention of cashing their tickets if he became the 12th Triple Crown winner in history. Even some of the people who had picked Empire Maker on logic would qualify their choice by saying they wouldn't mind if Funny Cide won.

"It would be history, wouldn't it?" said one betting man in the clubhouse who had tickets on both horses but thought Empire Maker would win. "It'd be great to see. Great for the sport."

Meanwhile, what began as a light, silvery rain had turned into heavy gray sheets, and thick streams of muddy water flowed along the horse paths in the stable area. Just beyond the end of the clubhouse, at the corner of Count Fleet Road and Man o' War Avenue, Funny Cide's barn was buttoned up against the weather and the prying eyes of visitors, fans, and cameramen alike. Workers from other barns and owners of other horses stabled at Belmont walked by, casting sidelong glances to spot the Derby and Preakness hero, but the barn's doors and windows were closed. A burly Wackenhut security guard, Bill Miller, stood outside the barn door. A man with slicked-back hair and dressed in business attire that suggested he might have an owner's license approached Miller and tapped him on the arm, asking him to convey a message to Tagg.

"Tell him to win it for all of us," he said earnestly.

"Sure, sure," Miller said. "But I'll tell you what, he was talking about the horse the other day, and he says there's not a doubt in his mind. Not a doubt in his mind."

"Well, that's good," said the man, nodding gravely. "I said a lot of prayers for him last night."

The man hunched his shoulders and walked on again toward the clubhouse. Miller watched him go and shook his head.

"I think he's going to do it," he said of Funny Cide. "He's definitely gotten bigger. The thing is, the weight he's put on, it's *muscle*."

He rubbed his hands together and smiled. "I got the big horse, right here," he said. "It's been fun. My wife has seen me on TV about a hundred times. I'm like a celebrity on a poor man's salary!"

The races were already under way by the time Khalid Abdullah's North American racing manager, John Chandler, arrived at the track, this time without the prince. He stood inside the clubhouse, water dripping from his trench coat, his royal-blue umbrella, and his *Daily Racing Form*.

"It's crappy weather, isn't it?" he said, shaking out his umbrella. "But Empire Maker will be fine in this," he added, smiling broadly. "He'll win. No problem."

At 5:05 P.M., the racing officials called trainers to bring over their runners for the day's 10th race, the last one before the Belmont. Barclay Tagg, wrapped in a tan trench coat, his face partially hidden under an olive-green trilby, ducked out of his barn office and into the rain, striding along at a pace that he hoped would discourage any reporters who might follow. He made his way down the horse path and into the rubber-floored tunnel that led from the stable area to Belmont's paddock. In about 10 minutes, he would saddle his 10th-race horse, a turf runner named Macaw. But there wasn't any need to spend the extra time fending off the rain or the crowds outside. Instead, he stepped into the relative sanctuary of Belmont's racing office, a small building near the paddock.

When he closed the door behind him, the other trainers and owners who had been conversing, swapping jokes, and watching the races on TV there grew hushed. One or two nodded in his direction, and then, while Tagg leaned against the racing secretary's counter and waited to head out to saddle Macaw, a few more came over one at a time, quietly wishing him luck and shaking his hand. They were reverent and spoke in low tones, as if Tagg, unexpectedly chosen for a tilt at racing's most sacred honor, was now clothed in a holy aura. He was in a place they had all, at one time or another, hoped they could be.

"So many people have gotten into this horse," Tagg said, "I'm going to feel guilty if it doesn't happen."

By 2003, the Belmont Stakes had been the graveyard of 17 Triple Crown attempts since 1944, when Derby and Preakness winner Pensive was beaten by a half-length in his try for the difficult triple. The losers' list includes some of the Thoroughbred game's most illustrious runners and sires: Carry Back, Northern Dancer, Majestic Prince, Spectacular Bid, Pleasant Colony, Alysheba, Sunday Silence, Silver Charm—all fell short in the Belmont. The closest anyone has come since Affirmed won it in 1978 was 1998 contender Real Quiet, who lost the Triple Crown by just a nose when Victory Gallop beat him in the Belmont.

The reasons a horse loses any race vary widely, but in the Belmont, the excuses often relate to the race's distance. The Belmont is one of the few American races run anymore at the marathon length of 1 ½ miles, a factor that generally works against modern horses bred primarily for speed instead of stamina. What makes it even more difficult is that it comes at the end of a grueling three-state, five-week series, and it is run over the largest track in America, whose long homestretch can lure riders into making a move too soon. Whether through a horse's aggression, a rider's impatience, a lack of fitness, a stamina deficit in the genes, or simple road-weariness, most Triple Crown attempts founder over that anomalous mile and a half.

There had always been some question about Funny Cide's ability, based on pedigree, to win at the Belmont distance. Empire Maker's more stamina-oriented breeding suggested he had a genetic edge when he stepped into the Belmont starting gate. But no one, and certainly not Empire Maker's jockey, Jerry Bailey, was taking it for granted that pedigree alone would lose Funny Cide's Triple Crown. Bailey thought the gelding had another, far more fatal flaw: his willfulness.

It was the same flaw that Tagg and Smullen had identified in Funny Cide, and it was a major reason that Tagg had worked so hard to keep his horse relaxed, away from the electric tension of the media and the fans. There was a fine line between competitive toughness and rank self-destruction, and much of Tagg's training had been about managing and reinforcing that line. To win the

Belmont, jockey Jose Santos would have to throttle Funny Cide down and ration his speed early in the race. If Funny Cide didn't want to relax and wait for orders, if the delicate negotiation between the 110-pound rider and his 1,000-pound horse failed, Funny Cide would simply burn himself up in the fight.

Bailey, on Empire Maker, aimed to help that fight along. When the gate opened, Santos put Funny Cide on the lead in an effort to control the pace and, if possible, slow it down. But within seconds, as Bailey predicted, it was clear that Funny Cide was arguing with his rider, pulling hard against Santos's hands. In an effort to slow his horse down, Santos was standing slightly upright, bracing himself against his stirrup irons and his horse's mouth. Bailey kept Empire Maker, who was relaxed and going easily, just alongside Funny Cide's right flank, egging the competitive gelding on against Santos's wishes. Funny Cide, with the rail on one side of him and a rival breathing down his flank on the other, wanted to shoot forward, but Santos kept an iron grip on him. He had managed to slow the pace down to 23.85 for the first quarter-mile and 48.70 for the half. But, as Bailey had hoped, the tension was wearing Funny Cide down. Bailey eased Empire Maker forward, needling Funny Cide a little more.

"He was pulling on Jose, and my horse was very relaxed, which is the whole key to going a mile and a half," Bailey said later. "I knew I had him."

And so it proved. When the field splashed into the turn for home, Jose Santos was scrubbing his hands along Funny Cide's neck, encouraging the horse now to release his pent-up run. He raised his whip and struck. But Empire Maker, who had been biding his time, simply cruised past him. Bailey hardly had to move his hands at all. Coming off the turn, the horses were nearly blown backward by the crowd's roar, or so it seemed to Bailey, now on the lead.

It was becoming apparent as the horses emerged, gray in the rainy gloom, that the popular hero was losing. Empire Maker had put one length of mud and daylight between himself and Funny Cide and was going comfortably. Funny Cide slogged on, but things were getting worse. Another runner, Ten Most Wanted, had been tracking Funny Cide and Empire Maker around the turn. When his rider, Pat Day, saw Empire Maker ruin Funny

Cide's Triple Crown and gun for the finish line, Day sent his horse after him. Ten Most Wanted raced past Funny Cide, but he couldn't chase Empire Maker down. When they finally reached the wire, Empire Maker had won, beating Ten Most Wanted by three-quarters of a length. Funny Cide, spent, finished more than four lengths behind them in third.

"This vindicates that he's the best horse," Frankel said of Empire Maker after the race. But the crowd, their romantic dream thwarted by cold facts, clearly felt robbed. As the elegant, graceful Belmont winner, once the favorite for the Kentucky Derby, was brought into the winner's circle, boos and insults rained down on him from the sodden and demoralized everymen who had filled the grandstand hoping to see Funny Cide win.

John Chandler, meanwhile, dashed toward the winner's circle, where he gave an uncharacteristically jubilant high-five to Juddmonte's Kentucky farm manager, Garrett O'Rourke. Empire Maker, the horse who had been supposed to win all along, the one whose long, deep pedigree and training had pointed him toward this kind of moment all his life, finally had done it. As far as his supporters were concerned, it was a final triumph of class and pedigree. It was, in short, the way things were supposed to turn out when you bred the best to the best for generations. The rules of the Thoroughbred universe had righted themselves.

Barclay Tagg watched from his box seat as Funny Cide's Triple Crown bid came unraveled in the Belmont mud. Scanning the field's progress around the vast Belmont oval, he held his binoculars as steady as if he were watching a claiming race at some minor-league track on a weekday. When the horses slopped across the finish line, Tagg watched for a little longer to see how Funny Cide pulled up, and then he lowered his binoculars and pushed back onto the crowded clubhouse aisle. The walkway was clogged with disappointed spectators trying to go home and angrily debating the Belmont results. Tagg's green trilby floated along through the crowd like a drowned man's hat carried along in a roiling river. He was tired.

"I feel bad for all the people who came out," he said when he reached the racetrack to pick up Funny Cide. "We were beaten by a good horse. I don't know what else to say. I am being honest. It's horse racing."

Upstairs, on the fourth floor of Belmont's clubhouse, the Sackatoga crowd was still partying.

"How can you be sad?" Jackson Knowlton said. "What a run. What a run. We never thought we'd be here. We weren't supposed to be here. He still won two-thirds of the Triple Crown, and third in the Belmont Stakes is not too shabby for a New York-bred."

Four floors below Sackatoga's last hurrah, there was one more race to run. The light was fading fast, and the rain was still falling. Eleven horses, bedraggled, wet, and steaming in the chilly evening air, walked cheerlessly around the muddy paddock path. Their owners huddled under umbrellas, their breath visible in the raw weather.

Bobby Frankel, out of the rain and celebrating his Belmont Stakes win, said something that those owners would have agreed with, if they could have heard him.

"You like to be right once in a while," he said of Empire Maker. "We're wrong so much in this business."

8 Family Values

EMPIRE MAKER RAN only once more before retiring to stud. Two months after the Belmont Stakes, when the Saratoga race meet opened, Frankel put him in the Jim Dandy Stakes. He was the heavy favorite but he lost by a neck to Strong Hope, a horse that had been a $1.7 million Saratoga auction yearling two years earlier. Various small physical complaints, including a recurrence of the foot bruise, derailed Juddmonte's plans to run Empire Maker again, and ultimately, the colt's connections determined that his potential value as a stallion was becoming their top priority. Empire Maker was whisked away to Khalid Abdullah's luxurious farm in Lexington, Kentucky, to begin the next phase of his career.

Empire Maker, who hailed from some of the world's richest, most productive bloodlines, merely added another decorative flourish to his family's already elaborate coat of arms when he won his races. His achievements were not exactly superfluous, but they were expected. Empire Maker's dam, Toussaud, was a daughter of El Gran Senor, a four-time champion. Toussaud had won at the highest levels herself, then retired to become one of the greatest broodmares of all time. Before Empire Maker was born in 2000, Toussaud already was the mother of four stakes winners; three of those had won Grade 1 stakes. She was named the industry's Broodmare of the Year in 2002, and, thanks to Empire Maker, again in 2003.

Empire Maker's sire was Unbridled, who pulled off a coveted double by winning the Kentucky Derby and the Breeders' Cup Classic in 1990. He earned a staggering amount, almost $4.5 million, during his illustrious racing career. Like Toussaud, he followed up with even more success in the breeding shed. He got a Kentucky Derby winner from his very first crop of foals when Grindstone won in 1996, and the list of champions and Grade 1 winners rippled outward from there.

It would have been disheartening, given all this genetic gunpowder, if Empire Maker hadn't turned into a high-caliber racehorse. Indeed, it was a little disappointing that he hadn't done better, hadn't won the Derby and even the Triple Crown as his owner and trainer had hoped. People undoubtedly would speculate for years over what would have happened if Empire Maker's foot hadn't had a bruise, if he hadn't missed that little bit of training time. It was extraordinary that so small a thing could trip up all those generations of breeding and talent, but that was racing. People would count Empire Maker unlucky in that regard, and those who could afford his $100,000 stud fee would be delighted to breed to this latest scion of Thoroughbred aristocracy.

Funny Cide's closest relatives, by contrast, were young and unproven. Like a teenage pop idol, Funny Cide had made his family nouveau riche in a hurry. His Triple Crown bid had imploded, but the gelding still scattered some stardust around as he rose from a $22,000 ridgling to Derby and Preakness winner. As a gelding, Funny Cide would not be able to do for his family what Empire Maker presumably would for his: continue the bloodline and reinforce its reputation as a legitimate source of big winners. What Funny Cide could do, immediately, was add value to some of his relatives.

Nearly every year, horses that were anonymous on the Friday before the Kentucky Derby suddenly became valuable when their son or half-brother crossed the finish line in front, as if King Midas had strolled through a couple of random barns and stopped occasionally to pat a nose.

· · ·

The 2002 Derby, won by War Emblem, was one such case. War Emblem's sire was Our Emblem, who came from a distinguished racing family. He stood at Claiborne Farm in Kentucky for four years, starting off with a $10,000 fee that seemed especially modest considering that his sire was the great Mr. Prospector, his dam was the undefeated champion Personal Ensign, and his siblings included three Grade 1 winners.

It was a stellar pedigree, and hopes were high for Our Emblem. His first yearlings, sold when everyone could still dream about the stud potential of his fabulous bloodlines, averaged more than $88,000 at auction. But when those yearlings started racing the following year, it quickly emerged that not many of them could run. Our Emblem got only three winners from his first crop of racehorses, and none of them developed into the crucial stakes winner that the commercial market values so highly. Buyers ran away in droves, and the stallion's average yearling price plummeted to just over $27,000. Claiborne, not surprisingly, decided it might be time to get out, and in November 2001 the farm found a willing buyer.

Maryland breeders Allen and Audrey Murray had heard the horse was on the market, and they were intrigued. They drove to Kentucky to look the stallion, liked him, and bought him for $200,000, figuring the horse's pedigree just had to be worth that much. He was still a young stallion with plenty of time ahead, and surely at some point those valuable genes would rise to the surface. The Murrays sent their new acquisition home to Murmur Farm in Darlington, syndicated him for $7,500 a share, and started advertising him with a $4,000 stud fee.

Within six months, two horses from Our Emblem's second crop of runners suddenly emerged as stakes winners. Named War Emblem and Private Emblem, both were pointing for the Kentucky Derby. The Murrays could hardly believe their luck. They decided they would raise Our Emblem's stud fee for the next breeding season to $7,500.

Then War Emblem won the Derby. Five minutes after he crossed the finish line, the Murrays' phone rang in Darlington. It was a California bloodstock agent, wondering whether the Murrays might be interested in selling their stallion to a Japanese buyer. It was the first of about 25 such calls that came in from a wide array of area codes, including the magic numbers of 859: Lexington, Kentucky.

The Murrays decided not to sell right then, gambling that Our Emblem's value might go up even farther if War Emblem won the Preakness. He did. Now, buoyed by War Emblem's winnings in the Derby and Preakness, Our Emblem was sitting atop the nation's stallion rankings. And, as the Murrays had hoped, the offers were getting bigger.

The Murrays didn't press their luck. In late May, they sold Our Emblem back to Kentucky for $10.1 million. The new owners were Kentucky's Taylor Made Farm and WinStar Farm, who agreed to stand the horse under joint ownership.

A week after the deal was struck, War Emblem stumbled coming out of the starting gate in the Belmont Stakes and lost the race. But his new buyers were philosophical about that. The thinking was that War Emblem was good enough to win the Derby and the Preakness, and a little bad luck in the Belmont did not reflect badly on his sire's chromosomes. Our Emblem's new stud fee for the 2003 breeding season was $35,000. War Emblem, incidentally, also was sold in 2002, reportedly bringing $17 million from a Japanese stud farm.

The Triple Crown races are not the only ones that can confer instant wealth on a horse's relatives. Any good horse anywhere reflects well on its family, raising values and presenting an unexpected opportunity to sellers who strike while the runner is hot. Take the case of Our Dani, a mare so nondescript that her owner, Dolphus Morrison, donated her to the Agricultural Sciences Department at tiny University of Louisiana at Monroe. Months later, when one of her fillies won a Grade 1 race at Saratoga, Our Dani was acting as a piece of teaching equipment. The Monroe students had bred the mare to the school's $500 Thoroughbred stallion as part of their course on equine reproduction, raising a foal, and preparing a young horse for sale. They got a bigger lesson than they bargained for. A Kentucky sales agency finally tracked the mare down to the university, told the astonished school what they had, and offered to sell Our Dani at auction for them. Sold at Keeneland, the donated mare brought $680,000 and provided the ultimate field trip.

In November 2002, Italian partners Marco Bozzi and Giuseppe Riccioni bought a mare at Keeneland for the paltry sum of $14,000. Almost exactly a year later, her 3-year-old colt Cajun Beat won the Breeders' Cup Sprint at odds of 22-1. The longshot paid $47.60 to his few backers in the Sprint, but the people who owned his dam got the real payoff. Bozzi and Riccioni put their mare in the next available auction, Cajun Beat won another race, and the Italians got $850,000 for his dam. It was the equine equivalent of a familiar dream: buy a $5 painting at a yard sale, and it turns out to be an original Van Gogh.

There are thousands of stories like this in Thoroughbred history, dating back to the day William Wildman, having bought Eclipse's sire for 20 guineas, sold him on for 1,000 guineas. The stories throw fuel on the fire of Thoroughbred buyers' hopes, and their common element is the home run horse.

In 2003, owner Kennard Warfield Jr.'s phone in Maryland started ringing soon after the Derby. Eight months earlier, Warfield had paid $30,000 for a filly he liked at a Maryland yearling auction. Then, the horse had been known only as a Personal Flag-Belle's Good Cide filly, but now she was the Kentucky Derby winner's half-sister. When Warfield bought his filly, Funny Cide was 2 and showing some talent on the profitable New York racing circuit, so Warfield felt even then that he had gotten his filly for a good price. Named Rockcide, she had turned 2, and Warfield thought she looked promising. Now everybody wanted her.

But Warfield, a racing man more than a seller, was inclined to keep his filly.

"She's training well," the 63-year-old Warfield said. "I bought her mostly for breeding purposes, but I hope she does well at racing, too. I just liked the bloodline."

Warfield was about the only one who could profit immediately from his connection to Funny Cide's female line, which seemed unusually determined to snuff itself out. Normally, the horse whose value appreciated most from its connection to a Derby winner was the Derby winner's mother. Belle's Good Cide could have used that push, too, because before Funny Cide came along she hadn't seemed like much of a mare.

When Funny Cide was born in 2000, Belle's Good Cide was owned by a new operation in Kentucky called WinStar Farm. The farm's owners, a telecommunications executive and a former trainer, essentially inherited the mare (and Funny Cide, in utero) when they bought the property. WinStar sent her to New York to have her foal for business reasons. The Kentucky Thoroughbred market is the most competitive in the world, and foals out of average mares such as Belle's Good Cide might not attract much attention from international buyers focused on winning the world's greatest horse races. New York's breeding program, however, offered a potentially profitable option. The state's restricted races for New York-breds carried fat purses; a foal out of Belle's Good Cide would be worth a little more if he were born in the Empire State and thus made eligible for those races. But Funny Cide wasn't all that remarkable when he was born, and so WinStar decided to sell the mare, who appeared to have little going for her. A Maryland breeder, Joan Boniface—who was, incidentally, Kennard Warfield's sister—bought her for just $3,500.

When Boniface sold Rockcide, her first foal out of Belle's Good Cide, for $30,000, that sale immediately made Belle's Good Cide a profitable mare for her new owner. Boniface had bred Belle's Good Cide back to Mojave Moon, a young stallion that stood at her farm, and in the early spring of 2003, Belle's Good Cide had that foal, a colt. Then disaster struck.

"She just took sick," Boniface said sadly. Boniface and her husband, Bill, rushed Belle's Good Cide to an equine hospital in nearby Pennsylvania, but to no avail. "She had a twisted gut. She survived the surgery, but she didn't do well, and we asked that they put her to sleep because she was in pain."

Two months later, her son won the Kentucky Derby.

Belle's Good Cide was just 10 when she died. Of her four foals, only two—the filly Rockcide and the Mojave Moon colt now named Homicide—have much chance to prove whether Belle's Good Cide was a fluke or a genuine gold mine when she produced Funny Cide.

With Belle's Good Cide dead and her only daughter in the hands of an owner who didn't want to sell, it would be natural for bloodstock agents to ferret out any sisters Belle's Good Cide might have had, in hopes of salvaging some value from the Derby winner's female family. But even that option quickly ran dry. Belle's Good Cide had 13 siblings, but only five were fillies, and four of those females either already had turned out to be dismal producers or were dead. The one that was left was only 2 and therefore a potential bright spot, but the poor production record of her other female siblings made her look like a longshot to produce another Derby winner.

Ironically, the people who got the most residual value from Funny Cide's Triple Crown performances were the ones who had dumped his dam for $3,500. WinStar Farm's owners, Ken Troutt and Bill Casner, had been as surprised as anyone when Funny Cide won the Derby and Preakness. Now they were reaping two important benefits. First, because WinStar Farm owned the mare when Funny Cide was born, they would go down in history as Kentucky Derby-winning breeders—an honor countless Kentucky horsemen would strive a lifetime and give almost anything to achieve. Second, Funny Cide's performance on the racetrack gave an immensely valuable boost to his young sire, Distorted Humor, who was just starting his career and stood at WinStar. It was an astoundingly lucky break for Troutt and Casner, who had had nothing at all to do with the mating that produced Funny Cide.

Troutt and Casner were brought together in the first place because of a lottery for a racehorse. Three decades before Funny Cide became a racing star, both men were small-time players at the old Ak-Sar-Ben Racetrack in Omaha, Nebraska. Troutt was an Omaha waterproofer and contractor who owned a small breeding farm and a few racehorses, and Casner was the trainer of a modest string of runners. They met one afternoon in the Ak-Sar-Ben racing secretary's office when it turned out they had both put in a claim for the same horse. Horses entered in claiming races are automatically up for sale, and when two or more people stake a claim on a horse, the racing secretary settles the deal by putting numbered pills, one for each potential owner, in a bottle, shaking it, and drawing the winner's number out.

Casner won the two-way shake, and he still remembers the

name of the horse: Great Bear Lake. Great Bear Lake turned out to be a nice sort of horse for the 25-year-old claiming trainer, a bread-and-butter runner who paid his way. More importantly, though Casner could not have known the significance at the time, Great Bear Lake gave Troutt and Casner something to talk about when they ran into each other in the Ak-Sar-Ben grandstand. Troutt eventually asked Casner if he would train a few horses for him, and Casner agreed. The new team "had a lot of fun and won some races," as Casner put it.

But Casner, who had worked at various racetrack jobs since his teenage years, began to think about leaving the hard racetrack life. His wife, Susan—whom he had met at the betting window where she was a teller—was pregnant with the first of two daughters, and Casner wanted more stability.

"I didn't want to bring those girls up on the racetrack," he said. "It's difficult to have any semblance of a family life on the race-track, especially at the level I was. I walked away from racing and went to Texas."

But he didn't walk away from his friendship with Troutt. And when Troutt, burdened by the expenses of his small breeding oper-ation back in Nebraska, decided to get out, too, he also moved to the Dallas-Fort Worth area, where Casner was a dealer for Snap-On tools.

"Kenny was an incredibly dynamic individual," Casner explained. "He thought large, and he taught me to think big. He had such energy and vision, all these tools. I felt like he was my opportunity to be successful in business. If nothing else, at the end of the day I knew he would give his all, and whether we won or lost he was going to try."

The two entrepreneurs started an oil business together, but it went bust in the 1980's.

"We were about two years old when the bottom fell out of the oil market," Casner said. "Our numbers were based on $18 a barrel. Oil had been at $27 or $28 and dropped to about $9, so we had to try something else."

That "something else" occurred to Troutt one night, and he called to pitch it to Casner. Deregulation in the telecommunica-tions business had created opportunities in long-distance phone service, and Troutt suggested forming a phone company. The result was Excel Communications, which grew from a one-room office into a company with annual revenues of about $1.3 billion. Excel went public in 1996 with about 10 percent of its stock, and it has since gone through a series of mergers that have made it part of Bell Canada. The stock that Troutt and Casner kept had made the former waterproofer and his claiming trainer worth untold millions, and that presented a nice way to get back in the Thoroughbred game at a new level.

In his time in Texas, Casner also had become friends with a band of racing brothers well known in Kentucky. Jack, J. R., and Art Preston owned a historic Bluegrass property they called Prestonwood Farm, where they stood Kris S., Distorted Humor, and a number of other stallions. Casner had raced a few horses in partnership with the brothers, and eventually he got Troutt involved, too. When the Prestons decided to sell their farm, it seemed only natural for Troutt and Casner to buy it.

Prestonwood Farm was a long, long way from Nebraska's windy plains and small-time stables. When Troutt and Casner bought Prestonwood in January of 2000, they got a turnkey operation on some of the region's most fertile land. They also got Distorted Humor and a package of broodmares that included Belle's Good Cide, already pregnant with Funny Cide.

"The horses that were part of the package we got from them gave us a big step up," Troutt acknowledged.

This time, they had a business plan on a grand scale—and the means to make it happen. They changed Prestonwood's name to WinStar, which had a lucky sound and referred to an incident in the 1800's when a meteorite fell on the farm. They expanded the farm to 1,450 acres, built new facilities, and bought a corps of expensive mares, each worth at least $500,000, to give their stallions the best possible chance at siring winners. From the beginning, Troutt and Casner focused on stallions and the commercial breeding market.

"Our main thing is to try to build stallions," Troutt said. "That's where the money is, and everything else supports that."

Troutt and Casner maintain two groups of mares, one consisting of about 50 mares whose foals are sold and another of about 30 whose foals race for Troutt and Casner's WinStar stable. Mares from the two bands don't cross over, so buyers can remain confident the farm isn't just selling its culls.

WinStar also applies some Excel-style business principles to the Thoroughbred venture. Troutt and Casner keep a substantial percentage of WinStar's syndicated stallions, just as they did when they took Excel public, so WinStar gets ample rewards from the stallions' successes. And, just as Excel sold its long-distance service through Mary Kay-style, person-to-person marketing, WinStar has spread its mares around the country to maximize product distribution. The plan, devised by farm president Doug Cauthen, is simple and effective: Put mares in foal to WinStar stallions, then send them to states like New York with strong breeding programs, and let the foals sell and race there. That advertises WinStar's stallions in regional markets to more buyers and also lets WinStar reap benefits through state breeders' awards.

One of the mares the farm sent to New York was Belle's Good Cide, whose 1999 mating had been planned by former Prestonwood farm manager Rich Decker and pedigree adviser John Prather.

Belle's Good Cide, a daughter of the stallion Slewacide, was a winner herself, but not an impressive one. Her real value, Decker thought, was in her pedigree.

"I liked her half-sister, Belle of Cozzene," Decker said. "And John Prather and I had talked about Slewacide as a good broodmare sire; we liked him because he was out of a Buckpasser mare."

Decker also liked Distorted Humor, though the young stallion's race record had caused many breeders to label him a pure sprinter unlikely to get horses of the Derby-winning kind. But Decker keenly remembered one of Distorted Humor's races, the Fayette Stakes, in which the colt was narrowly beaten going 1 ⅛ miles.

"I remember after the Fayette, I said to Art Preston, 'This is a dirty shame. Distorted Humor ran his eyeballs out, and he was 3 when the winner was 5, but no one's going to remember how good and close this race was,'" Decker said.

Decker and Prather agreed that Distorted Humor and Belle's Good Cide were a good match to get a versatile foal that combined some speed with some stamina. But by the time the mating was accomplished, both horses were in new hands, and Belle's Good

Cide was soon on her way to New York, a cog in WinStar's business plan. Troutt and Casner could have sold Distorted Humor, too, but the horse was young and, with his first runners due to hit the track in 2002, they opted to gamble on keeping him. One of those first runners was Funny Cide, who won $136,185 as a 2-year-old.

By the end of 2002, Distorted Humor was in close competition with another freshman sire, Elusive Quality, as the year's best debut stallions, as measured by the purse winnings of their young runners. In the end, a peculiar and unforeseeable circumstance 4,000 miles away from Kentucky tilted the balance in Distorted Humor's favor. One of Elusive Quality's best runners, Elusive City, was disqualified from two of his victories in England when racing officials discovered he had tested positive for a trace of omeprazole, better known in human medicine as the active ingredient in the antacid Prilosec. In horses, it is a component of GastroGard, a paste veterinarians commonly give racehorses to prevent stomach ulcers. The English Jockey Club agreed that Elusive City's drug positive undoubtedly came from GastroGard use while he was in training, but a positive drug test is a positive drug test. Elusive City was disqualified.

When Elusive City lost those two victories, he also lost $74,005 in winnings—and so, by extension, did his sire. With Elusive City's help, Elusive Quality had eked out a $14,898 lead over Distorted Humor on one of the Thoroughbred breeding industry's most important lists: the rankings of first-year sires, by progeny earnings. But when the English Jockey Club made Elusive City's DQ official at the end of the year, Elusive Quality plummeted to third on the freshman sires' list. Distorted Humor was now the top young stallion in the nation by a comfortable margin, with total earnings of $1,301,950.

Funny Cide had been an asset to Distorted Humor as a 2-year-old, but no one at WinStar imagined that the following season the New York-bred gelding would bring in more than $1.9 million, catapulting Distorted Humor into the top 15 of an even more competitive list: the general sires' list, which compared all North American sires of all ages. Distorted Humor was 14th on that list and keeping some elite company. Just above him in 12th was Storm Cat; Derby winner and highly successful sire Unbridled was posthumously listed 10th;

and the fashionable Kingmambo, whose sale yearlings so often seemed to bring numbers in the million-dollar range, was actually below Distorted Humor in 23rd place.

Take away Funny Cide's earnings, and Distorted Humor sank like a stone to 69th place, between West By West, who had since been sold to Turkey, and Honor Grades, a stallion that had died in 2002.

"We were definitely surprised," Troutt said of Funny Cide's emergence as a Derby horse. But, he added, it reflected well on their decision to keep Distorted Humor. Most important of all, it has increased the stallion's value. For a man with Troutt's entrepreneurial zeal, that could be the most exciting thing about breeding a Derby winner.

"The plan has worked well," he said. "It executed perfectly for us. That's the thing that's special to me. I'm a big believer in having a well-thought-out plan and supporting it with a lot of statistics so that you're not reinventing the wheel. The value this brought our stud, all the stuff we've been talking to our staff about, it's all starting to come true."

A lot has come true for Troutt and Casner in the 30 years since they met at Ak-Sar-Ben. Looking back on it, Casner recalled again the night that Troutt phoned to pitch his telecommunications idea to his friend.

"Listening to him, I knew it was an extreme longshot, but if we could make it work, it could be huge," Casner said. "And that was what both of us were looking for: that opportunity to hit the home run."

They hit two home runs. One made them rich, and the other put their names in racing lore forever. Both were a matter of business. WinStar's quick success was due partly to Troutt and Casner's Thoroughbred inheritance from the Prestons and partly to their own aggressive business strategy. Funny Cide was a product of both, but he was as unexpected and brilliant as the meteorite the farm was named for. His dust was gold for his sire and the new farm owners listed as his breeders.

"You always dream of that Kentucky Derby horse," Troutt said. "But never in my wildest dreams would I have thought we'd do it in our third year and with the first crop we bred. If a crystal ball had showed it to me, I would never have believed it."

When Funny Cide won the Derby, WinStar yearling manager Dale Benson couldn't help himself. He went back to his files of photographs, sifting through two years of the routine pictures WinStar always takes of its sale yearlings. He looked for the one they took of Funny Cide between May and August of 2001, when he had made a brief stop in Kentucky to be prepared for auction. The colt had had a little problem with skin fungus, Benson remembered, but that had cleared up all right. He had a tough streak, but he wasn't dangerous. There wasn't much else to recall about the yearling known then simply as Belle's Good Cide '00. Benson kept flipping through the files, and then he found it. He looked at the nondescript chestnut yearling in the photograph and came to the same conclusion he and everyone else had come to back in the summer of 2001.

"Not one of us would have picked him out and said, 'This is the one that will win the Derby,'" Benson said. "The first thing I thought after the Derby was, 'What did I miss?' I thought maybe I just don't know how to pick out a horse. But we all looked at him back then, and none of us remembered him as a great one. I looked at that yearling picture again, and he still just looked like a rangy yearling to me."

Nowhere is the importance of a good family more obvious than at a yearling sale, where buyers have little to go on but the brilliance of the untried prospect's relatives. On the catalog page, the color of money is black: specifically, the bold-face type The Jockey Club uses universally to designate a superior, stakes-winning horse in the pedigree. A buyer's eye automatically stops on horses' names in that heavy black type. The more of them he sees on a single pedigree page, the greater his confidence in the family's genetic ability to produce a winner for him—and the more he will be prepared to pay for access to that family's blood. Two otherwise identical yearlings will bring vastly different amounts if one has a page dripping with black type and the other has only a bare-looking tree of names in plain type. It stands to reason that better-bred horses will be more athletic and capable on the racetrack, but buyers are also mindful of Thoroughbred breeding's complex exceptions: The purplest pedigrees can sometimes hide a fatal flaw, and sometimes it's the fluke from a humble family that turns out to be the big runner.

Saratoga Springs was still celebrating one of those apparent flukes when Satish Sanan came back to the Fasig-Tipton yearling sale in August, trying again to buy a Derby horse.

Funny Cide, a gelding bereft of stud value, had nonetheless allowed his connections to hit a home run. Knowlton and his high-school buddies had funneled the Derby winner's popularity into Funny Cide Ventures, a marketing company that put bottles of Funny Cide beer on bars all over town, Funny Cide T-shirts on horseplayers' and tourists' backs, and "New York Loves Funny Cide" buttons on everything from seersucker lapels to Funny Cide baseball caps. The FunnyCide.com website—where, among other things, Funny Cide bobblehead toys were on offer for $24.95—was still getting thousands of hits a week. The upstate New York rock band Blue Hand Luke became "the official band for Funny Cide" and released a song called "Funny Cide" on a CD that had a picture of the Derby finish on it.

"Take advantage of this time," Knowlton told trainer Barclay Tagg. "This is a once-in-a-lifetime chance. It can open whole new worlds to you, but it won't last forever."

Nobody knew that better than Tagg. After his Belmont defeat, Funny Cide had shipped from New York to the Jersey shore for one of the summer's major races, the $1.1 million Haskell Invitational at Monmouth Park on August 3. His fans had hoped for redemption, but Funny Cide struggled home in third. Adding injury to insult, during the race he got hit in the face with a clod of dirt; by the time he got back home to Tagg's barn in Saratoga, his right eye was swollen shut and he had a fever, too.

"In the Haskell, we learned that no amount of branding of beer, wine, T-shirts, posters, pins, and whatever else you can think of can make an overachieving 3-year-old develop further than he is capable of," was the tart analysis from the *Daily Racing Form*'s national handicapper, Mike Watchmaker.

But across Union Avenue from Barclay Tagg's barn, at Fasig-Tipton's sale pavilion, there were plenty of people who would give a lot of money to be in the position Knowlton and his pals were in.

Whatever else Funny Cide did or didn't do in the rest of his life, he would always be a Derby winner.

Arriving at the auction on a Wednesday night, Satish Sanan was in a familiar position. He and his team had winnowed the 217-horse catalog down to just two colts that looked like they could fit Sanan's bill, which was simple if ambitious.

"This sale, we are concentrating on buying a couple of Derby horses," Sanan said. "We are looking for pedigree, ability to go the distance, and athleticism."

The first yearling on Sanan's short-list became obvious when he threw his bid in on Hip 105, a son of the hot young stallion Unbridled's Song and a moderate mare, Stephanie's Road. The colt's pedigree combined Unbridled's Song's proven speed with the stamina influence of Strawberry Road, the sire of Stephanie's Road. It probably didn't hurt that Strawberry Road was also Vindication's maternal grandsire, giving Sanan a personal reason for confidence in that family line.

But Hip 105 was Sanan's second choice of the two short-listed yearlings, and he bowed out of the bidding, letting someone else sign for the colt at $800,000.

The auction world's handicappers were betting that Sanan's top pick was the dark bay colt selling as Hip 107. That colt was out of Vindication's dam, Strawberry Reason, and he was by the expensive and successful stallion A.P. Indy, a son of Vindication's sire, Seattle Slew. That made Hip 107 a three-quarter brother to the 2003 juvenile champion and Derby should-have-been. He was an obvious candidate for Sanan's Padua Stables.

Virginia Kraft Payson, breeder of both Vindication and Hip 107, was ebullient about the younger sibling.

"We felt from the very beginning that this colt was a little bit ahead of Vindication at every stage," she said of Hip 107. Powerful, muscular, and nearly black but for the flashy white socks on his hind legs, the colt looked like a cannonball, and he walked like he meant serious business. His pedigree alone made him the center of attention, but he also backed up the printed page with his looks and aggressive stride.

A crowd had gathered around the walking ring to take a final look at Hip 107 before he went into the bidding arena. People pressed against the ring's wooden railings, leaning over to drink in the colt. By the ring's entrance stood two of Sheikh Mohammed's men, bloodstock agent John Ferguson and trainer Eoin Harty, occasionally shifting position to get a better view of Hip 107 through the crowd. Harty looked from the colt to his catalog page while Ferguson studied the horse intently. Spectators around them watched as the two men conferred. When Hip 107 disappeared into the pavilion, Ferguson and Harty stepped over to a closed-circuit TV near the walking ring. Hands in pockets, Ferguson waited for the right time to bid.

Inside the pavilion, Fasig-Tipton announcer Terence Collier began his spiel with what amounted to a serenade to Satish Sanan, describing the owner's great success with Vindication: a Breeders' Cup victory, a championship title—priceless accomplishments that raised Vindication's value far beyond his nearly $700,000 in earnings.

"Please," Collier said in conclusion, gesturing opulently to Hip 107. "Help yourself."

Sanan smiled faintly, acknowledging the complimentary nature of Collier's opening remarks. But he did not acknowledge the invitation to bid.

Auctioneer Walt Robertson boldly asked for $3 million to start things off, a sign of something the bidders already suspected: that Payson had set a lofty reserve on this colt. Bidding opened at a more realistic $500,000 but quickly shot past $1 million, at which point Ferguson turned away from the TV by the walking ring and gave a nod to his bid-spotter. To general amazement, Sanan hadn't made a move, and the bidding galloped along without him.

At $1.7 million, Ferguson, uncharacteristically, was beginning to look slightly uncomfortable. Collier, perhaps sensing consternation among the bidders, interjected to remind them, "This horse looks like a champion, and that's what you have to pay for them."

The bidding continued, but in smaller increments and without Ferguson, who had turned away from the walking ring, the TV, and his bid-spotter. The price on the board clicked up to $1.75 million, $1.8 million, $1.85 million, and finally to $1.9 million. But Ferguson's departure left no apparent live underbidder, giving these seemingly anonymous bids the quality of suggestions, rather than definitive offers. Faced with no competition, even the reserve stopped bidding at $1.9 million.

Robertson dropped the hammer. When the usual blue-blazered Fasig-Tipton official failed to appear with a receipt, it became clear that Vindication's impressive younger brother had in fact fallen short of his reserve price. It was a perplexing outcome for a yearling that seemed a less risky selection than Vindication had been. Two years earlier, when Sanan had paid $2.15 million for Vindication, Strawberry Reason had not had any runners of note. Now she had a proven champion. That champion's sire had since died, but her A. P. Indy colt on offer this time around was as closely related as possible to Vindication. He was not merely conformationally "correct" but also extraordinarily handsome with an Olympian's stride. On paper and on the surface, he looked like a sure thing. But he wasn't.

"Our team's consensus was that he was a nice horse, but he wasn't our top pick," Sanan said, by way of explaining his lack of interest. "And we knew the expectations of Mrs. Payson would be very high."

It was a diplomatic answer that glossed over a single factor that for some bidders had outweighed all of Hip 107's glowing attributes.

The colt, initially a top pick on almost every major buyer's list, had abruptly fallen from grace when several veterinarians found a white line with a slightly irregular outline, a denser white than the area around it, on their pre-sale X-rays. Its technical name was osteochondrosis dessicans, a disease in which cartilage in a young horse's joints fails to mature properly as part of normal bone development. In serious cases, the affected cartilage can actually split from the bone beneath it or even crumble, potentially making the area weak or unstable. Many cases of OCD can be surgically corrected, but the problem area's size and location can make a difference in prognosis—and therefore in a buyer's willingness to bid. In Hip 107's case, the problem did not seem to be severe. One veterinarian described it as "healing," suggesting that the problem might even be resolving itself, and another said it was "not significant" for soundness. Would the buyers agree?

By the time Hip 107 came up for auction, the big-money agents—but probably not the auction house, which would not necessarily review individual veterinary records—were aware of this flaw. One of them, John Ferguson, was fearless enough to place a bid on the colt, but even he was unwilling to offer more than a discount price in order to take on the OCD risk. Reading X-rays is to some extent a subjective exercise, and Payson, who had her own veterinary advice indicating that the horse was a finer skeletal specimen than some other vets were reporting, stood her ground and kept her reserve price at $2 million.

Clearly, Payson and the general market had not reached an agreement. But Patrick Biancone, a French-born trainer who had conditioned horses for Payson, stepped into the breach. As the auction rolled on, Biancone feverishly negotiated a private deal to buy the horse on behalf of a partnership. Payson would retain an interest in the colt she had so much faith in, Biancone would train him, and, if they were right and lucky, the colt would go on to great things.

"I used to have dreams about Vindication, and I never dream about horses," Payson said after striking the deal with Biancone. "I really thought he would be our Triple Crown horse in 2003. And we feel that this horse could be better than Vindication."

Standing outside among the gossips, opportunists, horse-traders, and glittering hangers-on who mingle behind the pavilion, a man who had already won his Kentucky Derby was bemused by such expensive intrigue. Jackson Knowlton, of Funny Cide fame, had been having a beer and swapping Triple Crown tales with local breeder Joe McMahon when Payson's $1.9 million colt went through the ring.

"When you can get a $75,000 New York-bred that wins the Derby and the Preakness, why would you ever pay more than $100,000 for a horse?" he said with a laugh.

The horse at the top of Sanan's two-horse short-list was Hip 136. This colt was by 1990 Derby winner Unbridled. The stallion was one of the most sought-after sires in the world, and his untimely death at age 14 two years earlier had put an even higher premium on his 2003 yearlings, who were the last horses he had sired.

Another horse named on the catalog page represented a cautionary tale for Sanan about giving in too soon at auction. Words of War, a classy racehorse who earned more than $680,000, was the mother of two nice runners. One of them, a Mr. Prospector colt later named E Dubai, had come up for sale at Keeneland in September 1999. Sanan had been in the bidding but threw in the towel north of $1 million; John Ferguson got the colt for Sheikh Mohammed for $1.35 million. E Dubai didn't win the Derby, but he got his share of glory and treasure, winning a pair of graded stakes races and making $800,800 for his owner on the racetrack. Sanan considered this a mistake on his part and categorized it with Fusaichi Pegasus as one of his most galling missed chances.

Not surprisingly, given the pedigree on offer, a number of market-movers liked the Unbridled colt, and the bidding shot rapidly upward.

Sanan tossed in an early bid just to catch his bid-spotter's attention and let him know, as Sanan put it, "we had a level of interest." His Padua Stables team had estimated that the Unbridled-Words of War colt would go for between $2 million and $3 million, and for the moment, having gotten his bid-spotter on the alert, Sanan was content to sit back and watch how things progressed. They progressed with great speed, the cast of players changing as agents and owners jumped in, were chased beyond their endurance, and dropped out, leaving the field to new or more stubborn bidders.

The price cruised past $2 million, and all the obvious players fell away. But the bids ticked upward in $100,000 increments as the battle settled down between two men in the pavilion, bidding with signs so discreet that only their spotters and auctioneer Robertson seemed to catch them. Whoever they were, the two rivals were in an unbreakable clench as the price rose: $2.4 million, $2.5 million, $2.6 million. At $2.7 million, one man balked.

When Robertson asked him for $2.8 million, one of the bidders revealed himself by shaking his head. It was B. Wayne Hughes, billionaire co-founder of the California company Public Storage. Robertson asked again for $2.8 million, and Hughes declined again.

"Would you like to reconsider?" Robertson asked. Hughes, his face reddening, shook his head for the final time.

John Ferguson, seated in a row between Hughes and Sanan, broke into a smile. As Robertson dropped the hammer, someone in the row in front of Ferguson leaned across to shake his hand, and a murmur went around the pavilion: "It's Ferguson."

They were wrong. The subtle winning bidder was Satish Sanan, who got all the way to the door before anyone noticed that he had the $2.7 million receipt for the most expensive horse in the sale.

Slipping out of the pavilion, Sanan ran into the Unbridled colt's consignor, Kentuckian Arthur Hancock III, who was on his way to thank Ferguson for the purchase.

"Well, I'll be darned," Hancock said, beaming, when Sanan's daughter, Nadia, set him straight. "Thank you very much! He's going to be a nice horse for you."

Hughes, waiting for his car outside, expressed no regrets.

"I went farther than I planned, but I knew that colt would be expensive," he said. "But, no, it's not painful. Remember: We've still got our money."

Sanan was lighter in the bank account, but, once again, he was leaving Saratoga with his pick of the yearlings. "We pulled up bidding on Fusaichi Pegasus, and we pulled up on E Dubai," he said. "You make mistakes, and I regret that. This sale, we came to buy a couple of Derby horses. Horses like that have to perform on the track, to prove it. We'll be patient and take our time with this one."

Was the $2.7 million Unbridled colt another, more fortunate Vindication? Only time, training, and the finish line would tell.

Genetically, at least, breeder Payson and trainer Biancone seemed to have the closest thing to Vindication that nature and selective breeding could provide. But which was right, the veterinarians' X-rays that warned buyers off, or Payson and Biancone's sense of a good horse?

"I am very much in love," Biancone said, melting into sentimentality over his new acquisition, just as Sanan had done two years earlier with Vindication. "I think this horse is more powerful than his brother, to be honest with you. I trained Strawberry Reason's sire, Strawberry Road, and this colt has a lot of him in him, a lot of that power. Now, the pressure's on me."

9 Delicate as Hell

OF ALL THE players gambling on a home run horse, the trainer is in perhaps the most uncomfortable position of all. He stands where an owner's optimism converges with a horse's actual talent, right at the intersection of hope and reality. His job, by definition, is to determine whether those avenues meet, or whether, as in many cases, the road of hope runs to a dead end.

Adding to the job's pressure is the fact that training a fit, rambunctious athlete is inherently risky. Whether because the trainer is an inexpert horseman, the horse is poorly made, the track is unsafe, or simply through the normal wear and tear of physical exertion, horses will develop injuries, and most of these will occur while the horse is in training. Some injuries are easily treatable, but some are not. Almost all require a substantial amount of time off, during which period the horse is not conforming to his owner's business plan. Not surprisingly, a trainer can quickly become a fall guy, and this is one of the reasons that many trainers—even successful ones—often seem congenitally pessimistic. As one trainer warily put it, immediately after one of his horses had not only won a race but also broken a track record, "A lot of things can happen, and only one of them is good."

Less than a half-hour after he won the Kentucky Derby with Funny Cide, Barclay Tagg was less jubilant than relieved, for reasons he tried to explain in the postrace press conference.

"Things go wrong with them so easy," he said of horses. "They're very, very frail, and we ask them to do a lot. We ask them to carry weight and run 40 miles an hour and train every day and live in a small stall full of dust and straw and hay, things like that. It's contrary to what nature really set them up for, and a lot of things go wrong with them.

"You just can't get too high on a horse, because anything can happen. I mean, the most *unexpected* things can happen. You'll think you have a big, fat, shiny, good-looking horse that's working beautifully and running beautifully, and you're setting him all up for something like this, and any day you walk in there at five o'clock in the morning and feel his legs, there could be something wrong with him that will just stop the whole thing. It's happened to me so many times in the last 30 years, you just can't let yourself get too high."

This, essentially, was the reason that 54-year-old Michael Dickinson, a somewhat hyperactive Englishman who also has been training racehorses for about 30 years, would not refer to the gray colt in his barn as a Derby horse, at least not yet.

"He's a nice horse," Dickinson said.

It was December of 2003, and the colt in question, a 2-year-old called Tapit, had recently caught a lot of attention by coasting home more than four lengths ahead of his nearest rival in Maryland's Laurel Futurity. It was only the second race of his career, and people who saw the result reflexively wrote his name on their list of Derby candidates. Dickinson, being a horse trainer, was more circumspect.

"Let's just say he's a nice horse who's got Derby potential," he said.

"At the moment, he has a 98 Beyer," he acknowledged, referring to Beyer Speed Figures, which were developed by handicapper and writer Andrew Beyer, and are used to standardize and compare different horses' performances. "That's a nice figure, but the top horse is a 105. And there will be lots more horses to come out yet."

Still, there were clearly things in Tapit's Laurel Futurity win that even a trainer could be optimistic about.

"Tapit ran that 98 in his second start in a common canter without the jockey even having to do anything with him," Dickinson said. "He was a bit rank and a bit green because it was only his second start, and he just cantered home. He just looked *class*."

Dickinson knew for certain after the Laurel Futurity that he had a potential home run horse in the barn, and now his main job would be to protect the colt while getting him ready for top races, including, if possible, the 2004 Derby. Dickinson immediately gave Tapit a break and announced that the colt would not run again until the spring of 2004, when he would be a 3-year-old and the Derby would be just three months away. He was trying to achieve a delicate balance with an asset that is as complex as a missile system and as perishable as a peach: a Thoroughbred racehorse on the Kentucky Derby trail.

"Class, speed, talent," Dickinson said. "They have to have all that. They've also got to be sound come Derby Day, and you've got to give them enough racing to get them experienced, and you've got to train them at 2. Half the problem with a Derby horse is getting them enough experience at 2, before they're really ready for it, and still having them sound on January 1 for the 3-year-old season. You have to race at 2 without breaking them down. It's difficult, and it could be that you fail either way. If you don't race, he's not going to win, and if you do race him, he's going to break down.

"Oh," he said, shaking his head, "they're delicate as hell."

Michael Dickinson is either a madman or a genius, or a little of both. That's what people in racing say. Stories about Dickinson's eccentricities abound, a favorite being the one in which he made his longtime girlfriend and business partner go buy a pair of stiletto heels and walk around a turf course before a big race, to see how firm the going was.

But there is method to Dickinson's madness, and his methods, however unorthodox, have made him especially adept at dealing with racing's most delicate instruments.

The stiletto story is true, and it reveals a few things about Dickinson's approach to training racehorses. It happened on October 25, 1996, the day before Dickinson was to saddle 8-1 shot

Da Hoss for the Breeders' Cup Mile at Woodbine Racecourse in Canada. It was astonishing in the first place that Da Hoss should ever have been in the $1 million race, which also included some of Europe and Great Britain's most talented runners. Da Hoss was a well-bred horse, but he had been plagued by significant problems almost from the moment he was born. He was not impressive as a yearling, partly because his right front foot turned out and partly because he was small—and, worse, an infection during his early months had eaten away part of a bone inside his hoof. Offered for sale at the 1993 Keeneland September yearling auction, he brought just $6,000 from a partnership calling itself Wall Street Racing Stables.

But it turned out that Da Hoss had talent, and in enough quantity to overcome his problems. When he was 2 and running at a blue-collar Arizona racetrack, he clocked a world-record time of 1:07.20 that caught the eye of Texans Jack, Art, and J. R. Preston. They promptly bought 85 percent of Da Hoss for $235,000 and sent him to Dickinson.

"We're pretty smart," as Art Preston explained it at the time. "We figured if he could break a world record he could run a little bit."

He could. Racing for the Prestons and Wall Street Racing, Da Hoss won stakes events from New York to California in 1995 and 1996. Dickinson firmly believed that Da Hoss's success was due mainly to the fact that he trained his horses over a forgiving wood-chip track instead of on a hard dirt track or a summer-baked grass course. If he'd had his daily exercise over the more usual racetrack surfaces, with his poor conformation and his damaged hoof bone, Da Hoss would surely have gone lame, Dickinson believed. Instead, trained gently and raced lightly, he won good races.

And that was how Dickinson ended up with Da Hoss at the 1996 Breeders' Cup at Woodbine, watching his partner, Joan Wakefield, step across the turf in red stilettos. The Breeders' Cup Mile is run over grass, which, compared to a dirt track, is more finicky and susceptible to change with the weather. That was a variable Dickinson could not ignore, especially in the Canadian autumn.

Dickinson is, he admits, obsessive about track surfaces. What he was looking for when he and Wakefield walked around the

Woodbine turf oval that morning was the best possible path for Da Hoss, the places where the course was consistently firm, not overly damp and sticky. Wakefield's stilettos were key to determining how soft the ground was at various points around the course: The deeper her heels sank, the damper the ground and the worse the going, from Dickinson's point of view. Together, he and Wakefield plotted out the best path, and when the race came, Dickinson told jockey Gary Stevens where to keep Da Hoss: close to the rail, where the going was optimal. Da Hoss won the Breeders' Cup Mile by a length and a half, and suddenly the stiletto story didn't sound *quite* as silly as it had a few hours before.

What Dickinson did two years later was nothing short of miraculous. After winning the 1996 Breeders' Cup Mile, the injury-prone Da Hoss missed the entire 1997 season with three successive injuries. Dickinson and his team nursed the world-class gelding back to health, and by early spring in 1998, he was back on track and training forwardly for a campaign his owners hoped would end with another tilt at the Breeders' Cup Mile in the fall. Dickinson, the Preston brothers, and the Wall Street Racing partners were looking forward to a promising season.

Exercise rider Jon Ferriday, another English expatriate, had only been working for Dickinson for two months when he got the assignment to ride Da Hoss.

"I remember Joan telling me he'd won $800,000, and I thought, 'Oh, shoot,'" he said. "It was pressure. And I can't handle pressure. If something went wrong while I was on him, it would be my fault. If a breeze was wrong, it would be my fault. At the end of every day when I got off him, it was, whew, take a deep breath, that's one more day over with."

And then in late April, just a couple of weeks before he was scheduled to make his first start since the 1996 Breeders' Cup, Da Hoss tore a tendon in his left front leg. Dickinson, Wakefield, Ferriday, and farm manager Manuel Piedra, who also groomed Da Hoss, were devastated. But the more he thought about it, the more Dickinson began to believe there was still a chance that the gelding could make it back to the races in time for the Breeders' Cup— though, as he himself acknowledged, "We only had a little bit of hope at the best of times."

Over the next six months, Dickinson and the stable crew at his Tapeta Farm training center devoted themselves to healing Da Hoss and bringing him back to the races. They started at a walk, with Ferriday touring Da Hoss around the farm's sweeping fields and wooded trails for an hour a day, as if the gelding were just a park hack. The program gradually extended to two long walks a day, then Dickinson added occasional jogging. Carefully, the team reassembled their frail house of cards. By late June, Da Hoss was ready for a brief gallop. Dickinson's hopes were buoyed when his veterinarian found no sign of the tendon problem on a post-exercise ultrasound.

The next few months would have been enough to bring on a nervous breakdown in even the most optimistic trainer. Da Hoss showed signs of muscle atrophy in a hind leg. His hocks, which had developed some arthritis due to old bone spurs, got stiff. In his faxes to the Prestons, Dickinson glumly informed them of the occasional setbacks, but he told them he still had his eye on the Breeders' Cup. It seemed completely insane, but no one wanted to tell Dickinson that. Piedra spent hours doing stretching exercises with the horse, massaging his muscles, and keeping him comfortable. Ferriday kept his game face on, too, galloping Da Hoss to Dickinson's orders.

By mid-September, Da Hoss had had seven of his 10 planned breezes, and he was showing his old competitive flame, trying to race against passing cars on the road alongside Dickinson's turf gallops. Dickinson had put the horse through most of his paces going uphill, an effort to get him fit without putting too much stressful, pounding fast work on Da Hoss's less than perfect legs.

Dickinson faxed the Prestons another update. "We're all holding our breath at the moment, and it will indeed be a miracle if he wins the Breeders' Cup again this year," he wrote. "But miracles do happen."

Three weeks before the Breeders' Cup, Da Hoss made his first start since 1996, winning a Virginia grass race by just under a length. It would be his only start before attempting to reclaim his Breeders' Cup title in the face of the world's most talented turf challengers.

When Da Hoss arrived at Churchill Downs for the 15th Breeders' Cup Championship Day, there were still plenty of people who thought Michael Dickinson was crazy. But even some of those must have heeded the trainer's reputation as a "mad genius," because Da Hoss went off at odds of just under 12-1.

The day before the race, Dickinson and Wakefield walked the course, just as they had done before the 1996 Breeders' Cup Mile, except that this time Wakefield had brought a pair of high-heeled boots for the purpose. They circled the course six times, meticulously plotting out Da Hoss's ideal path. Dickinson delivered his instructions to jockey John Velazquez, and then it was all out of the trainer's hands. When the 14-horse field sprang out of the starting gate on November 7, 1998, there was nothing Dickinson could do but watch as his fragile runner hurtled around the racecourse.

Dickinson's miracle almost came unraveled on the final turn of the one-mile race when Velazquez asked Da Hoss to make his move. It seemed too soon, the rally would fall short, the cards so carefully assembled over months were collapsing less than half a mile from the finish line. As the horses surged into the homestretch, Da Hoss grabbed the lead and kept on running, but the competition was gaining on him. All appeared lost when 15-1 shot Hawksley Hill battled to get his head in front of Da Hoss, but Da Hoss fought back, and the two runners shot past the wire almost together. Almost. The margin between them was the length of a horse's head, and the head that was in front belonged to Da Hoss.

Dickinson, who dissolved into tears when the race was over, hadn't put money on his horse.

"I'd already gambled so much on him," he said. "I had my whole life wrapped up in him."

That wasn't an exaggeration. Michael Dickinson's life is about keeping racehorses sound, and his 30-year quest to find better, safer ways to train them has contributed to his legend as a brilliant eccentric.

Dickinson is the son of two successful racehorse trainers in Yorkshire, England. He was raised in the saddle, galloping steeplechasers, breaking young horses, and foxhunting, a varied background that gave him a sort of liberal-arts education in horsemanship. Despite his too-tall stature, which caused one horseman to advise him to "stick to window cleaning," he became a successful steeplechase jockey as a young man, but he knew that career couldn't last forever. His head and heart both would eventually point him toward the more intellectual art of racehorse training.

His education in horses took a particularly inspiring turn when Dickinson was in his 20's and spent two summers at the Irish training center Ballydoyle, a Shangri-la for aspiring trainers. Ballydoyle was run by Vincent O'Brien, revered as a god among racehorse trainers and one of the men who would help build Coolmore into a global powerhouse. O'Brien is generally regarded in England and Ireland as one of the best trainers ever seen, and his record both with steeplechasers and on the flat is extraordinary. As a jumps trainer in the 1940's and early 1950's, he saddled three consecutive winners of England's famed Grand National, and remains the only trainer ever to do so—just one of his many achievements. When he switched to flat racing in the 1950's, he had even more success, much of it with Coolmore's enormously expensive Northern Dancer-line purchases. He won 43 English and Irish classic races, including six Epsom Derbies.

When Dickinson spent those two summers in the 1970's exercising horses for O'Brien at Ballydoyle, O'Brien was at the height of his powers; one of the horses in the morning exercise sets while Dickinson was there was Roberto, 1972's champion 3-year-old and Epsom Derby winner. And there were others, representing the best bloodlines and most talented racing prospects available anywhere in the world.

The quality impressed Dickinson, but he was even more taken by the great horseman's methods and facilities, which he knew were also critical to O'Brien's phenomenal success. It wasn't just that O'Brien got his horses to win; he got them to stay sound so they could keep winning. Comparing O'Brien with other trainers who had racing strings of several hundred horses, Dickinson said, "He is the best trainer in the world, for two reasons. One, he's the only one who never relied on numbers. He used to start with 25 yearlings every year, but he had 40 champions. And, two, he had very, very few injuries. In 28 years, they had only two break a leg. That's why he's the best.

"And he used to make money for his owners," Dickinson added. "Where he was really good is, the bad horses, he'd peak them, they'd win three races, and he'd sell them for a lot of money. That's not a bad phone call to make: 'Sorry, your horse is no good, but we'll win three races and sell him for three hundred grand.'"

O'Brien used traditional methods of training, such as giving horses long, slow gallops up hills instead of drilling them frequently at speed. But he was also an innovator, and he had the funds to explore his theories. In a part of the world where racing and training were exclusively done on delicate, all-natural grass courses and therefore at the mercy of the weather, O'Brien was one of the first trainers to experiment with all-weather training surfaces so that his horses would not have their conditioning plans delayed by frost or the notorious Irish rainfall. But the main feature at Ballydoyle was its peerless greensward of rolling grass gallops, which O'Brien believed was the superior facility for training horses. His experimentation and his rigorous interest in maintaining soundness in fragile racing Thoroughbreds struck a deep chord in Dickinson, and what he calls "my passion for grass gallops" started at Ballydoyle with Vincent O'Brien.

"If I'd seen Niagara Falls, the Great Wall of China, and the Pyramids on the same day, it wouldn't have had more effect on me than he did," Dickinson said. "It changed my life."

In 1978, Dickinson ruptured his liver in a steeplechase fall at England's Cartmel racecourse, and, on medical advice, he retired from the saddle. He took out a training license when he recovered from the injury, and he immediately became a phenomenon. From his base at the Poplar House training center he developed with his parents in Harewood, Yorkshire, Dickinson rapidly became one of steeplechasing's most successful trainers while still in his 30's. In 1983, just before his 34th birthday, Dickinson trained 12 winners on a single day at races around the country, a feat that landed him in *Guinness World Records*. It had happened the day after Christmas. He, his family, and their assistants had fanned out to racecourses throughout Britain, saddling Dickinson's 21 total runners that day (aside from the 12 winners, Dickinson's string had five seconds, two thirds, a fourth, and a seventh-place finish). *The Sunday Times* called it "the greatest training performance since they first tamed *equus Caballus*" and ran a photograph of Dickinson, dapper in a double-breasted overcoat with a white flower in the buttonhole, standing at one of the racecourses and looking both amazed and relieved.

Indeed, relief still appears to be the primary reaction to success for this trainer that *The Sunday Times* accurately described as "impressively confident but supremely self-questioning." There is a reason for this, and it has to do with the fragility of horses and of the whole training endeavor.

"The worst part of the training job is injury," Dickinson said. "It's horrible, the barn's depressed. It's dreadful when a good horse gets hurt. And then you have to make the phone call. An owner's had confidence in you, says, 'You're a good trainer, will you train my horse?' And you have to call up and say he can't run Saturday. Or he's off for three months, or six months, or a year. Or, worst case, he's never going to run again. I want to be the best trainer, but I don't want to make that phone call any more than I have to with a modern Thoroughbred."

To that end, he has made some explorations that his colleagues have often found highly peculiar. He has consulted with Olympic-level human trainers, whose discussions about human physiology and conditioning convinced him to focus more on long, slow work-outs than on speed-sharpening breezes. He turned toward interval training, which he used to great effect with Da Hoss. He regularly haunted veterinary conferences, listening attentively to detailed technical discussions. He brought in a veterinary researcher to conduct heart scans and breathing analyses of his horses. He consulted with a researcher at the Massachusetts Institute of Technology to determine the ideal banking for racetrack turns to prevent unnecessary stress on horses' legs. He bought an instrument called a penetrometer, a sort of high-tech stiletto heel, to measure various characteristics of the racing surfaces his horses would run over. He consulted Olympic equestrian Bruce Davidson to help with some runners' quirks. Sometimes Dickinson would have riders gallop his horses clockwise around the racetrack, rather than the counter-clockwise galloping that is universally used in training at North American tracks.

But Dickinson's unorthodox methods haven't always been success-ful. After rewriting the record books in English steeplechasing (he also became the sport's only trainer to saddle the first five horses across the finish line in the prestigious Cheltenham Gold Cup), Dickinson got every horseman's dream job in 1986 when Coolmore

205

co-founder Robert Sangster hired him. Sangster set his new star up at Manton, a purpose-built training center in Wiltshire, England. Suddenly, while still in his 30's, Dickinson had a large supply of the best available runners and nearly unlimited financial resources to pursue whatever technology, research, or specialized staff, feed, and equipment he thought could help those horses fulfill their potential. But the assignment lasted only one season. Sangster fired Dickinson after he had just four winners in 1986, saying only, "We were not able to communicate."

The young trainer headed for America and opened a stable at the Fair Hill Training Center in Maryland, where the grass gallops and all-weather track put him about as close to English conditions as he could get in the States at the time.

There were compelling reasons to come to America. Because the race purses were richer, a successful trainer in the States could make far more money than in England, for one thing. And, unlike England, America had a year-round flat-racing season that offered big purses even in midwinter. On the other hand, Dickinson felt, American racing stables were more focused on the bottom line, a pressure that sometimes tempted owners and trainers to push horses that needed resting. And American trainers were generally based at the racetracks, a situation that also lessened their ability to control their horses' environment.

Despite the appalling lack of winners, Dickinson's time at Manton whetted his desire to train on his own terms, at a facility designed specifically with racehorse training and racehorse happiness in mind. He had decided that it was no good training in an environment he could not control, though most American trainers have to.

Horse racing in the United States is largely an urban game, and few trainers want (or can afford) to stable at a distance from the racing venue, then go to the hassle and expense of shipping their runners to the track for races. Such off-track training facilities are not always available anyway, and very few trainers have the funds to build their own operations within easy reach of the tracks where their horses will run. So most trainers apply for stalls at the racetrack, pass the daily stall rent on to their clients, and keep their clients' horses on the backstretches of Belmont Park, Santa Anita,

206

Churchill Downs, and other major racing venues across the nation. The downside is that training hours are limited (usually from dawn until about 10:00 A.M.) and often crowded, especially at big tracks, where 70 or more horses might exercise simultaneously at peak times. The crowd is not only inconvenient, but also potentially dangerous. Horses that manage to throw their riders, for example, will often bolt unpredictably around the track, occasionally killing other horses in collisions.

Trainers stabled at racetracks also feel pressured to run their horses, because the racing secretaries—racetrack employees who schedule races and dole out stalls to trainers—allot stall space to trainers who will regularly help fill the track's events. Those who don't might get fewer stalls, or none at all, the following season.

"I want to run when I want to, not when the racing secretary wants me to," Dickinson said.

Most importantly from Dickinson's point of view, trainers have virtually no control, beyond the right of suggestion or protest, over the management of things important to their horses' health and safety, most notably the track surface the horses run and train over.

It is this last point, in particular, that drove Michael Dickinson to finally do something his American colleagues thought was truly mad, financially speaking: build his own private training center. Many trainers would like to take that bold step, but the madness lies in the expense of it, a fact that Dickinson makes ominous references to without actually disclosing the amount he has spent developing Tapeta Farm in North East, Maryland. He maintains, though, that the farm's unique and most important asset, a spongy, forgiving all-weather training surface whose exact composition Dickinson has patented and guards jealously, could not be duplicated and installed at a major American racetrack for less than $3 million.

But Tapeta Farm's all-weather surface is not the only training ground available to Dickinson's horses. He also has three different grass gallops, each seeded with particular grasses to make it suitable for weather changes. The three lanes are each 16 feet wide and laid alongside each other in a long straightaway that borders a hedge. One lane looks almost like standard lawn grass and is for good weather with moderate rainfall; the middle lane's grass has coarse, broad blades that Dickinson believes tolerate drought better;

and the lane next to the hedge, which Dickinson calls his "Noah's Ark gallops," is designed to hold up to torrential rainfall.

Dickinson pays close attention to his gallops. He aerates the dirt beneath them with a machine that drills narrow holes 12 inches deep, every four inches. He walks over the gallops himself every day in a kind of goose-step, swinging his leg up high and then driving his heel into the ground to test its firmness. At the end of every morning's training hours, his exercise riders walk the course, too, replacing the divots their horses' hooves have scooped out.

Although he also has a traditional dirt oval track, Dickinson prefers to exercise his string over the grass gallops when they require any fast work.

"Grass is the best, but you need a lot of it," he explained. "So you need an all-weather, basically to save the grass. There's cinders, chips, sand, shavings—there have been a zillion of them. But nothing beats good grass, really."

Most racetracks and public training centers have a viewing area, often a covered stand, from which horsemen watch their string's workouts, but Dickinson, predictably, found that view too limited to be truly informative. In order to get a better assessment of his horses' turf workouts, he built a long driveway alongside his gallops, and he bought a bright red Ford Aspire to serve as his mobile viewing stand. When his horses breeze, Dickinson has Piedra or another assistant take the wheel while he folds himself into the tiny backseat, winds the window down, and peers out through his binoculars. As the horses take off at the head of the gallops, Dickinson—who also has a two-way radio that communicates to earpieces the riders wear—calls "Go!" and Piedra speeds away. The Ford Aspire rattles along the road, giving Dickinson a perfect perspective on the entire breeze, as if he were racing along right with the horses. When the riders pull up at the end of their works, Piedra stops the Aspire, and Dickinson leaps out to talk to them about how the horses went. Combining what he saw with what the riders felt, he tweaks the horses' exercise regimens as needed.

"Racing really is about controlling as many variables as you can," he said. "But there are a lot more downs than ups. If I have good surfaces to train on and keep the horses sound—I can't do everything, but I can do that. When things go wrong, trainers at the racetrack blame the track superintendent, but I have to blame myself. At least I don't have to be beholden to a man on a tractor, that he harrowed it wrong or whatever."

Dickinson believes his control over—and obsession with—creating the perfect track surface has given him an important advantage in keeping his delicate racehorses sound. But by his own estimation, if he is ahead of the game, it isn't by very much.

"Other trainers control a few variables, and I control perhaps a few plus two variables, that's all," he said. "It's hard to do better than anyone else. It mainly comes down to the horse. Anyone can train a good horse. There's nothing brilliant about training. It's all routine. Day in, day out, we have to be consistent and not make mistakes. But that's almost harder than being brilliant, because you can never let your guard down. Businessmen can lock up at five o'clock on Friday and open up again at nine o'clock Monday morning, and everything's the same. But we can't do that. We have to be out there the whole time looking, because it's changing all the time."

Humans have been training horses for at least 3,300 years, and, surprisingly, their basic day-to-day method has not changed all that much. The Kikkuli text, written in the Hittite language around 1350 B.C., is the first known document describing a daily plan for training horses, with an emphasis on getting them fit. The text's origin shows how strongly the ancients valued horsemanship skills. A Hittite king supposedly commissioned the guidebook-style text from renowned horsemen of Mittani, an ally kingdom in northeast Syria that was among the first to attach horses to chariots and use them in battle. The chief author, Kikkuli, obliged with a series of clay tablets with cuneiform lettering that, in translation, plainly shows what Dickinson described several thousand years later: that training is largely about maintaining a good routine.

The Kikkuli text is divided into more than 100 days, with prescribed routines for each. The instructions are simple, precise, and rigorous.

"In fall, he turns the horses into the pasture," Kikkuli wrote of the horseman. "He hitches them up and trots them three miles and he races them over seven fields. Returning, he races them over 10 fields. He unhitches them and takes off their harness and waters them. He takes them to the stable and gives them a handful of wheat and two handfuls of barley and one handful of hay all mixed together. And they eat it all. When they have finished their fodder, he ties them up. When evening comes, he leads them out of the stables and hitches them up and he trots them a mile and races them over seven fields. When he trots them back he unhitches them and takes off the harness and waters them. He takes them to the stable and gives them three handfuls of hay and two handfuls of barley and two handfuls of wheat all mixed together. When they are finished with their fodder he muzzles them. When midnight comes he leads them out of the stable and hitches them up."

And so on, day after day, starting at dawn. There are occasional variations such as standing the horses in streams, "dousing" them with water, feeding "coarse grain," sweating them under blankets, and, on the 13th day, rubbing them with "fine oil."

Like his modern counterparts, Kikkuli was fond of feeding moistened oats, similar to the boiled oats many trainers still feed. He also recommended nutritional supplements: "Malted barley is soaked in a vat. He gives them one measure of salt water and one measure of malt liquid and they drink all." And he was meticulous about bedding, prescribing that the horses be stabled on a floor "strewn with straw," still the common bedding in many training barns.

It is interesting to note that in 1892, Jimmy Rowe, one of the era's most successful and acclaimed trainers, echoed some of Kikkuli's routine when he penned advice for aspiring horsemen in *The Live Stock Record.*

"On the days he gets his work," Rowe wrote, referring to a horse's workout at speed, "if he goes out early, I give him a couple of quarts of oats before; if he goes out late, he gets his usual breakfast. As soon as he is through on the track, I proceed to have him cooled out. Boys get to work rubbing him and drying him out, his mouth is sponged, and I allow him from eight to 15 swallows of water. Then he is walked about for a while, with clothes on if the day is cool, and as soon as he is cool he is taken to his stall."

But Rowe also added this warning for would-be trainers who are inclined to be dogmatic, and in his words he echoed a favorite theme of Dickinson's: "To lay down arbitrary rules for training a racehorse would be as futile an undertaking as to lay down such rules for rearing a child. From first to last, from the moment you first slip the bridle over an unbroken yearling's head till you lead him from the track after he has run his last race, everything that you do depends on the horse. Racehorses are as varying in individuality, disposition, and constitution as are human beings, and the training that one horse will thrive on will kill another."

One suspects that neither Kikkuli nor Rowe would be surprised to find that the modern racehorse trainer's life still involves working at all hours (though midnight galloping is impractical at the modern racetrack), exercising his first set of horses every morning at dawn, and the endless rotation of galloping, washing, and feeding. The fundamental goal of Kikkuli's training—that is, superior fitness and a practiced turn of foot—remains the same for Thoroughbred racehorse trainers, although conditioners like Dickinson now have an astonishing array of modern tools at their disposal: the digital stopwatch, legal therapeutic medications, joint injections, X-rays and nuclear scans to identify bone injuries, titanium surgical screws to fix them, and many, many others.

Injury has been the trainer's eternal enemy. In 1683, Gervase Markham, whose general horsemanship book included sections specifically about training racehorses, identified a number of mysterious problems whose names alone sound terrifying: knobs on the liver, greedy Worm, dropsie, truncheons. Some of the injuries racehorses could sustain had nothing to do with exertion, Markham believed, as in the case of hind-limb paralysis, which he attributed to the running of a "shrow"—a mouse-sized creature "whose head is extraordinarily long, like a Swine's head, and her Feet shorter on one side than the other"—over the horse's legs in the night.

But many of the ailments Markham described still occur with some regularity today. Like his modern counterparts, he struggled to treat horses who bled from the nostrils after exercise (he recommended boiling half a peck of oats, then putting them in a bag and placing them across the horse's back for 30 hours). He complained about horses' lack of stamina (rub the legs with "old Urine a quart, of Salt-Peter three Ounces, boyl them well together"). And Markham also saw exercise-induced swelling of the forelegs, which probably equates to the bucked shins commonly seen today in 2-year-olds just starting their training. For those, Markham prescribed a liniment of butter and beer, or butter and vinegar, or "piss and Salt-Peter." Bucked shins, caused by work-related stress on immature bone, were considered so inevitable by Rowe's time that he wrote, "They get sore sooner or later anyhow, and it is just as well to get all the little troubles and hindrances one can over before the racing begins."

The more things change in training, it seems, the more they stay the same. Rigorous veterinary research has helped to properly diagnose and treat many ancient ills in the equine athlete, but a trainer's core aims and problems are much the same for Michael Dickinson as they were for Markham and undoubtedly for Kikkuli, too.

But the sport of racing horses has changed dramatically. Today's owners are more bottom-line conscious than their forebears ever were, partly because the gambling industry and the parimutuel system, which pays a percentage of wagers back into the purse fund, have given owners unprecedented opportunities to recoup at least some of their investment. A new owner today is encouraged to set goals. He sits down with his trainer and writes a business plan, and one frequently hears such investors say, "You've got to run it like a business." Owners and trainers know that a home run horse, once you have found one, can become a legitimate business by himself, especially if he has a long and successful career as a stallion. Not surprisingly, they are eager to do everything they can to ensure they will find, develop, and maximize that animal.

But the trainers who have to find and manage a horse's talent are acutely aware that horses, unlike many business assets, cannot just be managed by smart planning. Horses are, in fact, highly unpredictable once you put a bridle and saddle on them and ask them to run. They are increasingly mass-produced, but unlike widgets, horses still have their own brains, temperaments, habits, and physical and mental failings.

Dickinson's training methods try to take all of that into account. His philosophy actually has old roots that run deep in the history of horsemanship, but it has become anachronistic in the fast-paced industrial era. His decision to open his own training center gave him the freedom to do something that is very difficult for trainers constrained by the American racetrack's relentless schedule and limited options: to combine old English training traditions with state-of-the-art veterinary technology and sports medicine.

Dickinson's Tapeta Farm covers 200 acres alongside a narrow county road in rural Maryland, hard against the Chesapeake Bay. From a distance, it looks much like any other horse farm in the country, but on closer inspection its design reveals the eternal whirring of its creator's highly organized and restless intellect. From the white cinder-block walls of the barns to the smallest grains of its training track, Tapeta Farm was planned to control as many contingencies as possible, to maximize physical and mental soundness in its equine inhabitants. The result combines technology, New Age therapy, and an attempt to cater to the horses' instinctive desires and habits.

Built by Pennsylvania Dutch workmen, the training barn has 40 roomy stalls and a number of features Dickinson touts in a brochure he sends to clients: roofless stalls that prevent horses from injuring their heads if they rear up, outside windows protected by a three-foot overhang so the horses can look outside during rainy or snowy weather without getting wet, an equine scale set into the floor so Dickinson can monitor his runners' weight changes, and an air-circulation design that, Dickinson says, provides six complete air changes a day. There are two electric sockets outside each stall "because we're always using gadgets," from hair clippers to the electromagnetic-field devices Dickinson believes speed healing.

"Most stables are designed just like a prison cell, especially on the racetrack," he said one morning as he zipped along the barn's wide central aisle. "They have one little window for the light. They're dark, they're dingy, and they're pretty boring. We tried to design ours like a hotel room. We put in good windows, that's a no-brainer. We made white walls. A lot of people have black because they don't want to see the dirt. If dirt's there, we *want* to see it, so we can get the power washer and wash it down. And white makes it brighter. The skylights are double-glazed, which stops the cold getting in during the winter and the heat in the summer. They are UV-pervious glass to let the sun's rays come in and kill bacteria."

Many of Dickinson's stalls also feature metal "friendship grilles" between them that let the horses see each other. He believes that this often helps give horses, natural herd animals, a sense of security and well-being.

"Anything we can do to reduce stress for the horses, that's what we're trying to do," he explained. "Man survived by hiding and throwing stones. The horse survived because he ran from his predators. By nature, he's a nervous type of thing. I'm trying to get him to relax as much as I can."

In order to promote relaxation and a more natural lifestyle for his charges, Dickinson offers them two to three hours of turnout time each morning—an impossibility at most racetracks, where space does not allow for large paddocks.

"Fresh air," Dickinson said. "You can't beat it. Maintains the integrity of the lungs. Two, they move around and get rid of stiffness, especially after a breeze. And if you turn them out for an hour before they go to the track in the morning, they train much better. Three, it's mental. They're much easier to ride. It keeps them happy, and anything to reduce the stress on them. Four, never underestimate the benefits of fresh, green grass. It's very good for them. It's got minerals and vitamins in it, it's better absorbed."

Dickinson's paddocks are grass, encouraging the horses to drop their heads and graze lazily, but even the grass is specially grown for Dickinson's purposes.

"It's a mixture that has bluegrass, rye, and clover in it, specially selected for its nutrition, organically grown, deep-rooted, with a lot of aerating, and no chemicals."

The fences are of wide tape (though not electrified) instead of board, because, as Dickinson put it, "I want the fence to break, and not the horse."

"And that," he said, pointing up to one of about a half-dozen tubular black devices along the top ledge above the stalls, "is a Quadra air purifier."

The air purifiers, which sell through The Sharper Image catalog for $349.95 each, are Dickinson's most recent experiment in effective racehorse management.

"They are designed for people in an enclosed room," he said. "It is a giant leap of faith by me, thinking they are going to work for horses in an open environment. We just got them this year. We clean them every day, and we've just started to analyze the results last week."

Dickinson's experimental nature has also caused him to create specialized diets for his horses. In addition to the standard fare of oats and hay, Dickinson also feeds such surprising things as raw eggs (including the shells) and Guinness stout, the latter a traditional staple of English and Irish racing stables. He is also a devotee of so-called nutraceuticals, as well as of homeopathic supplements from a company called Dr. Xie's Jing-Tang Herbal.

Manuel Piedra, Tapeta's general manager, feeds the stable three times a day, hand-mixing various powders and supplements into a row of feed tubs that hang along the barn walls. Each horse's ration is tailored for him, Piedra explained.

"The horses eat a little bit better than you and me," he said as he pushed a trolley, laden like a candy-striper's but with egg cartons and supplement bottles instead of chocolate, down the barn aisle. The white plastic bottles on Piedra's trolley were filled with chalky powders in various shades of yellow, brown, and white. There was thyroid medicine, an herbal supplement cheerfully named Stomach Happy for ulcers, and something called Jade Lady, whose label listed such mystifying ingredients as Chuan NinXi, Ophiopogon, and Gypsum-Shi Gao (Sheng).

"You can get special feed from companies, but Michael makes his own," Piedra explained. "He gives regular oats, then mixes them with honey and water and supplements. Some is for the ulcers, some is for helping the horses' joints."

He picked up a couple of bottles from his trolley. "This one is for helping with muscle problems, when the horses get tired and muscle-sore, and this one is to clear up mucus in the lungs. The Guinness goes to the light-weight horses and the good horses to keep them in good shape. The eggs are for the skinny horses. When you use the eggs, you have to use the Guinness, because the eggs are stinky, and the Guinness will help them decide to eat them.

"I think Michael is a better trainer, because he is more interested in his track," said Piedra, who worked at the racetrack before joining Dickinson's operation in the 1990's. "The people working on the racetrack, they're worried about just getting their horses out to train them. They're not as worried about if the ground is all right. A lot of trainers at the racetrack don't spend money like Michael to have a good program for the horses, eating the best and worrying about whether the horse has got ulcers or whether a horse who breezed today has mucus. Michael always worries about the horses."

The nagging worry that something is always about to go wrong is the fundamental reason Dickinson strives to control his horses' environment so precisely. The best example of that control, and of the extravagance Dickinson will go to in order to achieve it, is the farm's most notable feature: the all-weather training track.

"I'm in love with safe surfaces," Dickinson said, by way of explaining himself.

So in love that he named his farm after the springy all-weather material, which Dickinson trademarked as Tapeta, the Latin word for "carpet." The all-weather course stands out like a brown ribbon laid across the farm's brilliant green grass gallops. It snakes over a mile around one end of Tapeta Farm, within view of the Georgian-style house where Dickinson and Wakefield live. Theoretically, he can keep a constant eye on the all-weather track, and it wouldn't be at all surprising if he did, so guarded is he about its exact ingredients. He once sued a man he suspected had collected a sample with the intent to duplicate it.

The Tapeta track's base material is brownish-gray. Sprinkled through it are rubbery pieces in vivid shades of pink, aqua, purple, green, and yellow, as well as fibers that resemble horsehair. It is distinctly bouncy underfoot.

"You've got more chance of getting the formula for Coca-Cola than you have of getting the formula for my track," Dickinson said. "It has eight secret ingredients, and sand is one of them. It's patented."

Whatever the ingredients, the Tapeta surface, Dickinson insists, fulfills his requirements of resilience in wet conditions and kindness to the equine leg.

"You see how it comes back to you?" he said proudly, striding along the spongy track. "It bounces back up under you. When I was designing the all-weather, I wanted forgivingness for the front end of a horse, because that's where 80 percent of his weight goes. You've seen a human runner push off from the starting blocks? Well, a horse does that every stride with his rear end. You've got to balance the two: forgivingness for the front end and stability for the rear end. That's why a dirt track can never, ever be right. Dirt tracks haven't changed in the last hundred years. If you put too much sand on, then it's forgiving for the front end but too cuppy for the rear end. If you make the track too tight so that it's firm for the rear end, it's *too* firm for the front end. It's not the track superintendent's fault; he's working with a product that's a hundred years old.

"I thought it would take me three months to design a new surface. It took me four years."

Dickinson has a photo album that chronicles his attempt to develop what his Tapeta Farm brochure, in emphatic capitals, claims is the safest track surface in the United States. There were, he says, many false starts.

"After 52 different formulas, I thought I had it, and we started mixing it," he said of one batch that he spent $30,000 to develop and manufacture into 300 tons of material. "We finished mixing at 2:00 A.M. one morning. And it was just no good. That was the worst day of my life. The $30,000 didn't really seem to matter, but it was my *dream*, and now what was I going to train on? It was a dead surface, it was inconsistent, no bounce to it, it was just awful."

Dickinson started tinkering again, and he finally came up with the right product, a track surface that exercise rider Ferriday described as feeling like "a carpet or a sponge."

"On a regular racetrack, a horse's leg hits it, and you almost feel a sort of shudder," Ferriday explained. "On this stuff, they just flick over it."

Dickinson is so confident in the final result that he has offered to pay the surgery bills for any client's horse that comes up with a bone chip or fracture while training at Tapeta. These common injuries are the bane of every trainer's existence, the problems that transform talented, expensive horses into what Dickinson calls "wastage."

It's a term that comes up often in any conversation with Michael Dickinson about training. In a second-floor office overlooking the training barn's stalls, Dickinson keeps a white cardboard box labeled "WASTAGE." Inside are a decade's worth of news clippings, veterinary-journal articles, and statistical studies about the causes of specific equine injuries.

Dickinson, like most horsemen, attributes injuries to a wide array of factors: poor equine conformation, unforgiving track surfaces, heavier riders, the pressure to keep horses running or bring them back quickly from injury rather than give them long, expensive layoffs.

"A lot of it is money," he conceded. "That's America now. We're all the same, aren't we? Instant gratification. Owners don't believe that three months isn't long enough to treat something. To them, three months is forever. They want their investment earning. They're missing races while their horse is off. They say, 'We want to make Saratoga, we want to make Gulfstream.' Well, the beauty of American racing is that it's year-round, so if we miss Saratoga, maybe you come back at Keeneland in October or Churchill in November. But it's finance, it's impatience, and it's lack of understanding for the horse."

At the very least, Dickinson has tried to make Tapeta an example of his understanding about what horses want and need in order to perform their best. At most, he believes his system actually prevents wastage. He feels certain that his training methods and facilities have helped him prevent injury in his string.

"Oh, yes, definitely," he said. "That's the whole idea. There's nothing genius in it. It's all common sense. We proved it with Da Hoss."

There was a downside to the Da Hoss story. After the notoriously flawed gelding won his second Breeders' Cup Mile, Dickinson became known as something of a miracle worker. The reputation has caused him to become a port of last resort for injury-prone horses whose owners now have one more reason not to give up on them.

"After Da Hoss, the phone was red-hot, but the calls were from people who had broken-down horses," Dickinson explained. "But here's what none of them would ever do: give horses enough time, the broken-down ones. That's a big mistake. A guy called me the other day who had an Elusive Quality horse that came up with a tendon in September. They gave it a month off, and then they breezed it in November, and guess what? It broke down again. *Big surprise.* So the thing has broken down twice, it has a tear in its tendon on an ultrasound, and he's going on about how the plan is to have the horse jogging in January and cantering in February. Well, that's not the way that it works. It's not that I'm patient. It's that they're impatient."

There are rewards, of course, like the gelding named A Huevo. The obscurely bred runner had shown speed and talent, once even setting a track record, but at age 3, in 1999, he had bone chips in both his knees and both his hocks. His owner, Mark Hopkins, agreed to have the chips surgically removed, and in due time Dickinson began preparing A Huevo for a comeback. Nothing seemed to go right, and nagging problems kept forcing the gelding to the sidelines. Hopkins's patience finally wore thin, and he told Dickinson to find the horse a good home, but Dickinson responded by offering to train A Huevo for free. He and Wakefield were sure the gelding wanted to run, and, as with Da Hoss, Dickinson wanted to solve the puzzle. He kept A Huevo on the Tapeta program, backing off him when necessary, nursing him through the setbacks, then training him on again.

It took almost four years, but in November of 2003, A Huevo did something Hopkins never seriously believed he would do: He won a Grade 1 race, and he won it easily.

"They talk about him being the mad genius," a beaming Hopkins said of Dickinson as he stood in the winner's circle that day. "If anyone thinks this man isn't the best trainer on the planet—he's the only person who could have done this."

That was a rewarding training job, Dickinson admitted, and he takes pride in rescuing a horse from the wastage box.

"But I want to focus on prevention, not cure," He said. What Dickinson needed was for people to send him some young, undamaged horses whose futures were ahead of them instead of ones that needed fixing. He believed that a Derby candidate, in particular, could advertise his training talents and change his reputation from that of a miracle worker to a star maker.

If he could pinpoint a likely turning point in his career, he would place it on the afternoon of November 15, 2003, at Maryland's Laurel Park racetrack, about two hours before A Huevo set off Hopkins's exuberant celebration in the winner's circle. Dickinson had sent out a gray 2-year-old to win a smaller but important race. The colt's name was Tapit, and his win announced Dickinson's arrival on the Kentucky Derby trail.

The colt was well bred. He had sold for $625,000 at Keeneland's 2002 September yearling sale. His buyer, Verne Winchell, died two months later, but his family wanted to let their father's racing dream run.

Tapit was one of the last horses rider Jon Ferriday exercised before hanging up his boots to take over other, less physically wearing duties for Dickinson's stable. But he remembered that ride well.

"He was a bit of a boyo," Ferriday said. "But he had such a *flow* to him when he jogged. He wasn't quick and snatchy. He really moved, and he had a bit of a bounce to him, like an athlete. I thought, 'I *like* this horse.'"

"Oh, you can't really get too crazy about them," said Dickinson, the natural conservative. "He was just a nice horse, a sensible horse."

But Tapit had no particular problems. He was young and bursting with potential that Dickinson hoped would bloom in the spring of 2004, right around Derby Day. He would train him like any other horse, Dickinson said, but the first Saturday in May was certainly on his mind as a potential target date, if nothing went wrong.

"It's no different, except you've got the one date," he said. "That's slightly harder. It's no good having him fit a week later, is it?"

Tapit was not a miracle case; he was a contender. And if he could make it to the Derby with a chance, he probably would help bring Dickinson more good runners like him—not rescue cases, but fresh, sound runners. If Tapeta could resurrect A Huevo and Da Hoss from the scrap heap, what could it do for a sound and talented young horse? Maybe win a Derby. There was a lot to control between now and then, but it was a thrilling thought.

"The big win is worth everything," Dickinson said. "There is *nothing* like it. That's why I do it. There are so many downs, you just have to be brave and keep going."

Tapit's November 15 race had turned out to be big, in one way. "It proved I can train a 2-year-old," Dickinson said. "That's why it was an important day for me, a career-changing day."

If Tapit were to become a Derby winner, the changes could be even greater.

"It's difficult to explain how winning the Kentucky Derby can change your life," trainer Carl Nafzger wrote after saddling Unbridled to win the race's 1990 edition. "The day before you are training a good racehorse for a fine family and he's only part, albeit the most important part, of a stable of competitive runners.

"That was yesterday. Today, you have the Derby winner and, just that quickly, he belongs to everyone. . . . You realize anew that your world can never be quite the same.

"Winning the Kentucky Derby is something I wish every trainer and owner could experience," he added. "There's nothing quite like it. But, if you can't, there still are thrills enough to go around for everyone in this wonderful world of racing."

Dickinson concurred.

"I love racing," he said. "It's a great game, because it's first to the winning post. I love that winning post. We're all dreaming, aren't we, to be honest? And we do it because we love the horses. You've got to admire their courage. They're going out there and doing it for the fun of it. There are no $50 million contracts. There are no gold medals. You have to admire them for going out every time. And they're great to work with."

Then he leaned forward, as if imparting the game's secret.

"If you've got a healthy horse, you'll make money," he said. "The two go hand in hand. You look after the horse, and the horse will look after you."

Almost six months later, Michael Dickinson had Tapit right where he wanted him to be: at Churchill Downs. The gray colt's 2004 Derby campaign had consisted of only two starts, the Florida Derby in March and New York's Wood Memorial in April, and the results had been mixed. In the Florida Derby, bumped at the start and crowded in the running, Tapit finished sixth. Dickinson discovered after the race that the colt had a slight respiratory infection that would require some time out of training—a bad development on the Triple Crown's tight schedule. But when Tapit returned to the races almost a month later for the Wood Memorial, he won by half a length.

He returned to Tapeta and had his final pre-Derby breeze there in a workout jockey Ramon Dominguez described as "beautiful."

"I can tell he's just getting better," Dominguez said. "He's improving."

When Tapit arrived at Churchill Downs four days before the Derby, he appeared poised to fulfill his home-run potential. But, then, so did several other horses in a race as wide-open as a Kansas cornfield. The season's 28 graded Derby-prep races had produced 25 different winners, and there was no heavy favorite going into the Derby.

"There's eight or nine, maybe 10 or 12, who, if they run their best race, can win the race," one trainer said.

"Whoever hits the trifecta can buy a new Mercedes, and whoever hits the superfecta can buy a new house," said another.

Dickinson, in a manner of speaking, had bet the farm on Tapit. Asked by reporters if he planned to wager on his colt, he pointed out that he already had bet Tapeta Farm's reputation on him, and that was enough to have at stake.

Even after he shipped to Churchill, Tapit had not entirely left the farm behind. Before leaving Maryland with the horse, Piedra had packed a full supply of eggs and Guinness stout so Tapit's diet would remain unaffected by his trip to Churchill. Dickinson even sliced out a four-foot strip of Tapeta sod and shipped it to Kentucky. The barn staff unrolled the bright green turf outside Tapit's barn at Churchill so the colt could have his custom-blended snack every day, as usual.

But Dickinson could not, of course, bring Tapeta's most important feature and the one variable he had devoted his life to controlling: the racing surface. And on May 1, 2004, it was the surface that made all the difference to Tapit. Derby Day arrived with a gust of wet weather. There was a brief hour of sticky, humid sunshine in the midafternoon that raised racegoers' hopes that the Derby start would take place in good weather, but it was a false promise. About an hour before Tapit and the other Derby runners were to head to the paddock, sinister black thunderclouds blew in over Churchill, unleashing a deluge so heavy that people in the barn area couldn't even see the grandstand and twin spires across the racetrack. Thunder rattled the barns, the rain poured relentlessly, and trainers with Derby runners helplessly cursed the weather as the track condition deteriorated from "fast" to "sloppy," a situation many of their horses had never faced before.

The rain had petered out to mere sprinkles by the time the 18 Derby horses assembled for their walk to the paddock, but the damage had been done. While Piedra and Ferriday handled Tapit, Dickinson plunged his fingers into the nearly liquid track, still analyzing the situation, but to no avail. It was sloppy, and Tapit would simply have to handle it.

But he didn't. When the gate flew open at 6:12 P.M., Dickinson quickly saw that his colt, so meticulously prepared, was in trouble. Jockey Dominguez later said Tapit never accelerated well in the poor going, and his problems were compounded by traffic trouble in the large Derby field. Surrounded by jostling horses, Dominguez had to steady Tapit heading into the turn and then, racing on the outside, Tapit was caught five paths wide as they headed into the backstretch. He gained some ground as the field turned for home, but it was futile. This time, there was no miracle. Tapit finished ninth behind Smarty Jones, the first undefeated Kentucky Derby victor since Seattle Slew in 1977.

Dickinson's natural pessimism had, and least, prepared him to be philosophical about Tapit's loss.

"We're battered, bashed, and bruised, but we'll live to fight another day," he said after the race. "I trained him to breeze, not swim."

For Smarty Jones, the Derby deluge had been one more lucky break in a perfect campaign that made him a genuine home run horse. The colt came into the Kentucky Derby off a win in the Arkansas Derby, where the track had been labeled muddy, and rider Stewart Elliott confessed with a grin that he had been glad when the heavens had opened over Churchill.

"I said, 'Let it rain!'" he commented after the race.

Smarty Jones had won all six of his starts before the Derby, but until he won at Churchill, he had struggled to gain respect. He was bred in Pennsylvania by the septuagenarian husband-and-wife team of Roy and Pat Chapman, who had never raced at the sport's top level. The Chapmans had almost gotten out of racing altogether after their longtime trainer was murdered in a family dispute. They had only two horses left in their stable, Smarty Jones and an unremarkable runner named Some Image. They decided to keep

Smarty Jones in the first place, car dealer Roy Chapman said, because "my wife liked the look in his eye."

Smarty Jones got his start at Philadelphia Park instead of at a more fashionable venue such as Saratoga, Keeneland, or Santa Anita. His jockey, a former alcoholic plagued by weight troubles, had actually left the game for a while, but he returned to the saddle because, as he put it, "It's all I know." His trainer, John Servis, was not well known outside the second-tier mid-Atlantic racing circuit, where he had made a solid living but could not have expected to become a national celebrity.

The difference, they all readily acknowledged, was a single exceptional horse who had changed the trajectories of their lives, from mundane to mythic. It wasn't just a symbolic change, either. Smarty Jones's Derby win was worth $884,800 in purse money, and he also earned a staggering $5 million bonus sponsored by Oaklawn Park for winning its Rebel Stakes and Arkansas Derby as well as the Kentucky Derby.

Hailed as racing's newest working-class hero, Smarty Jones went on to win the Preakness by a record 11 ½ lengths, bringing his total earnings to $7.6 million. The Chapmans struck a merchandising deal and began fielding offers for his breeding rights, which were estimated to be worth between $35 million and $40 million. The stud negotiations, involving Kentucky's wealthiest and most prestigious breeding farms, were still underway when Smarty Jones made his bid to become only the second undefeated Triple Crown winner in history. His attempt fell one length short as, once again, the Belmont Stakes distance felled a Triple Crown hopeful. The Chapmans and Servis, watching from their clubhouse box, stood in stunned and heartbroken silence as 36-1 shot Birdstone ground down Smarty Jones's homestretch lead, then passed him. Even the winning owner was apologetic for ending the popular colt's run.

"I'm sorry, sorry, sorry Smarty Jones couldn't win," Marylou Whitney emphasized after her colt carried off the traditional blanket of white carnations. "We do love Smarty, and I think Smarty Jones has done more for the racing community and people who love horses. It gives everyone the chance to think, 'This could happen to me.'"

10 "I Owed Him"

THE ENGLISH LANGUAGE, Arthur Hancock III finds, is too blunt an instrument to precisely describe the feeling. He's been trying to pin it down in words for more than 20 years, since about 5:40 P.M. on the cloudy afternoon of May 1, 1982, when he realized that his horse Gato del Sol was going to win the Kentucky Derby.

It seemed impossible to Hancock, even as he watched it happening. His hands were too shaky to hold his binoculars to his eyes, but he didn't need them anyway when the 19-horse field came barreling into the homestretch. Here came Hancock's gray colt at odds of 21-1, mowing down the horses in front of him like a scythe through wheat. Gato del Sol had started the race by running last, but he swept past every rival and crossed the finish line 2 ½ lengths in front.

It left Hancock with a sensation he describes as "eerie."

"It's the only time in my life I felt a sort of out-of-body experience," he said. "I felt like I could float in the air."

This euphoric fulfillment of an ambition that had run through his family for three generations was difficult for Hancock to believe. No one knew better than the Hancocks how hard it was to overcome the thousand variables that can, and usually do, trip up Derby hopes in the breeding shed, the pastures, and the starting gate. To clear-eyed Thoroughbred professionals like Hancock and his father, Bull, before him—the people who make their living selling the dream of a home run horse—the reality is stark. It is almost impossible to win the Kentucky Derby. And yet Arthur Hancock III had done it.

"I really didn't think it was real until I saw that 'Official' sign," he remembered. "I figured some way or other someone would claim a foul or something. I just couldn't believe it. That's what I always wanted to do: win the Derby. But I really didn't think I ever would, or, if I did, I figured I'd be about 75. Because my dad never won it, and he was a great breeder. He had a lot of chances, but something happened to all of them."

Arthur Hancock III was never really made for the cut-throat commercialism of the Thoroughbred business. If he hadn't been a Hancock, of the Claiborne Farm Hancocks, he might never have been taken seriously enough to make a start in the game. Arthur, the namesake of Arthur "Bull" Hancock Jr., and that respected horseman's older son, initially seemed destined to inherit Bull's place as master of Claiborne in Paris, Kentucky. But children, like yearlings, are unpredictable, and Arthur turned out altogether differently from family expectations. In central Kentucky's khaki-and-loafers culture, Arthur was a vivid paisley. He was into music and parties and a few other things his glowering father found unseemly. He jammed with a legendary Lexington rocker called Little Enis, he sang at the local radio station, and he got into a bloody fight at a 1969 wedding reception. His father called him "a goddamn court jester" and once floored him with a right to the jaw when Arthur came home one night at 11:15 instead of 11:00 P.M. Bull nearly banned him from the Hancock house outright after the wedding brawl. But Arthur's pleading, inspired by what he is fond of referring to as "Mr. R. E. Morse," kept him at the family hearth.

Arthur finally did go into the horse business. In 1970, he took over Stone Farm, a 100-acre parcel that Bull leased to him, not too far down Winchester Road from Claiborne. The idea was that

Arthur would serve a sort of apprenticeship there, learning the hands-on practicalities of racehorse breeding in preparation for his turn at the Claiborne helm. Bull sent him 100 mares to look after, but he took them back in a rage when Arthur made a foxhunting trip to Ireland in the middle of the breeding season.

That Irish jaunt marked a turning point for Arthur and his younger brother, Seth, and, by extension, for Claiborne Farm. Arthur, seemingly too feckless to be entrusted with sole authority over the family's Thoroughbred tradition, was kept at Stone Farm, and Bull set Seth up in his own apprenticeship at Claiborne. The plan appeared to put the two brothers on a collision course over the family legacy. When Bull died of cancer in September 1972, it became clear that he had tried a compromise. His will put Arthur, 29, and Seth, just 23 and only months into his apprenticeship, in joint control of Claiborne. In recognition of their youth, Bull made three of his closest allies— Ogden Phipps, William Haggin Perry, and Charles Kenney—formal advisers to the estate, requiring Arthur and Seth to get their approval before making any decisions regarding the Thoroughbred breeding operation. The winter after his father's death, Arthur got the bitter news from the estate's executors during a meeting at Claiborne: The advisers wanted the conservative Seth in charge, not Arthur.

Arthur stormed out, and from that moment on, the two brothers were on different trajectories toward the same goal: winning the Kentucky Derby.

Seth, left with the blue-blooded clients and horses at Claiborne, was an almost immediate success, thanks to his gamble on syndicating Secretariat before the colt's 3-year-old campaign. He had neither bred nor owned Secretariat, but his agreement to secure the stud rights for Claiborne with a record syndication of just over $6 million made him a major beneficiary of the colt's runaway Triple Crown win in 1973.

Secretariat's Derby that May, which reflected so well on Arthur's younger brother, was another chilly reminder to Bull's namesake that he was well and truly out of the Claiborne picture. Inevitably, he recalled the vow he had made back in December 1972, when he had stormed out of the executors' meeting, humiliated and angry that they had wanted him to work under Seth. He first said it to a friend that night at a bar, where he had gone to lick his wounds and figure things out: "I'm going to win the Kentucky Derby, and I'm going to make Stone Farm bigger than Claiborne." Watching Secretariat win the Derby, and then the Preakness, and then the Belmont, watching his brother hailed for a spectacular syndication that now looked as astute as any of Bull's judgments, Arthur understandably was stung. But he kept working.

By 1978, the year he decided to breed Peacefully to Cougar II, Arthur had something to show for his labor at Stone Farm. He had bought land, gradually expanding the property to more than 2,300 acres. He was standing stallions. He had some good clients. In June 1980, when Gato del Sol was just a scrappy yearling galloping around a pasture with the other colts, Arthur sold his 101 shares in Claiborne to his siblings—Seth and sisters Clay and Dell—for $3.5 million.

He was still playing music and he still liked a drink, but Arthur was also becoming a serious Thoroughbred farmer. He worked from 6:00 A.M. to 6:00 P.M. every day of the week, and that earned him respect from old-school breeders who previously thought of him, if privately, as a wastrel. He was married and was starting a family, another sign, people thought, that he was heading down a better road. He sold horses, and horsemen thought they were raised well, even if they lacked the aristocratic bloodlines of Claiborne stock. The Stone Farm motto—"We're trying to raise you a good horse"—was suitably modest and solid, and it seemed to reflect a realization on Arthur's part that the Derby dream, though eternally seductive, was distant.

In 1981, he had about the worst kind of luck a horseman can have: a barn fire killed eight of Stone Farm's 2-year-olds and three of its broodmares. It was an uninsured $400,000 loss. Arthur saved two horses himself, but the barn collapsed on top of a 19-year-old broodmare named Theonia, the dam of the first good horse Arthur had raised at Stone Farm, stakes-winner Table Run. But one of the 2-year-olds that was not in the fire was Gato del Sol, and, in a twist that Arthur Hancock might have put into one of his own country-music songs, that colt was about to give him the Hancock family's first Kentucky Derby winner.

Today, more than 20 years after Gato del Sol's Derby victory, Hancock looks like his father's natural heir. He is a consistently successful seller at the top of the Thoroughbred market. He and his

regular partners, Robert and Janice McNair, bred 2000 Kentucky
Derby winner Fusaichi Pegasus, whom they sold for $4 million at
the Keeneland July yearling sale. He also was co-breeder and co-
owner of Sunday Silence, who won the 1989 Kentucky Derby,
Preakness, and Breeders' Cup Classic before going on to become
Japan's all-time leading sire. In short, Arthur Hancock has been a
resounding success both by the Derby standard and in the auction
ring, despite his scattered beginning.

His father's influence bubbles to the surface even in casual conversation, when Arthur is inclined to quote Bull's homespun wisdom about raising horses.

Ironically, the old Hancock way of doing things has gradually
become nonconformist as commercial needs have begun to over-
take the less profitable breeding methods of Bull's generation.
Claiborne, still one of the world's most respected nurseries and still
run by Arthur's younger brother, Seth, is an anachronism now, with
its old-money clientele who control some of the most venerable
and valuable American pedigrees. The farm is like a museum of
equine greats, filled not with Vermeers or Botticellis, but the beautiful results of the fine art of breeding. The names and bloodlines
of champions run like seams of gold ore through Claiborne's
broodmare band and stallion barn today. Seth Hancock has only
reluctantly increased the Claiborne stallions' book sizes to fit the
ruthless market forces, and the Claiborne stallions do not shuttle to
the Southern Hemisphere in the off-season.

Arthur is similarly conservative and, when he speaks of his
breeding philosophies, he is equally deferential to his father's theories about breeding horses for classic stamina, for example, rather
than for the firecracker speed and precocity that have been in high
demand in the Thoroughbred marketplace. Hancock stands on the
uncomfortable divide between immediate commercial demands
and classic aspirations, with one foot in the sale ring and the other
on the racetrack. It's tricky ground to stand on, especially if, like
Hancock, you wage a constant battle to keep the yin and yang of
your commercial and spiritual impulses in balance.

"I think a lot of people who breed horses, especially if you sell
yearlings, have to try to figure out what the market wants,"
Hancock acknowledged. "And they want speed and size, and, of

course, a good, correct individual. I'm a horse breeder, and I personally breed a horse trying to win the Derby. I've had some good luck there. But it's probably hurt me. That horse isn't necessarily going to sell very well."

Hancock laments that there is a conflict at all between what sells and what is classically good.

"There are a lot of things that go into it," he said mournfully. "To give you an example of what I'm talking about: breeding early and putting these mares under lights. All you're doing there is tricking nature. People are trying to squeeze the lemon, and you see it in all phases of this business. They're breeding stallions to all these mares, putting the mares under lights to 'program' them, trying to get them in foal February 20, just everything. Fattening up the yearlings and hothouse-raising them, so to speak, not letting them be horses. That's the materialism working its way into everything."

It was Hancock's pragmatic, commercial side that made him sell Gato del Sol to a German stud farm in 1992. But it was his spiritual side that made him do something entirely contrary to Thoroughbred breeding's modern business ethic in 1999. He bought the old Derby winner, who had utterly failed as a sire on both sides of the Atlantic, and flew the horse home to the farm where he was born, all because of a little more than two minutes and two seconds on the first Saturday in May, 1982.

The mating that produced Gato del Sol was not especially propitious from a business standpoint. One of the stallions Hancock had collected for his new stud barn at Stone Farm was Cougar II, a Chilean-bred runner who had come to America and become a champion. But, in the commercial breeding world, there are hierarchies of champions, and Cougar II fell into the least flattering one: He was a champion of grass racing, a division that is a throwback to Thoroughbred racing's beginnings in 17th-century England, when contests were run over several miles through grassy meadows.

It was picturesque and harked back to an ancient era, but grass racing required a quality that had fallen out of fashion in the modern American market: stamina. To many American buyers, "stamina" equaled "slow," both on the racetrack and in physical development, because many of the most talented grass runners were rangy animals who took a season or two to fill out and grow into their sweeping, ground-devouring strides. If you were looking to make a quick return on your purchase price, this was not the shape for you; you wanted something with the powerful, muscular hindquarters that suggested quick, profitable maturation.

231

Gato del Sol was not bred to be fast-looking, or even especially fast. But he was bred to win the Kentucky Derby, as far as Hancock was concerned. Hancock specifically had the Derby in mind when he matched Peacefully, a modest stakes winner, to his not very popular grass-running stallion.

"I thought that was a good cross to produce a horse that could go a mile and a quarter, I remember thinking that," Hancock said. "The first foal, as I remember, was a filly, and she couldn't run. But I always go back twice. If you believe in a cross, try it twice. Three times is too many, because it might not work. But try it twice. So I booked the mare back again to Cougar."

Even Hancock wasn't overwhelmed by the result. Gato del Sol was small, and this was not a good start.

"I wasn't really disappointed, because they change so much, but I would have preferred to see a big, good-looking foal," Hancock admitted. "You always like that. He wasn't that big, but he was a nice foal."

But not quite nice enough. When Keeneland's selection team came to Stone Farm on its rounds, reviewing horses to let into its prestigious July yearling sale, they were not impressed with Arthur Hancock's little Cougar II colt, and they told him so.

"He was a nice-looking yearling, but he was by Cougar, and maybe he just wasn't quite fashionably bred enough to go in the summer sale," Hancock said. Keeneland's decision made sense, but that didn't take the sting out of it. "When they wouldn't take him in the sale, I said, 'Well, we'll just keep him and race him.' I've always been kind of sensitive when somebody insults me, and they didn't mean to insult me, but I kind of thought I'd show them, you know."

Only one man predicted that Gato del Sol would make it to the Derby, and that man was not Arthur Hancock or his partner in breeding the colt, real-estate businessman Leone J. Peters. The prophecy came from an unlikely but appealing oracle—a longtime farm employee, Sam Ransom, whose claim to fame was that he had broken to saddle the great Count Fleet, winner of the 1943 Triple Crown. Ransom had worked at Claiborne, but when Arthur left the family farm, Ransom had followed him.

"Called himself Handsome Sam Ransom, Women's Pet and Men's Regret," Hancock said. "But he had a real sixth sense for horses. He always would say about Gato, 'This is a Derby horse.' He'd never said that about anything else.

"The next one he said it about was Risen Star," Hancock added, referring to a Secretariat colt that Hancock and Peters later bred who won the 1988 Preakness and then the Belmont Stakes by almost 15 lengths.

Gato del Sol was born black, as grays are, and he gradually lightened with age. By the time he was 2, he was the color of granite. He was maturing, but not as fast as some of his more precocious classmates. Gato del Sol was a grinder who lurked at the back of the pack, launched a single, long swoop in the second half of the race, and wore down the leaders. But he needed help from the front-runners themselves, in the form of a rapid pace that would tire them out, softening them up for his late assault.

Hancock first saw Gato del Sol's heart-stopping running style in the 1981 Del Mar Futurity in California.

"He was *way* back there, and I thought he had no chance," he remembered. "And then he just came flying."

Gato del Sol won that race. He followed up with creditable efforts throughout the winter and spring, finishing third and fourth, but he didn't win again, and this disheartened Hancock and Peters. But their trainer, Eddie Gregson, was unfazed. The horse needs more ground, Gregson told Gato del Sol's owners, and he'll get it in the Derby.

Although he hadn't won all year, Gato del Sol's performances were enough to keep him on the road to Churchill Downs, however tenuous his chances seemed to outsiders. In his last start before the Derby, in April, Gato del Sol returned to Kentucky for the Blue Grass Stakes, and loped home a well-beaten second behind the highly regarded colt Linkage. But Hancock, Peters, and Gregson liked what their colt got out of the race.

"He ran a good race, but he needed that race," Hancock said.

"His muscles corded up."

They sent him on to Churchill Downs, where not many people thought they had much of a shot. But Hancock found one who did on the Tuesday night before the Derby, at a traditional dinner in honor of the race and its entrants. It was Bill Shoemaker, who had the call on eventual 16-1 shot Star Gallant in the Derby.

"Who do you think is gonna win Saturday?" Hancock asked the jockey.

"I think you're going to win it," Shoemaker said. "You're the only horse in the race that can get a mile and a quarter."

Hancock was pleased with that assessment, but only for an evening. The following morning, in the lottery that decided the Derby's post positions, Gato del Sol came out a loser, drawing stall 18 in a field of 19 runners. No horse had ever won from that far off the inside rail. He would practically be running through the grandstand for the first quarter-mile of the race. Gregson figured Gato del Sol would lose a minimum of six lengths and a maximum of 12 by coming out of the gate about 80 feet off the rail. For a come-from-behind horse without a sensational turn of foot, as Gregson said to Hancock, "It's really an obstacle we can't overcome."

"I said, 'Well, there's no hope,'" Hancock said. "And everybody around us at the draw knew it, too. Everyone said, 'Aw, that's too bad.' Because no horse had ever won from that outside post. They had the draw in a tent, and there was a wooden pole in the tent. I kicked that pole—and I about broke my toe, for a couple of days I could hardly walk on it—because I thought what bad luck it was to get that draw. See, my father could never win it, and he had five horses that could have romped, but something happened to every one of them. I said, 'We're jinxed. The Hancocks are jinxed. It's over.'"

Dejected, Hancock went back to Lexington and retreated in a sulk to his bedroom. Lying in bed and thinking over his rotten luck, it suddenly occurred to him to wonder exactly how bad, in measurable distance lost, the far outside draw had been.

"Now, when I was at Vanderbilt, I did get an A in logic," he said. "I had a vague recollection that if you knew this distance and that distance, and they formed a 90-degree triangle, you could figure out the third distance, the hypotenuse."

He called up a close friend, attorney Paul Sullivan, and ran the problem by him.

"They called him the Math Whiz in school, because he was always real good at all that stuff," Hancock said. "I asked Paul, 'What is so bad about being out there? Can't you find out how much distance he loses by starting there?' Paul said, 'Yes, it's the Pythagorean theorem.' It's the base squared plus the height squared, and you take the square root of that to find out what that hypotenuse is."

Hancock told his friend he figured Gato del Sol would have to make up about eight or 10 lengths, or about 64 to 80 feet, due to his wide post position.

"He had a calculator, so he figured it," Hancock said. "We figured it was a quarter-mile from the gate to the turn, and that was like the height of the triangle. We were post position 18, and we figured each stall in the gate was about four feet wide, so we figured we were out about 80 feet from the rail; that was the base of the triangle."

When Sullivan punched in the calculation, the final number shocked both of them. Gato del Sol would only lose 2.4 feet from a post position that conventional wisdom said was impossible to overcome. Hancock couldn't believe it.

"He did it again: It was 2.4 feet," Hancock remembered. "By that time, I was sitting on the edge of the bed. Then he said, 'But there's a catch. You can't cut in real fast to the rail, because if you do, you'll lose the whole 80 feet. You've got to gradually come over.' Well, by this time I was *standing* on the bed. I called Eddie Gregson. Eddie was a real smart guy, Phi Beta Kappa at Stanford. He was all down about the draw, too."

Hancock went through the mathematical exercise again, this time with Gregson. By the time they ended their phone call, Gato del Sol's whole scenario had turned around, and his odds—at least to his owners and trainer—were looking much better. The key now was to get jockey Eddie Delahoussaye to ride the hypotenuse.

"You know, when you're out plowing a field with your tractor and you want to plow a straight line, do you know how you do it?" Hancock said. "You line up the muffler on that barn you can see off at the end of the row, and you'll have a perfectly straight line by the time you get there. You've got to look at something way off, something fixed. We told Eddie Delahoussaye, 'When you come out of there, just keep looking through the horse's ears at that turn, and don't come in.' He did it, too. If you look at the tape of the race, he didn't get over to the inside rail for a while, maybe an eighth of a mile.

"I remember some guy hollering behind us during the race. When they broke out of the gate I couldn't even look through the binoculars, my hands were shaking so hard. But I could hear this guy shouting behind us, 'Why won't that gray horse git on in thar?'"

Delahoussaye was riding according to strategy, and that put Gato del Sol in a position to contend for the roses. He was aided further by the only filly in the race, Cupecoy's Joy, who shot to the front and led through fast early fractions of 23 and 46 ⅕ seconds. Chasing the quick pace, the rest of the field was strung out in a narrow line, which helped Gato del Sol make his gradual path toward the inside rail without getting caught wide on the turn, on the edge of a bunched group of horses.

The race was unfolding perfectly for Hancock's slow gray bomber. As the field rolled out of the final turn, Gato del Sol came soaring by his rivals, picking them off until he was alone at the wire. He won by 2 ½ lengths, writing the most unlikely Hancock's name indelibly in the 108th Kentucky Derby results.

Gato del Sol never ran that well again. He finally retired in July 1985, at age 6, having won just seven of 39 starts. The one in May 1982 brought Hancock solace he probably could not have gotten any other way, the sense that his father would finally have been proud of him.

"I just feel blessed to have ever had that happen to me," Hancock said. "That feeling is still there. It's hard to put into words. It's a strange feeling. Did you ever have a dream where you can fly, and how great it is? And then you wake up, and it's so sad. Well, I didn't wake up from this dream."

But there are dreams and there are realities in the Thoroughbred industry, and the after-Derby reality was not kind to Gato del Sol. A prolonged losing streak after the Derby victory confirmed for many people that he was a fluke, and some began to refer to him unkindly as Gato del Slow. He ended his career with a win, but his failure to regain his Derby form had cemented breeders' viewpoints that his Cougar II bloodlines were not going to help him at stud.

Hancock was undeterred. "If nobody wants to breed to him, I'll take my own mares and come up with another Derby winner," he said.

Gato del Sol was retired to Stone Farm in July 1985, but the negative predictions about him came true. Within five years, it was clear he was not making it as a stallion, a failure that was worsened by a weak market for Thoroughbreds. When the telephone rang in January 1993, with an offer from Gestut Goerlsdorf in Germany, Hancock was not in a position to turn down the $100,000.

"He didn't do any good as a stallion, and we bred him to a lot of our better mares," Hancock said with a sigh. "I don't think he ever got a stakes winner. So we had the offer from Germany, and we figured it was the right thing to do to take it.

"I had something like 4,600 acres of land and bought all these mares. What was worth a dollar was worth 30 cents, and I had all this debt. It was the right thing to do. I learned a lot of the horse business from my dad, and he was a businessman. We're all businessmen, we have to be or we couldn't make it. That's the other side of the coin to the spiritual."

Still, it was with a twinge of disappointment that Hancock went to the barn to see his family's first Derby winner off when the horse van came.

"You know they say you can't eat your cake and have it, too," he said. "He won the Kentucky Derby for us. That's enough. Like Sam Ransom used to say, 'For the needy, not the greedy.' But I was disappointed that he hadn't done too well as a stallion. I remember patting him good-bye. I figured I'd get over there to Germany someday to see him. The plane was coming, and they needed to get him going.

"I wasn't *mad* at him for not making a stallion, but I was kind of disappointed in him. I thought, 'Well, you're going to have a good home over there, and maybe you'll do better there.' It was a good sale, and that's part of it. You're not supposed to fall in love with a horse, because they can break you. I was in love with Gato del Sol, yeah. But I kept a lot of the yearlings and didn't sell them so I could race them, and they couldn't run a bit. From that standpoint, I was just disappointed."

Hancock paused, thinking back to the day almost 10 years earlier when he had sent his Derby winner away.

"But they didn't run over there, either."

Failure and disappointment are the norm in the Thoroughbred gamble, and their consequences can be ghastly. According to a white paper issued in 2003 by the anti-slaughter Thoroughbred Retirement Foundation, it is impossible to determine exactly how many former racehorses go to slaughter each year, because no one, including the slaughterhouses, keeps statistics on the horses' former occupations. The TRF has determined that 754,300 horses were slaughtered in the United States, Canada, and Mexico in 2002. Sixty-two thousand of those were killed at United States slaughterhouses, where the most commonly "processed" breeds are Thoroughbreds, Arabians, and Quarter Horses.

Former racehorses, stallions, and broodmares meet the same fate overseas with some regularity once they are deemed unproductive. It is perhaps an expected consequence of industrialization that the worn-out item, no longer fit for its intended purpose, is sent to be recycled into a final useful product, its constituent parts rendered into oil, hide, and meat. But such ruthless efficiency has some painful effects. Horses of little consequence, economically speaking—geldings who are injured or past their running days, mares who are persistently barren, horses of unfashionable lineage that are losing in cheap races—are far more likely to end up at a slaughterhouse than well-bred horses with breeding promise. But even champions are not immune to the modern business's relentless hewing to the bottom line for its definition of "usefulness."

In 1979, the year that Gato del Sol was born, one of the sport's kings was entering what should have been a glorious, or at least a peaceful, retirement. His name was Exceller, and he would later be elected to Thoroughbred racing's Hall of Fame. But, sadly, what people remember most about Exceller now is the squalid nature of his death in a utilitarian breeding industry.

Exceller embodied the home run dream. Bought almost on a whim by Nelson Bunker Hunt for $25,000, he went on to earn more than $1.6 million. In 1978, he became the only horse ever to beat two Triple Crown winners when he won the Jockey Club Gold

Cup over Seattle Slew, who was second, and Affirmed, who finished fourth.

Exceller's owner, Texas billionaire Hunt—a son of the oilman
H. L. Hunt who tried from 1979 to 1980 to corner the silver
market with his brother Herbert—could have spent almost any
sum imaginable to acquire a horse when he went to the
Keeneland July yearling sale in 1974. He certainly thought he
would have to pay more than $25,000 to get Exceller, though he
wasn't even sure he wanted him. Hunt's adviser, Ted Curtin, an
Irish trainer and bloodstock agent, had seen the Vaguely Noble
colt outside the pavilion minutes before he came up for sale, and
he recommended they buy him, even though Hunt—who had
shares in Vaguely Noble—already had stables full of the stallion's
get. But the price was certainly right. Much to Hunt's surprise,
bidding stalled out on the opening offer of $24,000. The colt had
very upright pasterns, a fault conventionally believed to make a
horse more prone to damaging concussion on the legs, and other
buyers had gotten off him. So Hunt, who raced his best stock on
the more forgiving grass courses of Europe, stepped into the
breach and got the colt for $25,000, well below the auction aver-
age of $57,000.

Over the next five years, Exceller ran first in France and later in
the United States, and he became the richest horse ever to have
gone through an auction ring. With $1.6 million to his credit, he
had taken aim on the great Kelso's all-time earnings record when
he cracked a bone in his foot while finishing third in the Century
Handicap. Hunt retired him.

"The owners decided that he was too valuable as a sire to try and
race him again, although his foot is improving every day," trainer
Charlie Whittingham explained to the press when the decision
came down. "If he were a horse of less value, we probably would
go on with him."

Exceller's stud value, as marked by his syndication total, was a
record $15 million. Hunt syndicated the stallion in 40 shares,
keeping 10 himself and selling the rest for $375,000 apiece.
Exceller shipped from Whittingham's barn in southern
California to Gainesway Farm in Lexington, Kentucky, where his
fee was set at $75,000.

238

But Exceller's actual value at stud, as determined by his ability to get winners, turned out to be far less than his shareholders had hoped. By 1991 he had only a handful of stakes winners to his credit, and, at age 18, he appeared to have limited prospects. When an offer came from Swedish breeder Gote Ostlund, Exceller's shareholders did what in business terms was a prudent thing: They cashed out.

Exceller had a good start in his new home. In 1994, he was Scandinavia's second-leading sire of 2-year-olds, and the following year he was sixth on the general sire ranking. In 1996, he climbed a spot, ending the season as Scandinavia's fifth-leading sire. But in 1996 something happened that sent Exceller, despite his success, on an irrevocable downward spiral. His owner, Gote Ostlund, went bankrupt. Exceller became collateral damage when Scandinavian racing authorities responded to Ostlund's bankruptcy by banning him from all financial transactions in the sport—a move that was required under Scandinavia's rules of racing.

Unable to make any money from stud fees or sales of Exceller's progeny, Ostlund shipped the horse, now 23, to a small farm in central Sweden. Shortly thereafter, he called the farm's owner, Ann Pagmar, and told her to have the stallion slaughtered.

Few, if any, in the United States Thoroughbred industry had given Exceller much thought since his departure in 1991. But one small group did happen to think of him in 1997, and it is partly because of them that his story came to light. In April of that year, the National Museum of Racing and Hall of Fame's nominating committee, sifting through the sport's greats, put him on their ballot.

The reappearance of Exceller's name prompted a *Daily Racing Form* reporter, Mike Mullaney, who was working on a series of columns called "Whatever Happened To," to check into the nominee's whereabouts. What he found ended up on the front page of the *Daily Racing Form*'s July 20, 1997, edition, which landed at Arthur and Staci Hancock's Stone Farm early in the morning. Here is what they read:

"Shortly after Exceller came to me last year, the owner called and told me to kill the horse, because he couldn't pay for him," farm owner Ann Pagmar told the *Form*. "He said that since we weren't breeding Exceller, there was nothing else to do with him.

The owner didn't want to pay for a stallion license, and he wasn't paying me, so I offered to take Exceller, to buy the stallion license and breed him.

"He wouldn't give him to me, saying the horse shouldn't keep moving from one owner to another. The stud fees would help me get paid, but the owner was very stubborn. He wanted to kill the horse."

According to Mullaney's story, Pagmar stonewalled Ostlund, telling him over a period of several months that she could not carry out his wishes without written authorization. But in April 1997, the same month Exceller was placed on the American Hall of Fame ballot, Ostlund sent Pagmar the authorization. Exceller was slaughtered on April 7, 1997, at the age of 24.

"He told me to take Exceller to the slaughterhouse," Pagmar told the *Form*, "and I walked him over myself. I made an appointment because I wanted to get it over with quick, but they were very busy when we got there and we had to wait. Exceller knew what was going on; he didn't want to be there. Standing with him like that . . . it made me feel like Judas."

When she put down the harrowing account of Exceller's end, Staci Hancock immediately thought of Gato del Sol, now a failed and worthless stallion in Germany. It ate at her, and she began to prod her husband about it, too, reminding him every week: What about Gato?

"I'd say, 'Maybe he'll get a runner and something good will happen,'" Arthur Hancock recalled. "But nothing ever did, and she was really concerned. I was, too, but she was the force. She wouldn't let it go."

In 1999, the Hancocks called an agent in Bremen and asked him to make a private offer for Gato del Sol, who was then 20 years old. In the end, they bought him for $5,000. Quarantine fees and the flight home cost nearly four times that much.

"I remember the first time Staci brought it up," Hancock said. "We were sitting right there in the kitchen having supper. The first thing I thought was, 'Man, that's a lot of money. He'll be okay. Somebody will give him a good home. He'll be fine.' I thought it would be a nice idea, but it would cost a lot of money. And it did cost a lot of money, but I don't regret it.

"As you get in this business, you do learn that it is a business," Hancock said. "But it doesn't have to totally push out the love of the horse. It has to go hand in hand. You read about how some of these horses are sent for meat. My dad had a saying: One of the worst things in the world is the dog that bites the hand that feeds him. When you do that to horses that have tried to do well, that have run for you and tried to make it as a broodmare and failed and aren't worth anything, if you do that, that's kind of the dog that bites the hand that feeds it. They've tried. It's not their fault.

"Gato tried to be a stallion, he just didn't have it, genetically. Then he tried to be a stallion in Germany. He tried to win the Derby, and he won the Derby. He was a great horse and a great creature of God. As I said, it was the least I could do."

Gato del Sol returned to his birthplace in August of 1999.

Now almost entirely white, old Gato del Sol has the same job his Derby trophy has: to be admired. He has not covered any mares since he left Germany, and he doesn't appear to mind his retirement. On a snowy, windy February day two decades after his Derby win, he stood at the far end of his grassy, rectangular paddock, ears pricked in the direction of Arthur Hancock's SUV.

"There he is, down there standing out of the wind," Hancock said as he slid out of the driver's seat. "He's doing well."

Gato del Sol watched Hancock approach the paddock fence, then, with a quick toss of his head, he cantered up the hill at a stately pace. He looked dignified, Hancock thought. "That's the Derby in him," he said, proudly. "You know, I come over here sometimes and just stop by the fence. He never bites or kicks or anything, he's just that way. It's him and me together, and I can reminisce."

Gato del Sol is nearing the end of the average life span for a Thoroughbred stallion. But however long he lives, Hancock said, his Derby winner will have his paddock at Stone Farm. "I'm glad to have him back here," Hancock said. He reached a gloved hand over the fence and patted the great woolly neck that once wore that elusive blanket of roses.

"The money thing to do isn't always the right thing to do, but the right thing to do is always the right thing to do," he said. "With

241

Gato, bringing him back, it's like taking $25,000 and tearing it up, if you want to put it that way. But it was the right thing to do. And what's life for if you can't do that?

"If you have an older mare, you set aside some acreage in the back, you don't send her to the killer to make $300 or $400 or whatever they give for them. That's squeezing the lemon. If you take care of your horses, your horses will take care of you. If there's no more in this universe than just grabbing the dollar—and you've got to have it to make it, we all have to work for a living—but there's more to life than that. If there's not, it's not worth living."

Hancock's extraordinary gesture is not the only one of its kind in the Thoroughbred world. Back in 1982, some concerned citizens established the Thoroughbred Retirement Foundation, which has grown into one of the most active and successful retirement programs for ex-racehorses who are no longer sound, young, or talented enough to run. The foundation's supporters have included the late Paul Mellon, who devoted space on his Virginia farm for his own retired geldings and pensioned broodmares, and as of 2004 the TRF was caring for an estimated 600 horses at facilities in numerous states.

The TRF and similar rescue and retirement organizations, such as ReRun, the California Equine Retirement Foundation, and others, sometimes offer retraining and adoption programs, through which horsemen in other disciplines can pay a nominal fee to adopt former runners, provided they agree never to breed, race, or sell the horses. Through such groups, countless horses who otherwise might have headed to North American slaughterhouses have instead ended up at horse shows, parades, mounted-police programs, trail rides, at pasture, and even in Olympic-level competition.

Even stallions, traditionally more difficult to place, now have a retirement home, thanks to an organization called Old Friends, which operates a breeding-stock pensioning program in Midway, Kentucky. A few other horses, like the entirely infertile champion Cigar and a cheap claimer who was one of the horses to play Seabiscuit in a 2003 movie by that name, have found a home at the Kentucky Horse Park in Lexington.

But the slaughter problem, even for the industry's best horses, still exists. In 2003, another sad story emerged when Barbara Bayer, a reporter for Thoroughbred trade magazine *The Blood-Horse*, discovered that 1986 Kentucky Derby winner Ferdinand had died in a Japanese slaughterhouse. Ferdinand's Derby was perhaps most famous for the emotional return of jockey Bill Shoemaker to the Churchill Downs winner's circle at age 54, making him the oldest rider ever to win the Derby. But even that did not save Ferdinand once Claiborne Farm sold him to Japanese interests. After the distressing news of Ferdinand's death was published, Claiborne sent out a press release the next time it sold a horse to Japan, noting that it had included a clause in its contract requiring the overseas farm to give Claiborne the right to buy the horse back if he ever came on the market again.

It is not clear how binding such clauses really will be. But the relationship between a man and his horse, especially his home run horse, should be eternally binding, some insist. It is not a sentiment that is universally welcomed among the grinding wheels of industrial racehorse production, but it is one that almost everyone who benefits from a lucky, talented horse seems to feel at one time or another.

When Exceller retired, Nelson Bunker Hunt, who described the horse as "generous," clearly felt the glow his special horse had radiated.

"I've been in racing long enough to be philosophical," Hunt told the *Daily Racing Form* back in May 1979. "Funny how the best-laid plans go awry. I'll bet in the next 100 years there won't be another horse that beats two Triple Crown winners like he did. I feel fortunate to have had such a remarkable horse, and I'm looking forward to racing his foals."

Every owner looks forward to racing the foals. The commercial Thoroughbred industry is built on those delicate sands of hope and potential, which converge when a human with a competitive soul catches sight of a young, beautiful horse that has its entire career ahead of it. The modern Thoroughbred-breeding business has made those dreams more accessible to more people, from the breeder hoping for a big sale to the buyer with Derby aspirations. But few industries are entirely free of pollution, and the noxious byproduct of the Thoroughbred game is a ruthless adherence to profit motive. It has existed since the beginning of the breed, when English horsemen began paying extravagant sums to import Arabian stallions to create faster horses that could win more money, both in purses and in wagers won. But the money that today's home run horses can make, and bestow upon their owners, has made breeding's industrial machinery more corporate and callous, according to some of the Turf fraternity's more wistful members.

"I remember as a little boy, people like the Whitneys, Bill Woodward—my grandfather's clients—they loved horses," Arthur Hancock III said. "If something happened to a horse at Claiborne, they grieved like it was the family dog, because it was built on love of the horse, respect for the horse, and the love of the beauty of the sport. There's an old saying that it's 'the sport of kings,' and it always was, because it took a king to afford to be in it. But they loved their horses. Now, it's more of a business, it's more materialistic. You don't often see that same spirit, and I think that's bad for the whole industry."

It was not just an indescribable feeling that wafted Arthur Hancock from his Churchill Downs box to the most improbable destination of all, the Kentucky Derby winner's circle. It was Gato del Sol that got him there, and Hancock did not forget it when it mattered. Which gave him another good feeling that is somehow related to the emotion buyers get when they outbid a hard-nosed rival at auction, that sellers get when the bidding duel rockets the price up into the millions, and the breeder gets when a foal is born healthy and perfect: a deep satisfaction.

"I knew we'd done the right thing," Hancock said, leaning against the pasture fence that contained his retired Derby winner. "There's no telling what would have happened to him. If you don't have a feel for the horses, if it's just a commodity . . . It *is* a commodity, but . . ."

Hancock's voice trailed off, and he idly scratched Gato del Sol's neck, leaving tracks where his gloved fingers ran through the horse's thick winter coat.

"I think somewhere, when you do the right thing by them, it comes back to you for the good," Hancock concluded. "It's the right thing to do as opposed to the money. He won the Derby for us. I owed him."

BIBLIOGRAPHY

BOOKS

Alexander, David. *A Sound of Horses*. New York: The Bobbs-Merrill Company, Inc. 1966.

Blyth, Henry. *The Rakes*. New York: The Dial Press. 1971.

Case, Carole. *The Right Blood: America's Aristocrats in Thoroughbred Racing*. New Jersey: Rutgers University Press. 2001.

Crist, Steven. *The Horse Traders*. New York: W. W. Norton & Company, Inc. 1986.

Daily Racing Form. *Champions*. New York: Daily Racing Form, LLC. 2000.

De Moubray, Jocelyn. *The Thoroughbred Business*. London: Hamish Hamilton. 1987.

Finney, Humphrey S. *Fair Exchange: Recollections of a Life with Horses*. New York: Charles Scribner's Sons. 1974.

Hewitt, Abram. *The Great Breeders and Their Methods*. Lexington, Kentucky: Thoroughbred Publishers. 1982.

Hollingsworth, Kent. *The Wizard of the Turf: John E. Madden of Hamburg Place*. Lexington, Kentucky: The Blood-Horse. 1965.

Kikkuli. *The Kikkuli Text on the Training of Horses*, translated by Gerhard F. Probst. The Keeneland Association Library. Lexington, Kentucky: King Library Press, University of Kentucky. 1977.

Livingston, Bernard. *Their Turf*. New York: Arbor House. 1973.

Markham, Gervase. *Markham's Horsemanship.* 1683.

Nafzger, Carl. *Traits of a Winner.* Neenah, Wisconsin: The Russell Meerdink Company, Ltd. 1994.

Onslow, Richard. *Royal Ascot.* Wiltshire, England: The Crowood Press. 1990.

Prior, C. M. *Early Records of the Thoroughbred Horse.* London: The Sportsman's Office, 1924.

Smith, Nicholas Hanckey. *Observations on Breeding for the Turf.* London: G. Whittaker. 1825.

Taylor, Joseph Lannon. *Joe Taylor's Complete Guide to Breeding and Raising Racehorses.* Neenah, Wisconsin: The Russell Meerdink Company, Ltd. 1993.

Tesio, Federico. *Breeding the Racehorse.* London: J. A. Allen & Company, Ltd. 1958.

Tyrrel, John. *Running Racing: The Jockey Club Years Since 1750.* London: Quiller Press. 1997.

Walsh, J. H. *The Horse in the Stable and the Field.* London: George Routledge and Sons, Ltd. 1899.

Winter, Gordon. *The Horseman's Weekend Book.* London: Seeley Service. No date.

Xenophon. *Scripta Minora.* Translated by E. C. Marchant. Cambridge, Massachusetts: Harvard University Press 1968.

MAGAZINE AND NEWSPAPER ARTICLES

Biles, D., et al. "Keeneland Select Sale: Comments from the Players," *The Blood-Horse,* July 27, 1985.

Daily Racing Form staff. "Exceller is Syndicated for Record $15 million," *Daily Racing Form,* August 13, 1979.

Flake, Carol. "The Intensity Factor," *The New Yorker.* 1988.

Grisham, Don. "Lukas Organization Shooting for 80 Stakes Wins," *Daily Racing Form,* September 1, 1986.

Heckerman, David. "Chace-ing a Dream," *The Blood-Horse,* April 13, 1996.

Heckerman, David. "Perfect Harmony," *The Blood-Horse,* November 4, 1995.

Hollingsworth, Kent. "A. B. Hancock, Jr.: 1910-1972," *The Blood-Horse,* September 25, 1972.

246

Hollingsworth, Kent. "Quest for the Best," *The Blood-Horse*, July 27, 1985.

Hussey, Charles. "Country Homes—Gardens Old and New: Aldby Park, Yorkshire: The Seat of Lt.-Col. Geoffrey Darley, DSO," *Country Life*, November 9, 1935.

Keyser, Tom. "A Dash of Genius," *The Blood-Horse*, November 22, 2003.

Keyser, Tom. "Miracle Mile," *Breeders' Cup Souvenir Magazine*, 1999.

Mullaney, Mike. "Exceller Remembered as a Truly Class Act," *Daily Racing Form*. July 20, 1997.

Mullaney, Mike. "Unique Superstar Exceller Met Tragic End," *Daily Racing Form*, July 20, 1997.

Nack, William. "Another View from the Top," *Sports Illustrated*, May 8, 1988.

Nack, William. "The Bargain of a Lifetime," *Sports Illustrated*, March 19, 1979.

Nack, William. "Blood Brothers and Bluegrass," *Sports Illustrated*, October 30, 1989.

Senzell, Howard. "Exceller Takes Amazing Credits into Retirement," *Daily Racing Form*, May 10, 1979.

Simon, Mark. "All About Purses," *Thoroughbred Times*, March 23, 2002.

Sullivan, Tim. "This 3-year-old Song is Music to Their Ears," Cincinnati *Enquirer*, May 4, 1996.

Williams, Rhonda. "The Myrtlewood Heritage," *The Blood-Horse*, April 14, 1990.

Numerous articles covering the Triple Crown by *Daily Racing Form*'s Steve Andersen, David Grening, Marty McGee, Jay Privman, and Mike Watchmaker also were helpful.

WEBSITES AND ARTICLES

Cruickshank, Dan. "The Wages of Sin." British Broadcasting Company Online, *www.bbc.co.uk*

Saratoga Springs Historical Museum, *www.saratogasprings-historymuseum.org*

Down Royal Racecourse, *www.downroyal.com*
The Jockey Club, *www.jockeyclub.com*
Kentucky Horse Park's International Museum of the Horse,
    www.kyhorsepark.com
Thoroughbred Bloodlines, *www.bloodlines.net*
Thoroughbred Heritage, *www.tbheritage.com*
Thoroughbred Retirement Foundation, *www.trfinc.org*
UK and Ireland Geneaology, *www.genuki.org.uk*

ACKNOWLEDGMENTS

IF YOU'RE WRITING a book about the Thoroughbred world, there surely is no better place to work than the *Daily Racing Form*. My thanks go first to the two people there who made *The Home Run Horse* possible in the first place. Without Charlie Hayward's encouragement and direction, this book might have remained just an idea. The newspaper's chairman and my editor on this project, Steven Crist, contributed his deep knowledge of racing and a great storytelling sensibility. His involvement undoubtedly made the manuscript stronger and more fun to write.

I also am indebted to Robin Foster for applying her red pen and her literary talents to this story. Where I stumbled, she caught me, and her excellent sense of humor made me feel better about making the corrections.

Many thanks are also due to *Daily Racing Form* editors Rich Rosenbush and Irwin Cohen, whose assignments helped me find these stories and who allowed me space and time to work on the book. Thanks also to the newspaper's copyediting team, and especially to Ira Kaplan and David McDonough, for their skilled and tactful copyediting on the parts of this book that appeared previously in the newspaper.

Many pages of this book could not have been written without three formidable assets familiar to anyone exploring the history of Thoroughbred sport: Cathy Schenck, Phyllis Rogers, and the Keeneland Library where they preside. How did the Hittites train horses 3,000 years ago? What did 17th-century English horse breeders use to treat equine infertility? Cathy and Phyllis always managed to point me to exactly the right source among the library's several thousand volumes, and they provided many interesting and curious facts in this book.

Thanks also to those people who generously read drafts and offered suggestions. Two, in particular, deserve mention: Logan Bailey, whose knowledge of the Thoroughbred breeding industry and of central Kentucky make him one of the most interesting and informative people I have met in the business, and bloodstock agent Mike Brown, one of the most astute and clever commentators on the Thoroughbred market and its mores.

Each of the people mentioned above had an important hand in the technical production of *The Home Run Horse*. There are numerous others who generously provided the raw material—that is, the stories. Thanks to those who agreed to interviews and, in many cases, long meetings or visits to their farms. The breeders, owners, trainers, grooms, veterinarians, and other workers and players make the game go and give authors a rich field to write about. My particular thanks go to the owners and staffs at Taylor Made Farm, Tapeta Farm, Hill 'n' Dale Farms, Stone Farm, WinStar Farm, and Claiborne Farm; to Arthur Hancock III, Satish Sanan, Michael Dickinson, Buzz Chace, Dr. Bill Bernard, Cecil Seaman, John Prather, Barclay Tagg, Robin Smullen, John Ferguson, Preston and Anita Madden, Dr. John Chandler, Ric Waldman, Dr. Craig Van Balen, John Ward, and Bob Baffert. My gratitude also goes to two very fine companions: Wilson Shirley, whose bright intellect and sharp wit have always been a refuge, and Andy Serling, for his generosity in the matter of gin and tonics and for his exquisite sense of the absurd.

And, finally, to the friends who cheered me on and forgave my inattention in the months when I was writing: thank you.